- THE JAINS

  PAUL DUNDAS

  pp: 368, gloss., notes, biblio. & index

- STUDIES IN JAINA HISTORY AND CULTRE

  Disputes and Dialogues

  PETER FLUGEL

  pp: 494, index

- IMAGINING HINDUISM

  A Postcolonial Perspective

  SHARADA SUGIRTHARAJAH

  pp: 182, notes, biblio. & index

MOTILAL BANARSIDASS

SINCE 1903 IN INDOLOGY

Imagining Hinduism

Imagining Hinduism introduces a new and significant way of looking at Western constructions of Hinduism. Employing current postcolonial categories, Sharada Sugirtharajah examines how Hinduism has been defined, interpreted and manufactured through Western categorizations, from the foreign interventions of the eighteenth- and nineteenth-century Orientalists and missionaries to the present day. Her contention is that ever since early Orientalists "discovered" the ancient Sanskrit texts and the Hindu "Golden Age," the West has nurtured a complex and ambivalent fascination with Hinduism, responding to it in ways ranging from romantic admiration to ridicule. At the same time, she focuses attention on how Hindu discourse has drawn upon Orientalist representations in order to redefine Hindu identity and construct a monolithic Hinduism, both in the Indian and diasporic contexts.

As the first comprehensive work to bring postcolonial critique to the study of Hinduism, *Imagining Hinduism* is essential reading for an informed and critical understanding of how both Europeans and Hindus engage with Hinduism.

Sharada Sugirtharajah is Lecturer in Hindu Studies at the University of Birmingham.

Imagining Hinduism

A postcolonial perspective

Sharada Sugirtharajah

Routledge
Taylor & Francis Group
LONDON AND NEW YORK

MOTILAL BANARSIDASS PUBLISHERS
PRIVATE LIMITED • DELHI

Reprint, 2017

First published 2003
by Routledge
2 Park Square, Milton Park, Abingdon, Oxon OX14 4RN

Simultaneously published in the USA and Canada
by Routledge
711 Third Avenue, New York, NY 10017

Routledge is an imprint of the Taylor & Francis Group, an informa business

Typeset in Galliard by Bookcraft Ltd, Stroud, Gloucestershire

British Library Cataloguing in Publication Data
A catalogue record for this book is available from the British Library

Library of Congress Cataloging in Publication Data
Imagining hinduism
p. cm.
1. Hinduism–Study and teaching. 2. Orientalism.
BL1205.I43 2003
294.5'07'22–dc21 2003046539

ISBN : 978-81-208-4091-1

Digitally Printed at Replika Press Pvt. Ltd.

To the Mother

Contents

Acknowledgements

I wish to express my sincere thanks to many people who have, directly or indirectly, made possible the writing of this book. First, to Roger Thorp who showed a keen interest in my proposal and commissioned this volume. Although he is no more with Routledge, I owe him a deep sense of gratitude. After Roger's departure, Clare Johnson of Routledge was of immense help and I would like to express my thanks to her. I would also like to thank staff at the Orchard Learning Resource Centre – Debbie, Pauline, Jane, Sandy, and particularly Clare and Rachel – who made stock-room materials available. My sincere thanks, as well, to Dorothy for procuring the material I most needed. I owe a special debt of gratitude to my long-time friend Lorraine for her meticulous reading of draft chapters and insightful suggestions, and for the many hours of discussion and for her constant support all through the writing of the book. I am immensely grateful to Ralph Broadbent who came to my rescue whenever I ran into computer glitches and needed his help. I also wish to thank various members of my family in India, especially my sister, Savithri, who took such an interest in my research. I would like to express my sincere thanks to my copy editor, Dilys Hartland, for her understanding and patience. My thanks are also due to the *Journal of Feminist Studies in Religion* and to *Studies in World Christianity* for permission to republish my papers (with some changes) that have appeared in their journals. Finally, my deepest personal gratitude to my husband, Sugi, whose expertise in postcolonial studies and incisive comments on my work have helped me enormously to focus and tighten my arguments. I am also grateful to him for his unfailing encouragement and his intellectual and emotional support, but more importantly, for believing with me in women's *śakti*.

Introduction

"Hinduism" has long been a central feature in Western consciousness. Ever since the West first came into contact with it, the tradition has been defined and interpreted mainly in Western categories. Western responses to Hinduism have been varied, complex, and ambivalent, ranging from romantic admiration to ridicule. What this volume seeks to do is to investigate some of these representations from a postcolonial perspective. Taking a brief look at the emergence of the concept "Hinduism," it examines European orientalist and missionary constructions of Hinduism during the colonial period, and also examines how such representations impacted on Hindus in India and in the diaspora. The volume draws attention to how Hindu movements in the diaspora replicate orientalist articulations of Hinduism. In looking at these constructions of Hinduism, the volume aims to show how Hinduism came to be tailored to fit the varied hermeneutical and ideological positions of both Western and Indian interpreters, all of whom, on their own terms, tried to homogenize a loosely knit tradition and invest it with a tight structure, thereby making it static, fixed, and palatable. Before we proceed further, a brief note about the contentious terms, Hinduism and postcolonialism.

Defining the Other

Defining, naming or classifying the Other is not peculiar to any one culture. Rather, it takes place within, as well as with respect to, other cultures. Naming the Other becomes problematic when one party tries to domesticate the Other. The term "Hindu," which comes from the Sanskrit word Sindhu (the River Indus), was initially used by Persian-speaking Muslims to refer to those who lived in that geographical area near the River Indus, regardless of the residents' particular religious affiliation. In its earlier phase, the term was applied to all non-Muslims, and did not always carry a specific religious significance. It was used in more than one sense by Muslims, sometimes for adherents of a non-Islamic religion, sometimes referring to the local inhabitants, and sometimes used in a geographical sense (Thapar 1993: 79). The use of the term as a religious category became explicit when Muslim conquerors used it to refer to the religious practices of the inhabitants whom they encountered in that geographical region. It became a convenient label to describe and at the same time to differentiate themselves from the local inhabitants. The fact that the term "Hindu" had a geographic connotation did not imply that the indigenous people had no sense of religious consciousness or identity. On the contrary, the people were from diverse communities which had their own languages, social and religious identities, customs and modes of worship. The point is that the term "Hindu" did not suggest any of the uniformity that it came to acquire later. The appropriation of the term by Hindus themselves can be traced back to the fifteenth century, in the literature of *bhakti* sects influenced by Islamic thought. In Kabīr's verses one finds a reference to Hindus and *Turuṣkas* (Muslims), Kabīr himself being a product of both Hindu and Islamic cultures (Thapar 1993: 79). Initially perhaps the term was used by Hindus to distinguish themselves from Muslims, but there was no implication of Hinduism as a uniform system of religion in the Enlightenment sense. In other words, religion did not entail an adherence to a set of prescribed beliefs or a uniform creed, a single book or a single authority.

The Portuguese and the British referred to Indians as *Gentoos*, meaning "gentile" or "heathen," the British deriving their usage from the Portuguese. It is interesting to note that Vasco da Gama who arrived in Calicut in 1498, distinguished the outsiders resident there from the natives. The residents were classified as Muslims (Moors), and the natives as "Gentios," the presumption being that the latter were practising some primitive or archaic form of Christianity and needed to be converted to the true faith (Srivastava 2001: 578). The term *Gentoo* was used by the eighteenth-century orientalist Halhed, and it occurs in the title of his book *Code of Gentoo Laws*, published in 1776. Hindus, too, described others in their own terms, for example, they referred to foreigners as *meleccha*, meaning "impure."[1]

The use of the term "Hindu" in the latter part of the nineteenth century came to be associated with religious identity, when local inhabitants were required in the British census to state their religion. The notion of *Hindutva* (Hindu-ness) which emerged in the twentieth century has little to do with religion. It was propagated by Vinayak Damodar Savarkar who differentiated *Hindutva*[2] from Hinduism as a "religion," and all Indians regardless of their differing religious identities were subsumed under the newly constructed notion. In other words, Savarkar posited *Hindutva* as a unifying socio-cultural category. *Hindutva* has become the political ideological slogan of the present-day Hindu revivalists who affirm a Hindu India.

While the label "Hindu" does not give any clear indication of a person's particular religious affiliation, terms such as *Vaiṣṇava* (worshipper of Viṣṇu) or *Śaiva* (worshipper of Śiva) do. A *Vaiṣṇava* is a Hindu, but a Hindu need not be a *Vaiṣṇava* or *Śaiva*. For those within the tradition, the word

"Hindu" in "Hindu *Vaiṣṇava*" is redundant. The label "Hindu" serves as a useful marker, albeit an inadequate one. Not all Hindus are members of a sect. The label "Hindu" has been contested, even from within the tradition. There are dissenting voices such as those of the Ramakrishna Mission who are not comfortable using such a label. Furthermore, from the legal point of view, people of Sikh, Buddhist, and Jain origin are subsumed under the title Hinduism, much to the annoyance of the members of these faiths whose particular religious identities are not given their due regard.

The term "Hindu" in itself does not carry any particular religious significance as does the word Buddhist or Sikh, nor does it give any clue to the internal religious diversity. It functions as a convenient term encompassing the complex pattern of beliefs and practices, diverse scriptural, mythological, philosophical, and popular strands, ritual and caste traditions, and varied religious groups and movements within what has come to be called "Hinduism." It is a term that continues to pose more problems than answers. I don't intend to get embroiled in the contentious debate regarding the term "Hinduism" which has been problematized by contemporary scholars of religion. Suffice to say, some scholars see it mainly as a nineteenth-century Western construct while others contest such a claim.[3] Whatever the case may be, my point is that the notion of a monolithic Hinduism emerged in the colonial era. This is not to say that there was no sense of a discernible religious identity or framework in precolonial India in terms of which one could speak about the tradition. As Romila Thapar remarks: "Identities were, in contrast to the modern nation state, segmented identities. The notion of community was not absent but there were multiple communities identified by locality, language, caste, occupation and sect. What appears to have been absent was the notion of a uniform, religious community readily identified as Hindu" (Thapar 1993: 77). In the hands of British orientalists and missionaries the heterogeneous aspects of a complex tradition came to be treated in a monolithic and monolinear fashion. Put differently, orientalists and missionaries were largely instrumental in transforming a disparate tradition into a uniform and manageable system mainly to serve their own purposes. In this they were assisted by native pundits but on terms set by Western scholars. In other words, both orientalists and native pundits were joint collaborators in this hermeneutical exercise. The emergence, in the colonial era, of the modern concept of a homogeneous Hinduism is not without added significance. Early British administrators, such as Warren Hastings and William Jones, were also oriental scholars who were keen to know about India and its traditions and who embarked on a serious study and translation of Sanskrit texts in the belief that it would enable them to govern efficiently. Even a cursory glance at the production of oriental literature under the governorship of Warren Hastings, such as Halhed's *A Code of Gentoo Laws*, Charles Wilkins' translation of the *Bhagavadgītā*, and Jones' recodification of *Hindu Laws*, demonstrates the close link between colonial power and the production of knowledge. India was to be governed by her own laws which were seen to be located in her ancient texts, but these laws were to be ordered in a scientific way for the benefit of Hindus. The following chapters demonstrate how orientalists and missionaries fashioned a Hinduism largely in terms of their own conceptual frameworks, informed by such Enlightenment ideas as modernity, rationality, linear progress, and development, all being qualities which were seen to be deficient or lacking in Hinduism.

Postcolonial criticism as an interrogative tool

Postcolonialism is one of the latest theoretical categories to enter academic discourse. The literature on postcolonialism is vast and expanding,[4] and the debates from within and from outside are too complicated to be recalled here. The chief proponents of postcolonial theory are Edward Said,[5] Homi Bhabha[6] and Gayatri Chakravorty Spivak,[7] whose works have elicited lively and contentious debate in various academic fields from literature to anthropology to art history. Sadly, postcolonialism is a late comer to the field of religion and therefore the literature on the subject is rather thin.[8] As an interventionary critical tool, postcolonialism has emerged from a number of dominant modes of thought such as Marxism, poststructuralism, psychology and feminism, and it has also borrowed creatively from textual analysis and social scientific methods. Its method, too, is eclectic.

Postcolonialism, like its other kindred theoretical category, postmodernism, is fraught with definitional ambiguities, but this is seen by its practitioners as indicative of its potential strength rather than its apparent weakness. Each discipline has come up with its own definition of postcolonialism and has appropriated it to suit its own academic needs, and hence what postcolonialism means differs from discipline to discipline. It has come to acquire various shades of meaning according to the varied historical contexts in which it has emerged. Postcolonialism is not a monolithic or homogenizing category. Any attempt to look for a linear development of the term would be a futile exercise as it encompasses heterogeneous voices, theoretical approaches and historical contexts. The unique or remarkable feature of postcolonialism lies in its heterogeneity. It challenges established theories and conventions, including its own terminology which is not free from definitional problems.

Postcolonialism is not the end of colonialism. As with postmodernism, there is a perpetual interaction between the past and present. Postcolonialism is not a strict marker of historical epochs. It is a discursive practice that takes a critical look at histories, textual productions, and visual and aural representations. In its hyphenated form, "post-colonialism" indicates historical periodization, that is, the period after the demise of colonialism or the empire. In its unhyphenated form, "postcolonialism," it goes beyond historical periodization in that it identifies various forms of colonialism and neo-colonialism in newly independent and contemporary societies. "Postcolonialism," as McLeod neatly puts it, "is not contained by the tidy categories of historical periods or dates, although it remains firmly bound up with historical experiences" (McLeod 2000: 5). Just as the term "colonialism" is not confined to the colonial era, so too the term "postcolonialism" is not confined to the period after colonialism. Colonialism did not end with the colonized territories gaining political independence; newly independent nations continue to replicate the hegemonic values and structures of the colonizer. In brief, postcolonialism is not about chronological periodization nor is it about simply recalling the malevolent aspects of the empire and contrasting them with the integrity and innocence of natives and their culture. It initially emerged as an active confrontation with the dominant systems of thought during the colonial period, and later turned towards national governments which failed to establish democratic structures after their independence. Postcolonialism is a way of critiquing totalizing tendencies in Eurocentric as well as nationalistic modes of thinking and practice. To state it differently, postcolonial critique is not simply confined to interrogating Western representations of the "Other." It also interrogates nationalist discourses which endorse and replicate colonial attitudes and methods in order to subjugate their own people in the name of development and progress. Moreover, it draws attention to the complexities, contradictions, ambivalences, and tensions embedded both in colonial and nationalist discourses.

Postcolonial theory has been used in many different ways – as a methodological approach, as a resistant or oppositional strategy, or as a discursive category. As with any critical theory, postcolonialism is not without limitations, but nevertheless it is a highly useful category. The field of postcolonial studies being an amorphous one, and one with divergent meanings and nuances, I will mainly use the term as a hermeneutical tool to interrogate the colonial assumptions and intentions embedded both in Western orientalist and missionary approaches to Hinduism, as well as in Hindu responses to such articulations. Postcolonialism is concerned with "knowledge" produced both by the former colonizer and by the colonized, as well as by postcolonial subjects in diverse historical contexts including diasporic locations. My concern is not with chronological periodization but with the ideological orientations undergirding textual productions. Ideological agendas do not disappear with the formal passing of colonialism; they tend to resurface in representations and reading strategies even in the "post-colonial" era. The aim of postcolonial criticism is to interrogate textual, historical, ethnographic, visual and other representations of societies which were badly affected by the historical reality of colonial presence and domination. It is about how colonizers constructed images of the colonized, as well as how the colonized themselves made use of these images as a counter-tool to combat negative portrayals and to construct a new identity. Postcolonial theory is useful in that it reveals the link between knowledge and power and between representation and mediation, and highlights homogenizing, essentializing and universalizing tendencies in varied discourses, reading and interpretative strategies.

My aim is not to get entangled in the diverse and complex theoretical discourses on postcolonialism, but to make cautionary and selective use of categories such as orientalism, colonial patronage, palimpsest, classification, negation, affirmation, and so forth. In other words, I will be using postcolonial theoretical categories mainly as a hermeneutical tool in examining representations of Hinduism. How I intend to use them will be illustrated in each chapter.

About this volume

A brief outline of the chapters follows: the first, entitled "William Jones: making Hinduism safe," looks at the kind of Hinduism fashioned by the eighteenth-century British orientalist William Jones. It mainly examines his various discourses published in the 1799 six-volume edition of *The Works of Sir William Jones.* While acknowledging Jones' empathetic approach to Hinduism, the chapter seeks to demonstrate that Jones constructs a Hinduism that is still locked in its infancy, needing the help of the progressive European culture. To state it boldly, my contention is that Jones' "empathy" is that of a benevolent parent towards a child who has yet to grow into maturity. His approach to Hinduism reflects his romantic and theological presuppositions as well as his concerns as a colonial administrator. As with other orientalists, Jones invents a magnificent Hindu past and a degenerate present, and sets about recovering for Hindus their pristine past. The chapter illustrates how he domesticates Hindu texts and myths by rendering them in categories familiar to the West.

The chapter draws attention to Jones' representation of Hinduism according to his varied roles as a jurist, biblicist and poet. As a scholar-administrator of the East India Company, Jones engages in a civilizing mission of educating the natives in their own laws. He takes upon himself the task of refining Hindu laws along European legal lines and transforming heterogeneous Sanskrit legal texts into a fixed body of knowledge to serve the administrative needs of the colonial government. The chapter demonstrates that in so doing, Jones ends up replacing the original Sanskrit version with his own translation. In other words, the chapter shows that Jones, in his desire to be true to the original (or to restore the purity of laws), engages in an inherently self-defeating hermeneutical exercise.

As a poet, Jones inhabits a different world. He puts Hinduism on a par with classical European culture, drawing numerous parallels between the Hindu and the Greco-Roman world. The chapter draws attention to Jones' predetermined conceptual framework in terms of which he approaches Hinduism. Associating the East with "imagination" and the West with "reason," Jones feels free to delve into the world of Hindu mythology and make it accessible to the West. For Jones, poetry being the realm of imagination, he feels at ease in expressing his romantic yearnings for the exotic. He composes hymns to feminine deities (as well as male), seeking their blessings for the successful implementation of the colonial project. Jones even resorts to what, by his own standards, would be considered, as an "effeminate" way of speaking about his fondness for Kṛṣṇa, and about his admiration for epic figures such Rāmā, Arjuna and others.

As a biblicist, Jones places Hindu texts within the biblical framework, seeking confirmation for and primacy of biblical truth in Hinduism. It is through a biblical, monotheistic lens that Jones views the Hindu tradition. The chapter shows how his representation of Hinduism is informed by his discovery of an Indo-European family of languages and shared origins. It establishes that Jones constructs a Hinduism that is in line with his Mosaic view of history. His biblical, textual, and poetic depictions of Hinduism are not to be seen as mutually exclusive; rather they demonstrate how Jones sought to appropriate Hinduism on his own terms, albeit in different ways. In brief, the chapter demonstrates how Jones biblicizes, textualizes, and "feminizes" Hinduism.

The main focus of the second chapter, "Max Müller: mobilizing texts and managing Hinduism," is Müller's 1882 Cambridge lectures addressed to young British civil servants and published under the title, *India: what can it teach us?* I also draw on his various works and those of his letters relevant to my theme. As with Jones, Müller's representation of Hinduism has much to do with his own nostalgic search for the supposed lost origins of European culture. The chapter draws attention to how his construction of a glorious age of Hindus is shaped by his theory of Aryan race – a theory which he later rejected. Equating a linguistic affinity between Sanskrit and European languages with racial affinity, Müller looks in India for Aryan ancestors of Europeans. India is important for what it can teach Europeans about their "supposed" past.

The chapter illustrates how Müller takes on the task of discovering for Hindus, the "real" or "true" Hinduism which he locates in the Veda. He is keen to recover what he sees as the "original" meaning of the Veda, and restore it to its immaculate form. But the Veda, however, has only an archival significance for Müller. The chapter demonstrates that he values the Veda for its historical worth rather than for its theological or spiritual import. It also shows how Müller regards himself as a spokesperson for Hindus whom he sees as ignorant about the truth of the Veda. He therefore sees Hindus as needing to be educated about the real worth of the Veda. What he implies is that Hindus should not treat the Veda as a spiritual text but only as a historical document. The chapter draws attention to Müller's thesis, which is that the Veda being an infantile text cannot serve as a basis for reforming Hinduism from within. He seeks to construct a purified form of Hinduism modelled on Protestant Christianity, and takes upon himself the role of reforming or rather Protestantizing Hindus who are seen to be in a state of infancy, stuck in their idolatrous practices. The chapter shows that, as with Jones, Müller views the relation between

Hinduism and Christianity as the relation between a child and an adult – the Hindu child needing the benevolent help of the Protestant parent. The difference between Jones and Müller, however, is that while Jones subjects Hinduism to a monogenetic view of history, Müller applies a modified version of Darwin's evolutionary theory to the study of religions in order to show that Hinduism is a puerile religion. Although Müller has no problems in acknowledging that there is truth in all religions, he is keen to demonstrate the superiority of Christianity. He makes clear the hermeneutical aim of his science of religion, which is to compare and contrast religions and establish which of them is better than the others. The chapter illustrates how Müller formulates a Hinduism that fits with his evolutionary notion of a religion.

The third chapter, "William Ward's 'virtuous Christians, vicious Hindus'," examines the nineteenth-century Baptist missionary William Ward's four-volume text, *A View of the History, Literature, and Mythology of the Hindoos*, which had a profound impact on missionary thinking of the time. My aim is to bring to the fore the hermeneutical factors at work in William Ward's representation of Hinduism. The chapter shows how he employs a series of negations in order to construct a Hinduism that is devoid of any spiritual or moral worth. While for orientalists the ancient Hindu past is venerable, for Ward both the Hindu past and present are defiled and beyond redemption unless "heathens" are converted to Christianity. In other words, Hinduism is pagan and barbaric, totally the "Other," in need of Christian salvation. The chapter demonstrates how his representation of Hinduism as decadent and primitive (requiring the intervention of Western rationality) has been shaped by the ideas of nineteenth-century Enlightenment, and by the evangelical and pietistic traditions in Britain. This chapter is a slightly modified version of a paper published in *Studies in World Christianity* (Sugirtharajah 1999b).

The fourth chapter, "Decrowning Farquhar's Hinduism," investigates the late nineteenth-century missionary John Nichol Farquhar's portrayal of Hinduism in his seminal work *The Crown of Hinduism*. Unlike his nineteenth-century Baptist missionary counterparts, Farquhar does not regard Hinduism as totally as the Other, but rather sees it finding fulfillment in Christ, as the title of the book indicates. He is willing to admit that there is some truth in Hinduism but argues there is no power within it to energize it. His classification of religions along evolutionary lines remains problematic in that it posits a single universal standard of truth in terms of which Hinduism is judged. What this chapter demonstrates is that, although Farquhar calls for a sympathetic understanding of Hinduism, he offers a Christianized form of it. As with Müller, Farquhar is engaged in Christianizing Hinduism. In brief, in Farquhar's view Hinduism as it is is of no value to Hindus.

The final chapter, "Courtly text and courting *satī*," examines a contemporary Western woman scholar's representation of *satī*, namely, the death of a young woman, Roop Kanwar, that took place in Rajasthan in 1987 on the funeral pyre of her dead husband. *Satī* assumed a central focus in nineteenth-century colonial Bengal. It occupied an important hermeneutical position in Hindu-colonial discourse and came to be seen as representing the entire religious and cultural tradition of India. It came to be scripturalized, romanticized, sensationalized, and essentialized.

My intention is not to argue for or against *satī* but to look at how Julia Leslie represents it in her chapter "Suttee or *satī*: victim or victor?" in *Roles and Rituals for Hindu Women*. This chapter highlights the hermeneutical implications of Leslie's use of a heavily biased eighteenth-century patriarchal text to depict Hindu women as "positive constructs." My point is that her use of a single patriarchal text to establish the relevance of *satī* tends to make other liberating female and male texts and voices invisible. The chapter problematizes Leslie's empathetic approach to *satī*. Her attempt to recover the agency of Roop Kanwar is commendable but at the same time problematic in that Leslie's positive construct is closely linked to the notion of woman as self-sacrificing agent. In other words, what appears to be a positive construct turns out in effect to be a conventional patriarchal construct. Intentionally or unintentionally, she paints a picture of a static and unchanging tradition and a monolithic Hindu patriarchy. I also point out that Leslie's hermeneutic approach echoes to some extent the nineteenth-century Hindu-colonial debate on *satī*. Despite her good intentions of speaking for Hindu women, she seems to be engaged in recovering for them idealized patriarchal images of women. The chapter demonstrates that Leslie's hermeneutical strategy falls within the orientalist mode of interpretation. As do orientalists in the colonial era and in the contemporary period, Leslie turns her gaze to the classical past in order to demonstrate the relevance of *satī* for contemporary Hindu women. This chapter was originally published in the *Journal of Feminist Studies in Religion* (Sugirtharajah 2001).

The chapters in this volume are not designed with a linear progression in mind. Rather, they form a mosaic – each piece is part of the larger pattern yet at the same time has its own independent identity. In other words, the chapters can be read in relation to one another, as individual pieces or in a linear fashion. There is a thematic link through the volume, and the overall thrust of the chapters has to do with representation and the hermeneutical presuppositions at work in orientalist, missionary, and Hindu approaches to Hinduism. My aim has been to show that Western constructions of Hinduism are varied although they display certain common identifiable features. There is no one consistent approach to the East. A variety of attitudes ranging from contempt and ambivalence and from binarism to complementarity can be seen in the East and West's representation of each other. While nineteenth-century Baptist missionaries such as William Carey and William Ward denounce India and its spiritual heritage, orientalists such as William Jones and Max Müller sing praises of India's venerable past, while yet maintaining the superiority of the West. For these orientalists, the Hindu pristine past is a source of inspiration and is necessary for Europe's definition of its own identity. It represents

Europe's childhood. For Ward and Carey, however, Hinduism represents all that is dreadful and totally the Other in need of Christian enlightenment.

With regard to most quotations from primary sources (Jones and Müller) used in the volume, I have retained the spelling, punctuation, capitalization and italicization as in the original texts, except for diacritical marks. The elongated eighteenth-century "s" which occurs in William Jones' *Works* has been modernized.

This is an exploratory volume in that it examines both orientalist and missionary representations of Hinduism from a postcolonial perspective. As indicated earlier, postcolonialism has been hesitant to enter the field of religion, and not many scholars of religion have taken a keen interest in this approach. A closer look will reveal that there are some striking parallels between postcolonialism and Hinduism. Without stretching the analogies too far, what is apparent is that neither label lends itself to any fixed definition or set of prescribed ideas, or linear treatment. Neither owes its allegiance to any centralized authority. Both are inclusive in that they encompass divergent and even seemingly contradictory aspects. As this volume demonstrates, both categories continue to be contested in their respective discourses, and serve as convenient terms yet need to be used with caution.

Chapter 1

William Jones

Making Hinduism safe

> All I need to do is make a few alterations. I can add the right words here and there, and I can cut out the offending ones.
>
> (Sijie 2001: 78)

William Jones (1746–94), an exceptionally gifted Welshman of his time, occupies a distinctive place in the study of British orientalism. His oriental pursuits began even before he set foot on Indian soil in 1783. Born in London in 1746, and a product of Harrow and of University College, Oxford, Jones rapidly gained linguistic proficiency in diverse classical languages such as Latin, Greek, Hebrew, Arabic, and Persian. Later he learned Sanskrit in India, mainly for administrative purposes. He is known for a language (Sanskrit) that he was not initially keen to learn but found himself falling in love with. He is best known, however, for his "discovery" of an Indo-European family of languages, drawing attention to the close resemblances between Sanskrit and the classical languages of Europe.[1] His published works include the translation of the Persian *History of Nader Shah* into French (1770) and English (1773), and the *Grammar of the Persian Language* (1771). Among his translations, two stand out: Kālidāsa's Sanskrit play *Śakuntalā* (1789),[2] which made a profound impact on Europe, and *The Institutes of Hindu Law: or, the Ordinances of Menu* (or Manu; completed and published after Jones' death as *A Digest of Hindu Law on Contracts and Successions*), intended for the use of English judges in India. Jones was more than a linguist – he was a polymath, a man of extraordinary talents and wide-ranging interests that included music, poetry, philology, religion, botany, astronomy, history, politics, and law.[3]

Jones turned to the Bar in 1770 in order to make himself financially independent. It was law rather than his quest for the Orient that led him to India. He set off for the subcontinent in 1783 to take up a judgeship in the Calcutta Supreme Court. As with many middle-class gentlemen of his time, Jones went to India to improve his financial prospects with the intention of eventually returning to England with his wife Anna Maria, to a peaceful retired life on a country estate. Sadly, he died in 1794, at the age of 47, before he could realize his dreams.

Jones arrived in Bengal at a time when the colonial grip on India was being strengthened under the governorship of Warren Hastings, himself a scholar-administrator. Although imperialism was not the prevailing ethos at this time, a colonial government was being formed. In the late eighteenth century (between 1772 and 1792), under the governorship of Warren Hastings, Bengal witnessed the production of orientalist knowledge for the needs of the colonial government. Hastings initiated the study and translation of Hindu texts such as *The Laws of Manu*[4] in the belief that an accurate knowledge of India and Hindu manners and customs could be gained from ancient Sanskrit texts. Even before the arrival of "Oriental Jones," Warren Hastings' Judicial Plan of 1772 had clear rules regarding the governance of natives, namely that the natives ought to be governed and protected by their own laws which were to be found in their sacred texts rather than in local customs.[5] Hindu legal texts thus became the object of study and investigation. Hardly had Jones arrived in India than he was appointed the first President of the Asiatic Society in 1784 in Calcutta, with Warren Hastings as its patron, thus initiating the process of studying, translating, and codifying Hindu texts. With the formal establishment of the Asiatic Society, orientalism was becoming a corporate enterprise. The works of scholar-administrators came to be published in the prestigious journal of the Society, *Asiatick Researches*, thereby making them available to a wider audience. The orientalist project initiated what came to be known as "oriental renaissance" (Schwab 1984).

Jones was the product of an eighteenth-century England which valued "reason," yet there was in him a romantic yearning for the "primitive" and "natural" that finds expression in his poetry. As well as being a product of the Enlightenment he was a precursor of the Romantic movement in that his works were a major source of inspiration for romantic orientalism.[6] *The New Oxford Book of Romantic Period Verse* begins with Jones' prefatory note to "A Hymn to Na'ra'yena,"[7] followed by his invocation to the deity, thus emphasizing the significance of his works for Romanticism (McGann 1993: xxi–xxii).

My main concern in this chapter is with the hermeneutical factors at work in Jones' construction and appropriation of Hinduism in his writings. This chapter draws on Jones' various "Anniversary" discourses and essays from the 1799 six-volume edition of *The Works of Sir William Jones*[8] as well as his letters. I discuss Jones' representation of Hinduism under three headings: Romantic Jones, Biblical Jones and Juridical Jones. These three categories are not mutually exclusive, rather they impinge on one another.

Biblical Jones

"Gods of Indian and European heathens"

In his seminal essay "On the Gods of Greece, Italy and India," written soon after his arrival in India in 1784, Jones renders the Other in categories familiar to the West. He draws classical analogies between the mythologies and religious practices of the Greco-Roman and the Hindu world. What Jones is trying to demonstrate is that Europeans are not encountering a strange culture but their own culture in its primitive form. In other words, Europeans are rather rediscovering their own pagan past in Hinduism.

Jones' thesis is that there is a great likeness between the popular worship of Hindus and Europeans; both share similar characteristics, namely polytheism, but the difference is that while Europeans have progressed from idolatry to biblical monotheism, Hindus are stuck in their primitive state. Jones' theory of common origins allows him to compare and contrast cultures without being intimidated by them, yet at the same time to affirm the primacy of Christianity. He perceives Indians and Europeans as sharing a common ancestry (descendants of the biblical Noah). However, having migrated from a common center (Iran) to different destinations, they had departed from the rational religion or what Jones calls "the rational adoration of the only true God" which is clearly the monotheistic God of the Bible. In his essay "On the Gods of Greece, Italy and India," Jones remarks:

> We cannot justly conclude, by arguments preceding the proof of facts, that one idolatrous people must have borrowed their deities, rites, and tenets from another; since Gods of all shapes and dimensions may be framed by the boundless powers of imagination, or by the frauds and follies of men, in countries never connected; but, when features of resemblance, too strong to have been accidental, or observable in different systems of polytheism, without fancy or prejudice to colour them and improve their likeness, we can scarce help believing, that some connection has immemorially subsisted between several nations, who have adopted them: it is my design in this essay, to point out such a resemblance between the popular worship of the old *Greeks* and *Italians* and that of the Hindus; nor can there be room to doubt of a great familiarity between their strange religions and that of *Egypt*, *China*, *Persia* ... From all this, if it be satisfactorily proved, we may infer a general union or affinity between the most distinguished inhabitants of the primitive world, at the time when they deviated, as they did too early deviate, from the rational adoration of the only true God.
>
> (1799a: 229–30)

Jones is not dismissive of the Hindu pantheon of gods and goddesses but sees them as a sign of a primitive state common to many nations. He uses the term "heathen" both for Hindus and Europeans, to indicate their unrefined state. In fact, he does not see much difference between what he calls the "Gods of the *Indian* and *European* heathens." He states that "in one capacity or another, there exists a striking similitude between the chief objects of worship in ancient *Greece* or *Italy* and in the very interesting country, which we now inhabit" (Jones 1799a: 232).[9] He draws attention to the resemblances between Gaṇeśa and Janus, Manu and Saturn, Ceres and Lakṣmī, Jupiter and Indra, Śiva and Zeus, Durgā and Venus, Pārvatī and Juno, Rāma and Dionysus, and so forth. For Jones, both Hindu and Greco-Roman gods and goddesses are the products of imagination rather than of rational thought. Being in their primitive state, both Hindu and European "heathens" are not as yet capable of exercising their rational faculties. The outcome is that the biblical truth has been distorted into fable by imagination (ibid. 230). As Balagangadhara points out:

> Generally, the eighteenth-century thinkers argued that the origin of religion – especially the primitive or the heathen ones – had to do with the fact that they, the "others," hypostatized natural forces into gods with human and semi-divine attributes and embellishments, and thus inventing their pantheon. Being not yet capable of rational and abstract thinking, the early man used the fanciful imagination that he was endowed with. This was at the root of those fantastical creations and absurd stories that constituted his religious world. These mythologies … are the products of "mythical thought," standing opposed to which is "rational" or "scientific" thought.
>
> (1994: 132)

For Jones, Hinduism has more to do with imagination than with reason but this does not lead him to conclude that it is a false religion, although occasionally he refers to Hinduism as an "erroneous religion" (Jones 1799b: 22). He finds in it a less refined version of biblical truth. This does not imply that Hinduism is morally corrupt but only that it is still in a state of infancy. Unlike most missionaries of the time, Jones does not associate Hindu worship of deities with moral depravity. For William Ward, the Hindu god Kṛṣṇa appears a "lascivious character" who is detrimental to the moral health of his worshippers, whereas in his letter to Charles Wilkins (Cannon 1970: 652) Jones speaks of being "charmed with *Crishen*."[10] Jones' sympathetic attitude is the outcome of his hypothesis that Hindus are still in a state of of childhood – yet to grow out of their wild imagination and innocence. Therefore it does not make any sense to attribute the worship of images to their moral degeneration. He remarks: "It never seems to have entered the heads of the legislators or people that anything natural could be offensively obscene;

a singularity, which pervades all their writings and conversation, but is no proof of the depravity in their morals" (Jones 1799a: 261).[11] For Jones, Hindus are like the Israelites who needed rituals and ceremonies because of their childlike- ness. With the full manhood in the form of Jesus, these rituals are made superfluous.

Primitive monotheism to biblical monotheism

As we have seen, Jones identifies in the ancient texts of Hindus a distorted monotheism. Biblical monotheism functions as the one rational and enlightened faith to which all belong but migration to various places resulted in departure from the monotheism of the biblical religion. Jones is concerned to recover the "ancient purity" (Jones 1799a: 23)[12] contained in ancient Sanskrit texts, for they alone contain the uncontaminated monotheism. As Balagangadhara points out: "The rediscovery of India and its culture meant a discovery of an ancient culture, which was contemporaneous with the modern one. The ancients were not dead but merely found living in another part of the world. These ancients ... represented the childhood of man" (Balagangadhara 1994: 132). In other words, Romantic thinkers who saw Indian culture as representing the infancy of European culture, "did not go beyond or against the Enlightenment tradition – but merely extended it with a fanciful twist" (ibid.: 133). While European civilization had matured, Indian culture was still in its early stages. Its growth had stagnated and thus it became comparable with the dead Greek and Roman cultures. India's past was important for Europe's definition of its own identity. If at all there was any trace of purity in Hinduism, it was located in the Veda, and this came to be seen as the true "Hinduism" while the present was seen as a distortion of the past. Placing the Veda within the biblical time scheme, Jones was trying to demonstrate that the Veda was the earliest declaration of undiluted monotheism. As Trautmann points out: "It was specifically within a short biblical time-frame that India and the Veda acquired their heightened significance for Europeans as a window upon the original condition of mankind and of ancient wisdom" (Trautmann 1997: 193). Having securely situated Hindu texts within the biblical time-framework, Jones felt free to interact with them. They were not to be discarded as they revealed the primitive state of Europeans in their bygone days.

Hindu texts made secure

Jones' discovery of an Indo-European family of languages and shared origins meant that India and Europe were strangers no more. While this discovery disturbed the Western world, it led Jones and other orientalists to explore India and Sanskrit literature with great enthusiasm. It also meant that the antiquity of Hindu sacred literature could now be explained and affirmed without feeling intimidated or being put off by its strangeness. Jones, who subscribed to the biblical scholarship of the time that regarded biblical events as historical facts, saw the Book of Genesis as the definitive record of the history of the world, and regarded Moses as the first historian. This view of Genesis led Jones to place Hindu texts such as the Vedas, the *Bhāgavata Purāṇa* and Manu's *Dharmaśāstra* within the biblical framework (1799a: 245).[13] What Jones was implying was that these texts were important not so much for their own merits as for their validation of Christianity. Once he had established the primacy of biblical history, Jones was comfortable with Hindu texts. To put it differently, they were not seen as a threat to Christianity but as endorsing or corroborating biblical truth. Now that Hindu texts were divested of their independent agency, they were not impenetrable; they had been made safe, especially for Christians. For Jones, Hindu texts were not totally corrupt as William Ward (whom we will encounter later) perceived them. Rather, Hindu texts verifed for Jones the truth and primacy of the biblical revelation.

Hindu chronology through a biblical lens

One of the characteristics of colonialism is that it deprives the natives of their own sense of time and reinscribes time in terms of the colonizer's version of it. Jones divests Hindu chronology of its own lengthy time-sequence by "semitizing" it to suit his own conclusions. Eighteenth-century Western orientalists constructed Hindu notions of time and history largely from selective texts such as the *Mahābhārata*, *Purāṇas* and the *Dharmaśāstra* (Thapar 1996: 1).[14] Jones sees the Hindu concept of *yugas* through a biblical lens, thus reducing vast spans of time in order to show that Hindu chronology before Genesis can have no real significance. Jones does not dismiss the history of Hindus as of no significance. Now, having situated it within the Semitic framework, he believes it is possible to get glimpses of Hindu history, however fragmentary, from the Sanskrit literature which has been uncovered by the West. In the light of such an interpretative framework, anything before Genesis can have only metaphorical importance. Jones considers the biblical Flood, narrated by Moses, as the commencement of Hindu chronology. He compares the story of the flood in the *Bhāgavata Purāṇa* with the story of the universal flood in the Bible. Manu is warned of an impending flood and was saved by Lord Viṣṇu in his *matsya-avatāra* (fish incarnation). Manu and seven sages board a boat which is fastened to a horn on the fish's head, and are towed safely to the mountain top. When the the flood subsides, new creation begins. For Jones the story of Manu "seems evidently to be that of NOAH disguised by Asiatick fiction" (Jones 1799a: 237).[15] Manu is none other than the Noah of the Bible. Jones places the Purāṇic flood narrative within the biblical time-span, thus maintaining the primacy of biblical chronology:

> This epitome of the first *Indian* History, that is now extant, appears to me very curious and very important; for the story, though whimsically dressed up in the form of an allegory, seems to prove a primeval tradition in this country of the *universal deluge* described by MOSES, and fixes consequently the *time,* when the genuine *Hindu* Chronology actually begins.
>
> (Jones 1799a: 241–2)[16]

According to one of the four sources of Hindu mythology outlined by Jones, "Historical, or natural, truth has been perverted into fable by ignorance, imagination, flattery, or stupidity" (ibid.: 230).[17] The implication is that while the universal deluge is historical, the flood story in the *Purāṇas* is a distorted version of the historical truth embedded in the Bible. Jones appropriates the flood story to suit his conclusions, which is that biblical history is the reliable starting point of any meaningful understanding of history. It should not therefore be surprising to find the biblical narrative perverted in the *Purāṇas.* Attributing the story of creation in Manu's *Dharmaśāstra* to Christian sources, Jones compares the opening passage of Genesis with Manu's account of creation, in order to establish the primacy of the biblical version of creation. Jones remarks:

> That *water* was the primitive element and first work of the Creative Power, is the uniform opinion of the *Indian* philosophers; but, as they give so particular account of the general deluge and of the Creation, it can never be admitted, that their whole system arose from traditions concerning the flood only, and must appear indubitable, that their doctrine is in part borrowed from the opening of the *Birásit* or *Genesis* ...
>
> (1799a: 250–7)[18]

In his view, the sublimity of the Genesis account is greatly affected "by the *Indian* paraphrase of it, with which MENU, the son of BRAHMA, begins his address to the sages who sought to know how the universe came to be formed" (ibid. 1799a: 251).[19] Jones then goes on to compare the description of the flood in the *Dharmaśāstra* with the verses in the *Bhāgavata Purāṇa.* Commenting on the verses of the *Bhāgavata Purāṇa* which affirm the One Being in a magnificent way, Jones alerts readers that one may conclude these verses to be superior to the poetry and mythology of Greece and Rome, but that Mosaic diction excels: "Wild and obscure as these ancient verses must appear in a naked verbal translation, it will perhaps be thought by many, that the poetry or mythology of *Greece* or *Italy* afford no conceptions more awfully magnificent: yet the brevity and simplicity of the Mosaick diction are unequalled" (Jones 1799a: 252).[20] In other words, for Jones the poetry of the *Bhāgavata Purāṇa* has all the marks of a primitive culture, whereas biblical culture is refined.

Jones is keen to prove the authenticity of Mosaic history. He declares that "Either the first eleven chapters of *Genesis* ... are true, or the whole fabric of our national religion is false; a conclusion which none of us, I trust, would wish to be drawn" (ibid: 233).[21] Although the link between nations such as Egypt, India and Greece predates the advent of Moses, Jones asserts that "the proof of this proposition will in no degree affect the truth and sanctity of the *Mosaick* History, which, if confirmation were necessary, it would rather tend to confirm" (Jones 1799a: 276).[22] He goes on to say:

> There is no shadow then of a foundation for an opinion, that MOSES borrowed the first nine or ten chapters of *Genesis* from the literature of *Egypt*: still less can the adamantine pillars of our *Christian* faith be moved by the result of any debates on the comparative antiquity of the *Hindus* and *Egyptians*, or of any inquiries into the *Indian* Theology.
>
> (ibid.: 277)[23]

Jones' interest in Hindu mythology is more than a matter of curiosity. He reads Hindu mythology in terms of universal history, starting with the Book of Genesis. In situating the flood narrative in the *Purāṇas* within the biblical time-framework, what Jones is demonstrating is that Sanskrit literature is not inimical to the Bible. On the contrary, it is seen as confirming the historicity of the deluge and Moses. By forcing the Indian *yugas* into the biblical time-span, Jones makes the new orientalism project secure, and thereby shows that Hinduism is no threat to Christianity, and that one can safely admire Hinduism and accept the "antiquity for Sanskrit literature" as it endorses "the Bible against the skeptics upon their own, rationalistic terms" (Trautmann 1997: 74).

It is interesting to note that Jones' predecessors, such as Alexander Dow and Nathaniel Brassey Halhed, were open to the prospects of the long-drawn out Hindu chronology. Jones' Mosaic ethnology is not something new; it is a replication "of a very old ethnological paradigm" common to Jews, Christians, and Muslims, and for which universal validity is sought (Trautmann 1997: 53). In other words, the roots of universal history are seen to begin with Noah and his descendants. Jones writes:

> Whatever the comparative antiquity of the Hindu scriptures, we may safely conclude that the Mosaick and Indian chronologies are perfectly consistent; that Manu son of Brahma was the Adima, or first created mortal, and consequently our Adam; that Manu, child of the sun, was preserved with seven others, in a bahitra or capacious ark from our universal deluge, and must therefore be our Noah; ... and the dawn of

> true Indian history appears only three or four centuries before the Christian era, the preceding ages are clouded by allegory or fable.
>
> (Jones 1799a: 326–7)

By making Hindu chronology fall in line with biblical narratives, Jones is able to foreground two things: proof of the authenticity of biblical events, thus silencing critics who raised doubts about the historical validity of Mosaic history, and the benefits of studying "pagan" literature. He finds historical accounts in the Old Testament confirmed by outside sources. The *Purāṇas*, in Jones' view, offered independent evidence of the truth of the biblical narrative of the Flood. He draws several parallels between biblical and *Purāṇic* figures. Manu is identified with Noah, and the first Manu, the progenitor of the human race, with Adam. Jones tries to fit Viṣṇu's *avatāras* into the biblical framework. The *avatāras* of Viṣṇu, Jones states in his Third Anniversary Discourse, "relate no less clearly to an Universal Deluge, in which eight persons only were saved ... we may for the present assume, that the *second*, or *silver*, age of the *Hindus* was subsequent to the dispersion from the *Babel*; so that we have only a dark interval of about a *thousand* years" (1799a: 29). The first three *avatāras* of Viṣṇu are associated with the flood in the *Purāṇas*, and the story of the *matysa* (fish) *avatāra* has strong resemblances with the biblical Flood. Jones compares the *narasiṃha* (man-lion) *avatāra* with the biblical Nimzoa; the demon king, Bali, who was vanquished by Viṣṇu in his *vāmana* (dwarf) *avatāra*, with biblical Bel; Rāma, the seventh incarnation of Viṣṇu, with the biblical Raamah. As Trautmann explains, this reconciliation of Hindu chronology with that of the biblical one was achieved by flattening out lengthy spans of time signified by Hindu *yugas*:

> In this manner the whole series of avatars of Viṣṇu can be forced into the diluvian and postdiluvian chronology, and Sanskrit literature can be read as reporting the same historical events as does Genesis. But this reconciliation of Indian chronology with the biblical chronology is only possible by simultaneously rejecting the vast spans of time that make up the *yugas*, *kalpas*, and *manvantaras* of Indian time cycles. The four *yugas* are squeezed into the Ussherite chronology, rejecting the traditional figures for their duration (4,320,000 years for the entire cycle of four ages), or the traditional dating of the beginning of the Kali, namely 3102 BC ...
>
> (Trautmann 1997: 58–9)

Dismissing or rather erasing Hindu notions of *yugas,* Jones offers his own reading of the *yugas*. He reckons that "the duration of the Historical ages must needs be very unequal and disproportionate; while that of the *Indian yugs* is disposed so regularly and artificially, that it cannot be admitted as natural or probable" (Jones 1799a: 244).[24] In other words, such a "geometrical progression and technical arrangement excludes all ideas of History." Jones remarks that "men do not become reprobate in a geometrical progression or at the termination of regular periods" (ibid.).[25] Jones is aware that these remarks may find disfavor with ardent supporters of Indian antiquity but insists that the truth must be stated, which is, that the Veda does not predate the Universal Deluge but it only can have allegorical significance:

> I am sensible, how much these remarks will offend the warm advocates for *Indian* antiquity; but we must not sacrifice truth to a base fear of giving offence: that the Vedas were actually written before the flood, I shall never believe; nor can we infer from the preceding story, that the learned *Hindus* believe it; for the allegorical number of BRAHMA and the theft of the sacred books mean only, in a simpler language, that *the human race was become corrupt*; but that the Vedas are very ancient, and far older than other Sanscrit compositions, I will venture to assert from my own examination of them, and a comparison of their style with that of the *Purans* and the *Dherma Sastra*.
>
> (Jones 1799a: 245)[26]

Jones mythicizes certain aspects of Hinduism and historicizes those aspects that are relevant or crucial to the validation of Christianity. Jones' Mosaic ethnology accepts "Hindu flood mythology as history" and rejects "Indian cyclical time as mythology" (Trautmann 1997: 59). Jones seems to subscribe to the belief that "mythological history as articulated in the biblical criticism of the late eighteenth and early nineteenth centuries, which entailed the view that myth was not mere fable or unworthy fiction but 'the oldest history and the oldest philosophy'. Events in the Bible are in a mythic mode and miracles become the paradigm of reported historical events" (Majeed 1992: 35). In his discourse on the "The Chronology of Hindus," Jones remarks "that the *three first* ages of the *Hindus* are chiefly *mythological*, whether, their *mythology* was founded on the dark enigmas of their astronomers or on the heroick fictions of their poets, and that the *fourth,* or *historical*, age cannot be carried farther back than about two thousand years before CHRIST" (Jones 1799a: 309).[27] In other words, any account of history before the Christian era can be of no real significance as such accounts are regarded as fictitious. The Hindu notion of *yugas* posed problems for Western scholars in the seventeenth and eighteenth centuries as it contradicted the prevailing conceptions of biblical time. Orientalists such as Halhed saw some virtue in Hindu yugas but there were others, such as George Costard, a clergyman as well as writer, who wanted to "show that Sanskrit and its literature are more recent than Moses and that only the Bible is a reliable guide to early history." In Western geological discussions, doubts were raised regarding biblical chronology. There was a raging debate "over the claims of the great antiquity for Sanskrit literature" in Britain and France, "creating between them a situation in which new orientalism was allied to skepticism and against orthodox belief" (Trautmann 1997: 73–4).

In orientalist reckoning, cyclical time did not "recognize historical change; and in the absence of a sense of history there was no differentiation between myth and history" (Thapar 1996: 4). Thapar challenges the notion that cyclical time excludes other categories of time. From an eschatological point of view, "there is an evident difference of form between linear and cyclical time. But not only does cyclical time have a genesis and a predirected termination (as does linear time), it can also encompass segments of time consisting of historical chronologies. Cyclic time does not preclude other categories of time ..." (ibid. 1996: 8–9).

Interestingly, one of the Hindu texts to find its way into St Paul's Cathedral in London is Jones' translation of *The Laws of Manu*, to which he devoted most of his judicial career in India. The cathedral houses a magnificent statue of Jones in standing position, resting his hand on *The Institutes of Hindu Law*. The front pedestal of the statue displays details of a complex scene – two mysterious figures on either side, one holding a torch and the other a lighted lamp, and in the middle is a woman in a sari holding a three-faced image of God in his three forms (*Trimūrti*). There are scenes from Hindu mythology – a four-armed Viṣṇu in his *kūrma avatāra, devas* and *asuras* churning the ocean for the nectar of immortality, and so forth. The message is that Hindu mythology is not as strange as it appears, and that the truths of Christianity can be confirmed in Hindu scriptures. As Trautmann notes, "the scene as a whole, therefore, is presented not under the aspect of a depiction of pagan idolatry but as a benign, independent record of the truth of the biblical story of the universal flood" (Trautmann 1997: 80).

Romantic Jones

The discovery of Sanskrit literature

As with other orientalists, Jones subscribes to the notion of India's glorious past and degenerate present. In his Third Anniversary Discourse, he speaks favorably of India's past – its civilization, scriptures, religion, art, language, and literature. Although Hindus may appear degenerate now, they are heirs to a magnificent civilization – "that in some early age they were splendid in arts and arms, happy in government, wise in legislation, and eminent in various kinds of knowledge ... " (Jones 1799a: 25). He speaks about the greatness of Indian civilization, drawing attention to its three inventions: apologue, decimal scale and the game of chess, and to works on grammar, logic, rhetoric and music which testify to their "fertile and inventive genius" (ibid.: 33). In the essay "On the Literature of the

Hindus" by Goverdhan Caul (translated from Sanskrit to English by Jones), which contains Jones' brief commentary on diverse Hindu scriptures from the Veda to popular literature, he affirms the richness of Indian culture and its value for Europeans (Jones 1799a: 358). Hindus may have fallen from their glory but they possess a rich classical past, as rich as the Greco-Roman culture. India's ancient past is now comparable to Europe's classical past. He compares Indian poets such as Vālmīki, Vyāsa, and Kālidāsa with Greek poets and philosophers such as Homer, Plato, and Pindar. Jones speaks of the Sanskrit language as being "more perfect than the *Greek*, more copious than the *Latin* and more exquisitely refined than either" (ibid.: 26).[28]

Jones' representation of Hinduism needs to be seen in the light of his predetermined conceptual framework which links the East with "imagination" and the West with "reason." In his Second Anniversary Discourse Jones states: "To form an exact parallel between the works and actions of the Western and Eastern worlds, would require a tract of no inconsiderable length; but we may decide on the whole, that reason and taste are the grand prerogatives of *European* minds, while the *Asiaticks* have soared to loftier heights in the sphere of imagination" (Jones 1799a: 11). He acknowledges their excellence in music, poetry, and painting, but when it comes to reason, the West excels in science and Asiaticks are "mere children" compared with Western nations (ibid.: 15). Having constructed this main distinction between the East and West, Jones feels free to explore the delights that the world of Sanskrit literature can offer. He shows an enthusiastic appreciation of Hindu literature, declaring: "Their lighter Poems are lively and elegant; their Epicks, magnificent and sublime in the highest degree; their *Puranas* comprise a series of mythological Histories ... and their *Vedas* ... which is called *Upanishat,* abound with noble speculations in metaphysicks, and fine discourses on the being and attributes of God" (ibid.: 33).[29] As was Warren Hastings, Jones too was highly impressed by the *Bhagavadgītā* and believed that if Europeans desired "to form a correct idea of *Indian* religion and literature, let them begin with forgetting all that has been said on the subject, by ancients or moderns, before the publication of the Gītā" (ibid.: 363).[30] While Jones rated the *Gītā* highly, Max Müller, despite being the product of the German Romantic tradition, did not share Jones' keen admiration of it. In fact, he lamented that a text of little importance had come to occupy an enormous significance in the West. In Müller's reckoning, "It was a real misfortune that Sanskrit literature became first known to the learned public in Europe through specimens belonging to the second ... period" (ibid. 1892: 90). The *Gītā*, in his view, was the product of a degenerate period whereas the Veda was the product of an uncorrupt period. To put it differently, with the discovery of the Veda, the *Gītā* mattered little. In one of his 1882 lectures to British candidates for the Civil Service, Müller refers to the *Gītā* as "a rather popular and exoteric [sic] exposition of Vedantic doctrines" (Müller 1892: 252). Early orientalists had to begin with *smṛti* texts such as the *Dharmaśāstras, Bhagavadgītā* and other classical works in Sanskrit as "at that stage of Sanskritic studies no authentic text of the Vedas was available, nor was Vedic Sanskrit known" (Chaudhuri 1974: 136).[31]

The world of Sanskrit literature is a revelation to Jones for what it revealed about Europe's primitive past. He reconstructs a romantic image of Europe – the lost innocence of childhood and adolescence – in his composition of hymns to Hindu deities, and his translation of Jayadeva's *Gītā-Govinda* and Kālidāsa's *Śakuntalā*. For Jones, the poetry of the *Bhāgavata Purāṇa* is significant for its "wild and obscure" verses (Jones 1799a: 252).[32] Like Müller, Jones does not disregard the devotional literature of Hindus. Rather, he seems to be as drawn to the devotional mysticism of *Gītā-Govinda* in which he finds uncorrupted passion and the love of a devotee for his deity. As with other orientalists, Jones is enchanted by the "mystic East" which he regards as the feminine self of Europe, now recoverable through Hindu mystical love poetry and non-dualistic Vedāntic mysticism. Whether it be mystical devotion, or union, both defy reason, so they tend to be expressed in an allegorical or symbolic fashion. Since Jones regards metaphors and allegories as belonging to the realm of "imagination," he is not looking for the "rational" religion, but the one that reflects Europe's own romantic past.

Jones' romantic admiration for Sanskrit literature stands in sharp contrast to the denunciation of it by missionaries and others. While for nineteenth-century Baptist missionaries (whom we will encounter later) Hindu texts represent all that is dreadful and unchristian, for Jones they corroborate biblical truth (see Biblical Jones). To state it differently, Hindu texts are not dangerous, rather they uncover the story of the lost childhood of European culture. Jones finds Sanskrit literature more appealing than Greek literature: "I am in love with the *Gopia*, charmed with *Crishen*, an enthusiastick admirer of Ram" and "a devout adorer" of Yudhiṣṭhira, Arjuna, Karṇa and all other warriors in the epic Mahābhārata, "who appear greater in my eyes than Agamemnon, Ajax, and Achilles ... when I first read the Iliad" (Cannon 1970: 652).[33] Jones speaks of Kṛṣṇa endearingly in his letter to Warren Hastings. He compares his sadness at the departure of Hastings to Arjuna's at the ascent of Kṛṣṇa from earth: "I long to see the Geita,[34] of which you gave me a taste in this room. The ascent of Crishen from earth was not more afflicting to Erjun than your departure will be to [me]" (Cannon 1970: 660).[35]

Jones, as a poet, affirms all that is ridiculed by Utilitarians (James Mill) and missionaries (William Carey and William Ward) and others. They see Hindu veneration of feminine deities as a mark of effeminacy and moral depravity, especially the passionate *bhakti*, devotion expressed towards Kṛṣṇa by devotees who saw themselves as *gopīs* pining for Kṛṣṇa. Jones is drawn to the very thing that the Baptist missionaries loathed – the erotic mystical love of Rādhā and Kṛṣṇa which is the subject of a twelfth-century Sanskrit lyric poem *Gītā-Govinda* which Jones translated. Unlike Baptist missionaries, Jones does not make a direct link between eroticism and moral depravity; he sees it as a sign of a "primitive" state common to all cultures in their early stages. While William Ward, as we shall see later, denounces any fervent outpouring of *bhakti* such as he witnessed on the streets of nineteenth-century Bengal, Jones treats the passionate love of Rādhā and Kṛṣṇa as "a mystical religious allegory, though it seems on a transient view to contain only the sentiments of a wild and voluptuous libertinism" (Jones 1779a: 445). He takes care to tone down sensual passages in the poem knowing that it would offend European notions of propriety. It is by subduing and domesticating the sensual imagery that Jones introduces *śṛṇgāra rasa* (erotic pleasure or love*)* to his European audience. In his paper to the Asiatic Society in 1791 "On the Mystical Poetry of the Persians and Hindus," he remarks: "The loves of CRISHNA and RADHA, or the reciprocal attraction between the divine goodness and the human soul, are told at large in the tenth book of the *Bhagavat,* and are the subject of a little *Pastoral Drama*, entitled *Gitagovinda* .... After having translated the *Gitagovinda* word for word, I reduced my translations to the form, in which it is now exhibited; omitting only those passages, which are too luxuriant and too bold for an *European* taste ..." (ibid. 1799a: 462). Jones exercises a similar caution in "A Hymn to Durga." He prefers the fierce goddess in her gentler aspect, as Pārvatī, but not in her terrifying aspect as Kālī. Pārvatī succeeds in awakening *kāma* or sensual desire in the ascetic Śiva by her austerities. In other words, she tames the ascetic Śiva by drawing him into the world of marriage. Realizing that certain types of love-making may appear odd to his European readers, Jones subdues the erotic element in his hymn to Durgā. The passionate love-making of Śiva and Pārvatī that shakes the entire fabric of the universe is rendered in a hushed tone:

> The rest, my song conceal:
> Unhallow'd ears the sacrilege might be rue.
> Gods alone to Gods reveal
> In what stupendous note th' immortals woo.
> (Jones 1799c: 328)

Jones prefers to present the Hindu feminine aspect in a sober manner to please the classical taste of his European audience. He adopts a similar treatment in his translation of Kālidāsa's *Śakuntalā*. Jones is keen that "the play not be performed in its entirety to a Calcutta audience of the East India Company officials and their wives, nor that the expanded version be read in England" (Thapar 1999a: 200). As Thapar points out: "Orientalism was trying to define and comprehend the culture of the colonised in European terms. Thus the colonised are viewed as civilised, but their civilisation may take some unpalatable forms, and these can be corrected or deleted" (ibid.: 201). As we shall see later, a reprint of Muddhupalani's erotic epic *Radhika Santwanam*, celebrating the love of Rādhā and Kṛṣṇa, was banned by the colonial government backed by some Hindus, as it was seen as endangering the moral health of the natives.

East and West – philosophical affinities

If in the sphere of mythology Jones finds resemblances between Hindu and Greco-Roman classical gods and goddesses, in the philosophical realm Jones finds parallels between Greek and Hindu thought. He draws classical affinities between Sanskrit and Greek, compares Grecian and Indian philosophical schools – Gautama with Aristotle, Jaimini with Socrates, Vyāsa with Plato, and Kapila with Pythagoras (Jones 1799a: 360–61).[36] Jones speaks highly of the *Vedānta*, comparing it with Plato and Pythagoras – the latter two are seen as deriving "their sublime theories from the same fountain with the sages of *India*" (ibid.: 28).[37] Although Jones views both Indians and Europeans as deriving their sublime theories from a common source,[38] his "views were dominated by the idea that India itself was not the original home of the religious and philosophical tradition of the West, but rather represented an old offshoot of an original source common to both East and West" (Halbfass 1988: 63).

Jones finds the Vedāntic notion of *mukti* (liberation) very appealing. "The Mucti, or *Elysian* happiness of the *Vedanta* School," he states "is far more sublime; for they represent it as total absorption, though not such as to destroy consciousness, in the divine essence" (Jones 1799a: 272).[39] In his Eleventh Discourse "On the Philosophy of Asiaticks," Jones speaks approvingly of Vedānta but also cautions against premature evaluation of it. Pointing out that he requires sufficient proof in order "to profess a belief in the doctrine of the Vedanta, which human reason alone could, perhaps, neither fully demonstrate, nor fully disprove," he warns against treating lightly "a system wholly built on purest devotion" (ibid.: 166). His discourse ends with a non-dualistic affirmation: "[The] spirit, from which these created beings proceed; through which having proceed from it they live; toward which they tend and in which they are ultimately absorbed, that spirit study to know; that spirit is the Great One" (ibid.: 174). As with other orientalists, Jones posits Śaṅkara's Vedānta as the cardinal philosophy of Hindus – one that unifies the diverse strands within Hinduism.

Jones' deist tendencies come to the fore when he relates to the spirituality of the East. In Vedāntic mystical thought, he finds echoes of Platonic mysticism. Jones' interest in Hindu mystical thought is apparent in his hymns to Nārāyaṇa and Sūrya. Whether it be Hindu law, mythology or philosophy, Jones makes them safe by rendering them in terms familiar to his European readers. Employing the Pindaric ode, in his "A Hymn to Na'ra'yena" (1785) Jones invokes in a Miltonic fashion the mysterious and abstract power immanent in all creation but which is at the same time beyond all names and forms.

The opening lines of the poem affirm, in Jones' own words, "the sublimest attributes of the Supreme Being" (Jones 1799c: 367).

SPIRIT of Spirits, who, through ev'ry part
Of space expanded and of endless time,
Beyond the stretch of lab'ring thought sublime,
Badst uproar into beauteous order start,
Before Heav'n was, Thou art:
Ere spheres beneath us roll'd or spheres above,
Ere earth in firmamental ether hung,
Thou satst alone; till through thy mystick Love,
Things unexisting to existence sprung,
And grateful descant sung.

(ibid.: 369)

While in his hymns to goddesses Lakṣmī and Gaṅgā Jones addresses the personal (*saguṇa*) aspect of the divine, in his hymn to Narayena the focus is on the non-personal (*nirguṇa)* aspect. In other words, he moves from the sphere of *bhakti* (devotion) which implies a personal relationship with one's deity, to the sphere of mystical thought. Although not a deist himself, Jones' deist leanings[40] are apparent in this poem. He speaks of the immanence or the all-pervading presence of Viṣṇu in the whole of creation, as Viṣṇu's name implies, yet Jones takes a deist position in that he makes a distinction between the Creator and the phenomenal world. In other words, as Freeman points out, Jones "superimposes deism upon the Eastern nondual idea that the Supreme is an energy not a work." He does not see "that the Creator itself is this energy" but applies it only to the creation (Freeman 1998: 148–9). In the hymn's prefatory argument, Jones remarks: "the whole Creation was rather an *energy* than a *work*, by which the Infinite Being, who is present at all times in all places, exhibits to the minds of his creatures a set of perceptions" (Jones 1779c: 367). Yet Jones is also drawn to non-dualism, as can be seen in the concluding section of the hymn – the dividing line between the object and subject collapses. Jones describes his delight in being absorbed in the divine. He states:

My soul absorb'd One only Being knows,
Of all perceptions One abundant source,
Whence ev'ry object ev'ry moment flows:
Suns hence derive their force,
Hence planets learn their course;
But suns and fading words I view no more:
God only I perceive; God only I adore.

(ibid. 1799c: 373)

Freeman draws attention to the orientalist application of the concept "sublime" to ancient Sanskrit texts which came to acquire greater importance in Western esthetic philosophy in the eighteenth century. Jones' use of the term "sublime" indicates the inability to fathom Sanskrit texts of antiquity with "labouring thought." In other words, the Sanskrit texts challenge Enlightenment notions of discursive reasoning and logic which are seen to unlock the meaning embedded in texts. As Freeman points out: "When the British writers superimpose the nondualism they find in the Sanskrit 'sublime' onto their Enlightenment tradition the effect is one of profound ambivalence, revealed in the simultaneous attraction to and repulsion from the state they are calling sublime" (Freeman 1998: 142).

Jones credits Hindus with some degree of rationality when it comes to belief in rebirth. Despite his rather conservative belief with regard to Genesis (Jones 1799a: 233),[41] Jones finds the Hindu notion of rebirth far more rational and appealing than the Christian notion of punishment. In his letter to Earl Spencer, Jones states: "I am no Hindu; but I hold the doctrine of Hindus concerning a future state to be incomparably more rational, more pious, and more likely to deter men from vice, than the horrid opinions inculcated by Christians on punishments *without end*" (Cannon 1970: 766).[42] Jones' ambivalence becomes evident when one compares the Hindu notion of *Trimūrti* with the Christian Trinity. While classical comparison between Hindu and Greek systems of thought are legitimate and permissible, any comparison between the Hindu *Trimūrti* and the Christian Trinity is seen as undervaluing the sublimity of the Christian doctrine. Jones draws attention to missionary misconceptions of the Hindu notion of the *Trimūrti* and the Christian Trinity. He was displeased with missionaries trying to impress on Hindus that they "were even now almost *Christians*" because they equated the Hindu triad (Brahmā, Viṣṇu and Śiva with the Christian trinity (Jones 1799a: 277).[43] He clarifies that the "*Indian* Triad, and that of *Plato* ... are infinitely removed from the holiness and sublimity of the doctrine, which pious *Christians* have deduced from texts in the Gospel, though other *Christians*, as pious, openly profess their dissent from them" (ibid.: 277–8).[44] Jones then goes on to state that "each sect must be justified by its own faith and good intentions" and "that the tenet of our church cannot without profaneness be compared with that of the *Hindus*, which has only an apparent resemblance to it, but a very different meaning" (ibid.: 278).[45] Likewise, for that matter, any comparison between Kṛṣṇa of the Purāṇas and Jesus of the Gospels is untenable. Furnishing a brief outline of Kṛṣṇa story recorded in the *Bhāgavata Purāṇa*, Jones asserts the historic authenticity of the Christian story: "This motley story must induce an opinion that the spurious Gospels, which abounded in the first age of *Christianity*, had been brought to *India*, and the wildest parts of them repeated to the *Hindus*, who ingrafted them on the old fable of CE'SAVA, the APOLLO of *Greece*" (ibid.: 278–9).[46]

Hindu goddesses and colonial enterprise

Within a short time of his arrival in India, Jones began to compose a series of nine hymns to Hindu deities. All of the hymns appeared in the 1799 six-volume edition of Jones' *Works*, but some of them were published earlier in 1785 in the *Asiatick Miscellany*.[47] Of the nine hymns, five are addressed to female deities (Lakṣmī, Sarasvatī, Durgā, Gaṅgā, Bhavānī), and four to male deities (Kāma, Indra, Sūrya and Nārāyaṇa). In the prefatory argument which precedes each hymn, Jones describes the nature and function of the deity being addressed, and also draws analogies between the Hindu and Western classical pantheon of gods and goddesses.

My main concern is with how Jones appropriates Hindu goddesses in his hymns, and the kind of Hinduism he constructs in the process. I focus on three of his hymns, two of which are concerned with pragmatic matters (British rule in India), whilst one is about recovering for Hindus their glorious past. As pointed out earlier, Jones feels free to approach the feminine in his poetry, for in his conceptual framework, both poetry and the feminine are linked with "imagination." It is ironic that Jones seeks the favor of the deities of "pagans" in order to legitimize colonial authority. In his "A Hymn to Lacshmi" (1788), Jones addresses the goddess as a Hindu would: "Thee Goddess, I salute; thy gifts I sing" (Jones 1799c: 357). His appeal to Lakṣmī is informed by what the goddess represents and her usefulness in establishing the colonial rule. Lakṣmī symbolizes good fortune, peace, happiness, wellbeing, and harmony. She is widely worshipped by Hindus of all backgrounds, especially by the merchant caste during the autumn festival of lights, Deepāvālī (the beginning of New Year for some Hindus). In Vedic literature Lakṣmī is associated with royal power, and it is fitting that Jones, as one who belongs to the nation of shopkeepers, has chosen such a deity for legitimizing the colonial project. All that Lakṣmī signifies is much needed for the successful implementation of colonial rule. In keeping with the prevailing mood of the time, Jones, too, sees British rule as a sign of divine providence. He implores Lakṣmī to instruct the "erring Hindu mind" muddled by "priestly wiles" and urges the Hindu to look to the British who have come to establish a just and benign rule – with "the wand of empire, not the rod." Obviously Jones sees the British government as a blessing for the natives who are still too much in their infancy to be able to manage their own affairs and who are therefore in need of the benevolent support of the colonial parent. As a lawyer, Jones seeks to govern the natives by their own laws in which he feels Hindus need to be tutored (see Juridical Jones). In the concluding part of this hymn, Jones represents Hindus as "pagans" implying that they are still in their primitive state. Although the natives err, they are not without feelings and "*though pagans, they are men*" (emphasis mine).

> Oh! Bid the patient *Hindu* rise and live.
> His erring mind, that wizard lore beguiles

Clouded by priestly wiles,
To senseless nature bows for nature's GOD.
Now, stretch'd o'er ocean's vast from happier isles,
He sees the wand of empire, not the rod:
Ah, may those beams, that western skies illume,
Disperse th' unholy gloom!
Meanwhile may laws, by myriads long rever'd,
Their strife appease, their gentler claims decide;
So shall their victors, mild with virtuous pride,
To many a cherish'd grateful race endear'd,
With temper'd love be fear'd:
Though mists profane obscure their narrow ken,
They err, yet feel; though pagans, they are men.
(Jones 1799c: 365)

In the prefatory Argument to the hymn to Lakṣmī, Jones adopts a utilitarian approach to Hindu beliefs and practices. Clearly, his appropriation of Hindu deities is informed by the commercial interests of the empire and its mercantile success. He tells his British audience that the Empire cannot afford to ignore "the wild fables of idolaters" whose "industry" is financially beneficial to the colonial government. Jones remarks:

> We may be inclined perhaps to think, that the wild fables of idolaters are not worth knowing, and that we may be satisfied with misspending our time in learning the Pagan Theology of old *Greece* and *Rome;* but we must consider, that the allegories contained in the Hymn to Lacshmi constitute at this moment the prevailing of a most extensive and celebrated Empire, and are devoutly believed by many millions, whose industry adds to the revenue of *Britain*, and whose manners, which are interwoven with their religious opinions, nearly affect all *Europeans*, who reside among them.
> (Jones 1799c: 356)

As with the previous hymn, "A Hymn to Ganga" (1785) is concerned with the implementation of the imperial project in India.[48] In these two hymns Jones figures both as an orientalist and as a benevolent colonial administrator. One of the marks of colonialism is that it makes the vanquished participate in their defeat and offer their gratitude to those who dispossessed them. Jones takes the role of the dispossessed and speaks on their behalf. He speaks in the guise of a Hindu, playing the role of a grateful native who welcomes the arrival of the British and Britain's desire to govern Indian subjects by their own laws. In the prefatory Argument to the hymn, Jones seeks Goddess Gaṅgā's approval of British rule in India. Gaṅgā, the river goddess, is conceived as the mother – the one who nourishes, protects, purifies, and sanctifies all those who seek her help. He attributes this work to a "BRAHMEN, in an early age of HINDU antiquity" who is no other than himself, and "who by a prophetical spirit, discerns the toleration and equity of the BRITISH government, and concludes with a prayer *for its peaceful duration under good laws well administered*" (Jones 1799c: 383). In treating this hymn as the work of a brahmin pundit of antiquity, Jones not only legitimizes the colonial project but also continues to foster dependency and control. In other words, he is presenting brahmin pundits as willing collaborators in the establishment of British rule in India. In the last stanza Jones implores the Goddess Gaṅgā to be kind to the British rulers who have come from colder regions to govern the natives by their own Sanskrit laws. Britain requires Gaṅgā's grace and consent as much as the natives, for whom Gaṅgā has salfvific significance:

> With growing gifts thy suppliants bless,
> Who with full sails in many a light-oar'd boat
> On thy jasper bosom float;
> Nor frown, dread Goddess, on a peerless race
> With lib'ral heart and martial grace,
> Wafted from colder isles remote:
> As they preserve our laws, and bid our terror cease,
> So be their darling laws perserv'd in wealth, in joy, in peace!
>
> (Jones 1799c: 392)

It is obvious that Jones is seeking to justify the British presence and involvement in Indian affairs by petitioning the Goddess Gaṅgā. In his ambitious epic poem *Britain Discovered* (1787), which he did not live to complete, Gaṅgā fears that the establishment of British rule will result in the destruction of her religion and culture. She fears that the victors "will possess themselves of her banks, profane her waters, mock the temples of the *Indian* divinities, appropriate the wealth of their adorers, introduce new laws, a new religion, a new government, insult the *Brahmens*, and disregard the sacred ordinances of *Brihma*" (Teignmouth 1804: 484). Jones introduces a benevolent Druid who dispels such fears by recommending "the government of the *Indians* by their own laws" (ibid.: 487–8). What is ironical is that while Jones is very keen not to impose alien laws on Indians, he does not seem to mind outsiders ruling the natives by those natives' own laws. Moreover, he considers that these laws need to be discovered and made intelligible to the natives. As the natives are not as yet ready to govern themselves, they require the British to implement these laws so that the natives are given a fair trial (see Juridical Jones).

A theme which recurs in the orientalist representation of Hinduism is that of the venerated past and degenerate present. Jones sets himself the task of recovering for Hindus their uncontaminated past. In the "Hymn to Surya" (1786), he regards himself as the first non-native to learn Sanskrit, "the language of the gods," and to draw from oriental knowledge in all its pristine glory. Referring to himself as the one who has come to unlock hidden treasures, Jones utters:

> He came; and, lisping our celestial tongue,
> Though not from *Brahma* sprung,
> Draws orient knowledge from its fountain pure,
> Through caves obstructed long, and paths too long obscure.
> (Jones 1799c: 353)

In this hymn's prefatory argument, Jones uses terms such as "heathen" and "idolatry" to draw attention to the superstitious practices of both Hindus and Europeans. He engages in a comparative exercise by drawing an analogy between the Sūrya of Hindus and "the Phoebus of Europeans." Jones' interest is primarily in the classical past of Hindus which sits well with the classical past of Europe. He writes: "A PLAUSIBLE opinion has been entertained by learned men, that the principal source of idolatry among the ancients was their enthusiastick admiration of the Sun; and that, when the primitive religion of mankind was lost amid the distractions of establishing regal government" (ibid.: 345). He distinguishes between what he considers as idolatrous worship of the sun, and the "sublime Theology of the Philosophers, whose understandings were too strong to admit popular belief, but whose influence was too weak to reform it" (ibid.: 345). In Jones' view, what the "heathens" attributed to the Sun, the "wiser ancestors had attributed to the one eternal MIND" (ibid.: 345). In other words, Jones affirms the mystical conception of the One – "Sūrya" symbolizing the "Eternal Mind" – but treats the Hindu worship of the sun god as a product of primitive religion. Nevertheless, there are rich treasures lying beneath the "low thoughts" which he seeks to recover:

> Yes; though the *Sanscrit* song
> Be strown with fancy's wreathes,
> And emblems rich, beyond low thoughts refin'd,
> Yet heav'nly truth it breathes
> With attestation strong,
> That, loftier than thy sphere, th' Eternal Mind,
> Unmov'd, unrival'd, undefil'd,
> Reigns with providence benign:
> (Jones 1799c: 353–4)

Unlike William Ward and John Farquhar, Jones does not condemn "idolatry" but regards it as a degenerate form of the pure religion enshrined in the Veda. It is a puerile practice that is confined to the primitive civilization. To put in another way, Jones perceives idolatry as belonging to a state of childhood, and considers that the "noble savage" needs to grow but needs the help of the evolved civilization which, in this case, is Europe, to enable it to arrive at a state of maturity.

To briefly sum up this section, these hymns represent Hindus as still taking delight in their "pagan" state and seeking gratification in their idolatrous practices. Although Jones sees that Hindus need to be delivered from this "effeminate" state, he finds the diligence of these "pagan" Hindus favorable to the commercial wellbeing of the empire. We see Jones as an orientalist engaged in recovering for Hindus their lost glorious past; as a grateful native seeking the blessings of the deities for the success of the imperial project; as a benign colonial administrator engaged in legitimizing the commercial interests of colonial government in the making; and as an oriental scholar-administrator concerned with educating natives in their own laws. These are not discrete roles but overlap with one another.

Juridical Jones

Oriental and colonial pursuits

One of the tasks of postcolonialism is to draw attention to the link between knowledge and power in the orientalist quest for knowledge of Eastern cultures. Postcolonialism seeks to show that the orientalist yearning to know other cultures is not simply a quest for disinterested knowledge but is intertwined with a variety of factors. Jones' interest in Sanskrit and his desire to bring out a new compilation of Hindu laws cannot be divorced from his colonial duties as a judge of the Calcutta Supreme Court. In other words, these were not simply the oriental pursuits of a scholar, undertaken with no ulterior motive. Along with others, Jones was not only reconstructing a body of knowledge about India and its religious and cultural traditions but treating them as an authoritative source of information upon which both the colonizer and colonized could draw, with the former having control of it.

Jones' oriental desire not only "to know *India*" but to know it "better than any other European ever knew it" came to be profitably used for the administrative needs of the colonial government (Cannon 1970: 751).[49] This is clearly encapsulated in his letter to Earl Cornwallis, seeking the earl's approval for the translation of *The Laws of Manu*. The earl's acceptance of his "offer to direct and translate his work" and granting Jones the freedom to appoint Hindu pundits to assist him in this task (Jones 1799b: 65),[50] is a significant indication of the growing link between orientalism and colonialism. In short, Jones' interest in Hindu laws is not an innocent engagement but one that is undertaken with the specific objective of domesticating Hindu laws in order to serve the needs of the empire. Assuming that Hindus believe in the sanctity and authority of a fixed a body of Hindu laws, Jones, in his letter to Earl Cornwallis, draws attention to the importance of Hindu laws. Indicating that the laws as they are appear are "obscure" but will gain clarity when they are recodified, Jones expresses his intention of translating the entire code:

> I have the pleasure of sending to the Governor General in Council, a system of Hindu laws, believed to be of divine authority, and, in my opinion, of the greatest importance. Having observed, that every page of the new compilation, by the Pandits employed by the Government, was filled with texts of Menu, I thought it best to translate the whole code of that ancient legislator; because I knew, that many of his laws, which appeared obscure when detached would be perfectly clear when connected.
>
> (Jones 1799b: 65–6)[51]

Not all oriental pursuits can be linked to the administrative needs of the colonial government, though some are. As a lawyer of the Supreme Court, Jones took upon himself the responsibility of recodifying Hindu laws. The English translations of two treatises on Hindu laws were undertaken and published under the following titles, for administrative purposes: Nathaniel Brassey Halhed's *A Code of Gentoo Laws* in 1776 and *A Digest of Hindu Law on Contracts and Successions*. The first was commissioned in 1773 by Warren Hastings, and the second was undertaken by Jones with the approval of Cornwallis in 1778, but completed by Henry Thomas Colebrooke and published after Jones' death. Jones found the translation of Halhed unsatisfactory as it was rendered into English from a Persian translation and was therefore lacking in authority (Cannon 1970: 797–8).[52] Jones' aim was to construct an authoritative text, translating directly from Sanskrit into English, thus investing the text with "a fixed form" (Derrett 1968: 250).

Although Jones was involved in literary pursuits, he spent most of his life in India on codifying Hindu laws, in the belief it would benefit both the colonial government and the natives. Even his learning of the sacred language, Sanskrit, was not without administrative implications. In fact in "A Discourse on the Institution of a Society," Jones saw the diversity of languages as "a sad obstacle to the progress of useful knowledge" but "the attainment of them is, however, indispensably necessary" to unlock their mysterious treasures (Jones 1799a: 5). Initially Jones left the study of Sanskrit to Charles Wilkins, but with Wilkins' departure for England, Jones embarked on learning Sanskrit himself, mainly for administrative purposes; soon he was entranced by it. He undertook the study and translation of Hindu laws because he wanted to be independent of native pundits whose interpretations he did not trust. It was only by neutralizing their agency that Jones sought to bring Hindu laws within the control and power of the colonial government, thus rendering the natives powerless.

Hindus and their laws

One of the characteristics of colonialism is that it employs the trope of the child in order to render the Other dependent on the colonial parent. That is to say, the "Other" is constructed as passive and therefore in need of assistance and protection. While Jones is keen to dispel the myth of "oriental despotism" by showing that Indians are in possession of divinely sanctioned laws and emphasizing that Hindus should be governed by their own laws (seen to be located in their ancient Sanskrit texts), at the same time he sees these laws as excluding even the notion of political liberty and also lacking the rationality of Western legal and ecclesiastical systems. In other words, the Hindu notion of authority is seen as deficient as it does not rest on the rational principles undergirding Western systems of judiciary. In his "Tenth Discourse, on Asiatick History, Civil, and Natural," Jones represents Hindus as politically immature, needing the protection and benevolence of the British government. In other words, Hindus are still too much in their infancy to appreciate the value of political liberty. Furthermore, in same discourse, Jones draws attention to the disastrous effect of despotism on Asiatic nations, in crippling and debasing "all those faculties which distinguish men from the herd" (1799a: 149). The implication is that Hindus are not in a fit state to govern themselves. An approach such as this sanctions colonial intervention and the establishment of British rule. Jones states in same discourse:

> In these *Indian* territories, which Providence has thrown into the arms of *Britain* for their protection and welfare, the religion, manners, and the laws of the natives preclude even the idea of political freedom; but their histories may possibly suggest hints for their prosperity, while our country derives essential benefit from the diligence of a placid and submissive people, who multiply with such increase …
>
> (Jones 1799a: 150)

Although back at home in England Jones advocates political and civil liberty, he does not apply the same principle to the colonies. True, he is against slavery and endorses eighteenth-century liberal ideas, but he considers that British rule is Divine Providence and that the natives placed under British rule need to be treated fairly and governed by their own laws. Jones embarks on a civilizing mission to the natives. He undertakes the task of refining and tailoring Hindu laws which, in his view, would benefit both the ruler and the ruled. Jones takes upon himself the role of a benevolent parent who is willing to tolerate the natives' childish religious practices. He declares in his "Charge to the Grand Jury," at Calcutta, on 4 December 1783: "The object then of the court … is plainly this: … that the natives of these important provinces be indulged in their own prejudices, and civil and religious, and suffered to enjoy their own customs unmolested" (Jones 1799b: 3).

Jones sees it as the moral duty of the British government to render proper justice and offer security to its subjects, to make concession to their harmless whims and indulgences so that the natives will come to recognize the benevolence of the British government as a blessing. Jones, in unequivocal terms, affirms Britain's dominion as beneficial to its subjects:

> Be it our care, Gentleman, to avoid by all means the highest imputation of injustice among those, whom it is the lot of *Britain* to rule; and, by giving them personal security, with every reasonable indulgence to their harmless prejudices, to conciliate their affection, while we promote their industry, so as to render our dominion over them a national benefit: and may our beloved country in all its dependencies enjoy the greatest national blessings, *good laws duly administered in settled peace!*
>
> (Jones 1799b: 15)[53]

It is interesting to note that while England in Jones' own time (and even now) had no written constitution or laws, laws were seen as an absolute necessity for the colonial subjects. The colonized needed to be governed by a written code in the name of democracy whereas this did not apply to the colonizers in their own country. Jones considered the written law as "generally hostile to the absolute rights of persons" whereas the unwritten law or common law as exemplifying "the true spirit of our constitution" (Teignmouth 1804: 212).[54]

Hindu laws: sublime and ridiculous

Jones tends to equate brahminical laws with the ecclesiastical laws of the Christian church, pundits with bishop's officials, and brahmins with Hindu priests (not all brahmins are priests) (Derrett 1968: 234–5). As with most orientalists, Jones adopts a textual approach to India and its traditions. He applies Western Protestant hermeneutical principles to Hindu laws and seeks to transform them into a uniform and fixed body of law. First of all, Jones assumes that a thorough textual knowledge would enable the British to govern efficiently. He treats *The Laws of Manu* as an authoritative text that would unlock the prevalent customs and manners of Hindus. Assuming that textual prescriptions are actual descriptions of reality, Jones calls for a literal adherence to textual or *śāstric* injunctions in order to ensure just governance or rule of the natives. In his preface to *The Institutes of Hindu Law*, Jones states that unless laws are related to "manners," they do not serve any purpose:

> It is a maxim in the science of legislation and government, that *Laws are of no avail without manners* ... that the best intended legislature provisions would have no beneficial effect even at first, and none at all in a short course of time, unless they were congenial to the disposition and habits, to the religious prejudices, and approved immemorial usages, of the people, for whom they were enacted; especially if that people universally and sincerely believed, that all their ancient usages and established rules of conduct had the sanction of an actual revelation from heaven ...
>
> (Jones 1799b: 53).

In the same Preface Jones also outlines what he sees as the "beauties" and "blemishes" of Hindu law. The law is seen as riddled with superstitions, ruthless priestcraft, obscure theology, meaningless ceremonies, yet containing redeemable features such as benevolent and exalted thoughts and sentiments about humankind. It is interesting to note that Jones spent almost all his working life in India on a task he considered crucial to the welfare of Britain, but one which paled into insignificance with the onset of an Anglicist administration. Jones remarks:

> The work, now presented to the *European* world, contains abundance of curious matter ... with many beauties ... and with many blemishes, which cannot be justified or palliated. It is a system of despotism and priestcraft, both indeed limited by law, but artfully conspiring to give mutual support, though with mutual checks; it is filled with strange conceits in metaphysicks and natural philosophy, with idle superstitions, and with a scheme of theology most obscurely figurative ... ; it abounds with minute and childish formalities, with ceremonies generally absurd and often ridiculous; the punishments are partial and fanciful ... nevertheless, a spirit of sublime devotion, of benevolence to mankind, and of amiable tenderness to all sentient creatures, pervades the whole work ...
>
> (Jones 1799b: 61–2)

Jones then goes on to state that the style of the legal texts has "a certain austere majesty" and inspires "a respectful awe" (ibid.: 62). While he acknowledges the divine source of Hindu laws, these laws do not necessarily constitute "true revelation," which is reserved for the biblical revelation. Nevertheless, as in his hymns to Hindu goddesses (Lakṣmī and Gaṅgā), Jones considers the laws as being of immense value both to the material and political welfare of Europe and to the subjects of the British Empire whose diligence contributes to the wealth of Britain. Clearly Jones' interest in Hindu law has much to do with its administrative and commercial value. He represents the natives as more than pleased with the British rule and who do not expect anything more than the freedom to carry on with their absurd religious practices and customs. Jones in his preface to *The Institutes of Hindu Law* states:

> Whatever opinion in short may be formed of MENU and his laws, in a country happily enlightened by sound philosophy and the only true revelation, it must be remembered, that those laws are actually revered, as the word of the Most High, by nations of great importance to the political and commercial interests of *Europe*, and particularly by many millions of *Hindu* subjects, whose well directed industry would add largely to the wealth of *Britain,* and who ask no more in return than protection for their persons and places of abode, justice in their temporal concerns, indulgence to the prejudices of their own religion, and the benefit of those laws, which they have been taught to believe sacred, and which alone they can possibly comprehend.
>
> (Jones 1799b: 62–3)

Justinian model for Hindu laws

One of the ways of domesticating the natives is to invade their textual spaces, thus denying them their own agency. Jones prescribes the Justinian model for the Hindu laws in order to wrest them from the control of native interpreters. This way, he thinks, can prevent any fraud or imposition by pundits. In his view, it is only by constructing a "fixed body of knowledge" that natives can be prevented from tampering with it. In proposing a Justinian model for the codification of Hindu laws, Jones is allowing himself a freedom to tamper with the indigenous text, a freedom which is not granted to the native interpreters. In his letter to Lord Cornwallis, Jones states:

> The great work, of which Justinian has the credit, consists of texts collected from law books of approved authority which in his time were extant at Rome ... It would not be unworthy of a British Government, to give the natives of these Indian provinces a permanent security for the due administration of justice among them, similar to that which Justinian gave to his Greek and Roman subjects.
>
> (Jones 1799b: 75)[55]

Jones' proposal to shape Hindu laws along Justinian lines implies that Hindu laws as they stand are beneficial neither for the colonizer nor the colonized. First, in making Hindu law fall in line with European legal categories, Jones is codifying Hindu law in terms alien to its own śāstric principles (Derrett 1968: 232–50).[56] He imposes uniformity on loosely knit textual injunctions compiled by diverse lawgivers. In his view, the laws as they stand lack any discernible coherence and serve no good purpose. They need pruning and tailoring to meet the needs of the colonial government. While orientalists are keen to govern Hindus by their own laws, the laws are not acceptable as they are. They need to be structured and made uniform in order to avoid any ambiguity or fraud. The aim is to transform the law books into a manageable and uniform body of knowledge as this would enable colonial administrators to check any inconsistency or ambiguity in the pundit's interpretation of law. Once this is achieved, pundits would be obliged to conform to the newly constructed code, thus allowing administrators to keep a check on false interpretation. Although Jones desires to rule the natives according to their own *śāstric* injunctions, he violates the very principles he wants to affirm.

Second, the decision to translate and codify Hindu laws has little to do with restoring their original character. The impulse behind translation is not so much to be true to the original as to convert them into a homogeneous and fixed body of knowledge. Jones is more concerned with constructing what he assumes to be a better and more authoritative code. He is replacing the multiple indigenous voices that went into the making of the laws, with one authoritative voice. In other words, he replaces brahminical authority with colonial authority and thereby makes the British administrators "patrons of the *śāstra*" (Derrett 1968: 225). The English translation is invested with more authority, thus dislodging the original Sanskrit version. Jones, like other orientalists, is working under the assumption that he is restoring Hindu laws to their original status, that it is only by going back to the origins that the Ur-text can be located and the purity of the laws recovered. As Cohn points out:

> Jones and others had the idea that there was historically in India a fixed body of laws, codes which had been set down or established by "law givers," which over time had become corrupt by accretions, interpretations, and commentaries, and it was this jungle of accretions and corruptions of the earlier pure codes which was controlled in the present by those Indians whom the British thought of as the Indian lawyers. An Ur-text had to be found or reconstituted, which at one and the same time would establish *the* Hindu and Muslim law as well as free the English from dependency for interpretations and knowledge on fallible and seemingly overly susceptible pandits and maulavis.
>
> (Cohn 1996: 29)[57]

Jones and the pundits

The relationship between the colonizer and colonized is never an easy one; it is fraught with ambivalence. In colonial discourse, ambivalence "describes the complex mix of attraction and repulsion that characterizes the relationship between the colonizer and colonized. The relationship is ambivalent because the colonized subject is never simply and completely opposed to the colonizer ... Ambivalence also characterizes the way in which colonial discourse relates to the colonized subject, for it may be both exploitative and nurturing, or represent itself as nurturing, at the same time" (Ashcroft *et al.* 1998: 12–13). In oriental discourse Sanskrit pundits are seen as necessary for the production of knowledge about the natives, but at the same time they are mistrusted and seen as a nuisance. Orientalists required the help of pundits as well as their endorsement of the codification of Hindu laws. Both pundits and Western orientalists were joint collaborators in the orientalist project, but the final authority rested with the latter. Without their assistance and endorsement, the orientalist project would have been a futile exercise. By officially appointing them to assist them in their task, the orientalists acknowledge their importance while at the same time they distrust their interpretations and seek freedom from native intrusion. In his letter to Earl Spencer dated 4 August 1787, Jones remarks: "I have the delight of knowing that my studies go hand in hand with my duty, since now I have read both Sanscrit and Arabick with so much ease, that the native lawyers can never impose upon the courts in which I sit" (Cannon 1970: 742).

Pundits both frustrate and gratify Jones.[58] In a letter to Charles Chapman dated 28 September 1785, Jones remarks that he "can no longer bear to be at the mercy of our pundits, who deal out Hindu law as they please, and make it at reasonable rates, when they cannot find it ready made" (Cannon 1970: 683–4). He makes clear his mistrust (of the pundits) in his letter to Lord Cornwallis: "if we give judgement only from the opinions of the native lawyers and scholars, we can never be sure that we have not been deceived by them" (Jones 1799b: 74). Even the written opinion of the pundits, however learned it may be, is to be suspected for it can be misleading: an "obscure text" may be treated as authoritative whereas the same text could have a different interpretation. Jones remarks in his letter to Lord Cornwallis:

> It would be absurd and unjust to pass an indiscriminate censure on a considerable body of men; but my experience justifies me in declaring, that I could not with any easy conscience concur in a decision, merely on the written opinion of native lawyers, in any cause in which they could have the remotest interest in misleading the Court: nor, how vigilant forever we might be, would it be very difficult for them to mislead us; for a single obscure text, explained by themselves, might be quoted as express authority, though perhaps in the very book from which it was selected, it might be differently explained, or introduced only for the purpose of being exploded.
>
> (Jones 1799b: 74)[59]

Jones renders the pundits incapable of demonstrating any accurate understanding of their own laws, and takes upon himself the task of interpreting these laws for Hindus. Furthermore, in his view, the laws themselves lack clarity and accurate information which make it difficult to render proper justice to the subjects. Referring to laws relating to Hindu oath-taking by different castes, Jones states in his "Charge to the Grand Jury" (1787) that "the brevity of this text has made it obscure, and open to different interpretations. The subject is, therefore, difficult for want of accurate information" (Jones 1799b: 15). He then proceeds to point out that "*Hindu* writers have exalted ideas of criminal justice" but any meaningful interpretation of it is impossible because the laws are introduced in a figurative style (ibid.). For Jones, these reasons justify the translation of Hindu laws for the benefit of the natives. Taking a textualized approach to oath taking, he suggests in his "Charge to the Grand Jury" (1787) that "we must not forget to remind all *Hindu* witnesses from time to time, that false evidence even by their own *Shastras*, is the most heinous of crimes ... such, after all, is the corrupt state even of their erroneous religion" (ibid.: 22).

The ultimate authority on how laws are implemented rests with colonial administrators, and more often than not, pundits had to interpret śāstras on terms required by orientalists. Both texts and pundits are domesticated and thereby rendering them harmless and beneficial to colonial rule. When the unfamiliar is made familiar there is no more the threat of the "Other." Jones prides himself on his ability to speak the sacred language of Hindus and to interpret their laws. He speaks of the pundits' admiration of his work and its usefulness to the subjects of the empire. Jones figures as a benevolent colonial parent in charge of colonial children:

> I speak the language of the gods, as the Brahmens call it, with great fluency, and can engage in superintending a Digest of Indian law for the benefit of twenty million of black British subjects in these provinces: the work is difficult and delicate ... the natives are charmed with the work, and the idea of making their slavery lighted by giving them their own laws, is more flattering to me than the thanks of the Company and the appreciation of the King, which have been transmitted to me.
>
> (Cannon 1970: 885)

In oriental discourse pundits are treated as both unreliable interpreters and benign men. As with Max Müller, Jones speaks warmly of his pundits. For example, he calls Jagannātha Tarkapāñcānana a "venerable sage" (Cannon 1970: 923). Jones shows his familiarity with the language of brạhmin pundits and speaks of being held high in their esteem. In his letter to Earl Spencer dated 19 September 1788, Jones states: "I read and write Sanscrit with ease, and speak it fluently to the Brahmans, who consider me as a Pandit" (Cannon 1970: 813) In his essay "On the Literature of the Hindus," Jones remarks on the benevolence of the British government which encourages Hindu pundits to share their śāstric knowledge with colonial administrators. Referring to the diversity of Hindu texts which pose problems to Europeans, Jones states, "we have the pleasure to find, that the learned *Hindus,* encouraged by the mindfulness of our government and manners, are at least eager to communicate their knowledge of all kinds, as we can receive it" (Jones 1799a: 362–3).

Concluding remarks

By way of conclusion, I would like to bring to the fore some aspects of Jones' representation of Hinduism, applying theoretical categories such as the trope of the child and palimpsest.

The trope of the child

The trope of the child functions as a discursive strategy in Jones' construction of Hindus as "submissive" and in need of nurturing. In representing natives as lacking any sense of political freedom and as incapable of understanding and implementing their own laws, Jones renders them impotent. Such a strategy legitimizes colonial intervention in the interests of the colonial subjects. The colonizer becomes the benevolent parent to whose care the child is entrusted. The relationship between the colonizer and the colonized is that of the parent and the child, and the rules that govern the relationship are set by the colonial parent. Once this pattern of relationship is in place, the parent exercises authority for the benefit of the child who lacks the tools to manage its affairs. In other words, the trope of the child becomes a convenient strategy to define the place of the Other and neutralize the ambivalent relationship between the ruler and ruled. Although the production of knowledge involves the joint collaboration of the colonizer and colonized, it is not an equal partnership. On the one hand, Jones needs the approval of the native pundits for his translation of Hindu laws, but on the other, he wants to be independent of them.

Both orientalist and colonial discourses employ the trope of the child to categorize the Other as innocent and childlike. Such an approach permits Jones to relate to the Other without feeling intimidated by the Other. It allows for a sympathetic and tolerant attitude to the cultures of the colonized and at the same time lets the colonizer take a dominant role in the interests of the colonized. The culture of the colonized is placed in a permanent state of childhood whereas European cultures are regarded as constantly evolving. If there is anything of value in oriental cultures, it relates to their glorious past. As with other orientalists, Jones frames an untainted timeless orient and a decadent present. The orient is frozen – immune to any historical change – whereas the West is perpetually developing. Orientalist interest in the ancient past of Hinduism has much to do with the light it can shed on Europe's own forgotten origins. Jones' construction of a splendid Hindu past is simultaneously a construction of the lost childhood of European culture. The trope of the child becomes a handy hermeneutic strategy for defining Europe's own self-identity in relation to India's past. Jones' search for a pristine Hinduism is in fact a romantic yearning for Europe's own pagan past.

The trope of the child is used as a strategy to bring the unfamiliar within the orbit of the familiar. Furthermore, the trope of the child serves to emphasize sameness and difference, thus neutralizing the contradictions and ambivalences that mark the relationship between the colonizer and colonized. As Ashcroft remarks: "The trope of the child, both explicitly and implicitly, offered a unique tool for managing the profound ambivalence of imperialism, because it absorbed and suppressed the contradictions of imperial discourse itself" (Ashcroft 2001: 36). Jones renders the strange familiar by constructing analogies between the Hindu and European classical past. By highlighting the "pagan" past of both Hindu and European cultures, Jones brings Hinduism within the sphere of the known. These cultures are not to be denounced, for they represent the state of childhood. The difference, in Jones' view, is that Europeans have moved on from paganism to rational worship of the one true God whereas Hindus are still in their primordial state. Jones' comparison of Hindu and Greco-Roman cultures challenges missionary representations of Hinduism by showing that Christians too were inheritors of a "pagan" past. But, unlike most missionaries of his and a later time, Jones does not see Hinduism and Christianity in oppositional terms. While his classical comparisons call for a sympathetic attitude towards Hinduism and a raising of its profile, these analogies tell us much about Jones' own construction and appropriation of Hinduism. In other words, Hinduism is important insofar as it relates to Europe's origins, Europe's own primeval past. Hinduism assumes an extraordinary significance, not so much for its own features as for the documentation it provides for the historical authenticity of the biblical religion. As we have seen, Jones offers his own reading to allay any fears that his Christian audience might have about Hinduism.

In Jones' view, as we have seen, Hinduism is largely linked with imagination, but this does not mean that it is a false religion; rather it signifies a state of infancy when rational faculties have not as yet been developed. To put it in another way, for Jones it is not a question of Hinduism being true or false – as it is for the missionaries of the time – but of "biblical truth" being distorted by whimsical imagination. It is not a wilful distortion but one that is caused by the exercise of one's wild imagination which clothes revelation in allegory and mythology. Jones links reason with historical facts, and imagination with mythology and fable. Once history is separated from mythology, we are left with imagination which can offer delight to the senses but not to the reasoning mind; it is on this reasoning that Jones turns to Hindu mythology in order to bring newness and freshness to tired neo-classical poetry. In his view, one can discern fragments of biblical truth in Hindu mythology, albeit in a twisted form. In other words, Jones constructs a Hinduism that validates biblical truth, thus making Hinduism an acceptable religion to a Christian audience. He fashions a Hinduism that is Bible-friendly even though, in his view, there is much in Hinduism that belongs to the world of imagination.

Jones' theory of common origins neutralizes the opposition between East and West, between Hinduism and Christianity, and makes the experience of the "Other" a less threatening one. For Jones, as we have seen, the East is not the "original home" of European culture. On the contrary, the East owes its origin to an "original source" common to India and the West. From a theological point of view, the original habitat of all humankind is biblical monotheism. In Jones' reckoning what is embedded in Hinduism is a primitive form of biblical monotheism. For Jones, biblical monotheism/revelation is the origin of religion and it suffered distortion because of a migration of people from one common center to different places. Seen in the light of Jones' theological framework, universal history begins with Genesis. Mary Hodgen, who has examined the views of the seventeenth- and eighteenth-century anthropologists, draws attention to two competing views that were prevalent before Jones' time – monogenetic and polygenetic. The former was in conformity with the Mosaic history propounded in Genesis, while the latter conflicted with the Genesis account (Hodgen 1964: 223). The monogenetic view held that "mankind in the beginning was the creature of a single creative act, at a single moment in time, and at a single spot on the earth's surface. Of one blood and one inheritance, he was therefore physically, ethnically, and socially homogeneous. Diversity, his present condition, was something that had come upon him" (ibid.). The polygenetic view, by contrast, held that "mankind was the outcome of plural creative acts, at plural moments in time, and at plural geographical stations" (ibid.). Jones subscribed to the dominant monogenetic view of history since it was the orthodox one. Scriptural assumptions were accepted as historical confirmation of the Genesis account of history. The first eleven chapters in Genesis were seen to hold "the lost key to the lost lock of the cultural riddle" (ibid.: 225). The solution to cultural diversity was to be found in the monogenetic view of history propounded in Genesis. This meant turning to the past to recover Europe's lost history or origins. Jones' search for the past and his reading of history is, as we have seen, informed by the monogenetic notion of history which sees the entire human race as proceeding from one center and migrating to different places, resulting in cultural differences.

The kind of Hinduism that emerges in Jones' hymns to Hindu deities is already settled by his hermeneutical presuppositions which identify the East with "imagination" and the West with "reason." It is in his poetical works that Jones lays bare the "exotic" treasures of the Hindu world in a manner agreeable to European modes of thinking. Being a poet himself, Jones was drawn to Hindu mythology which he felt would revitalize tired neo-classical

English poetry. Hinduism offered something exotic which had enormous literary potential and Jones did not hesitate to use Hindu mythological images to enhance and reanimate European poetry, thereby introducing these to Europe. Hindu mythology offered him the raw material to reconstruct the lost childhood of Europe. The hymns have much to do with Jones' engagement with his own romantic past through the medium of Hindu mythology. They are about the recovery and celebration of a past that is reminiscent of Europe's primitive self or Other. For Jones, Hindus represent the feminized self of Europe, and their literature offers a delightful insight into the world of primitive Europe. As we have seen, Jones resurrects the feminized self of Europe's past in his hymns to female deities and in his translated works (*Śakuntalā, Gītā-Govinda*). His hymns to various the goddesses celebrate the many aspects of the feminine power or *śakti*, and the natural world.

It appears that for the poetic Jones the Hindu feminine deities have a stronger appeal than does the patriarchal god of the Bible. In other words, distancing himself from the monotheistic patriarchal god of the Bible, Jones effortlessly glides into the world of the divine feminine. The hymns demonstrate a lively sense of devotion and an affirmation of the feminine. It is not to the Hindu male divinities that Jones turns to ask favors, but to the Hindu female divinities, especially the gentler ones such as Lakṣmī and Gaṅgā. He implores the blessings of Lakṣmī, to facilitate the establishment of British rule in India, and he requests the mother goddess Gaṅgā to be kind to those who have come from colder climes. While Anglicists, Utilitarians and Evangelicals are engaged in masculinizing the "effeminate" men of Bengal, who worshipped the mother goddess, Jones, in his poetry, is engaged in feminizing the imperial project, but at the same time adopting a patriarchal stance when it comes to Hindu laws. It is interesting that Jones affirms that which his colonial counterparts denounce. At one level, we see the subversion of colonial masculinity in the sense that Jones seeks the approval and protection of feminine figures. But it appears that such a subversion can only take place in the realm of poetry and not in the religious and political spheres. Jones finds it is safer to approach the feminine in poetry than in religion which Jones associates with reason. To phrase it differently, Jones relegates the feminine to the poetic domain where it is seen as appropriate to affirm the feminine, for both poetry and the feminine, in his reckoning, have to do with imagination.

It is in his hymns that Jones moves with great spontaneity and delight in the world of Hindu mythology, demonstrating a sound knowledge of it. Unlike nineteenth-century missionaries such as William Ward and John Farquhar, whom we will be discussing later, Jones is not dismissive of Hindu myths. Whereas the former see Hindu myths as detrimental to the betterment of Hindus, for Jones they are a source of inspiration, and he uses them freely to revive and enhance eighteenth-century English poetry. Jones' profuse use of Hindu mythological allusions indicates their acceptability, but on his own terms. Just as he situates Hindu chronology within the biblical framework, he places Hindu myths within the English literary tradition to make them harmless for his European audience.

It appears that for Jones, Hindu deities and their myths are of interest not for what they are in themselves but to the extent that they resemble the Greek and Roman deities. While Jones is appreciative of Hindu classical culture and challenges biased representations of the East, he largely appropriates Hinduism on terms agreeable to European tastes. Jones' classical analogies serve to mitigate the disparaging accounts of Hinduism and raise its stature. By using these classical parallels, Jones makes oriental culture and religion accessible to the West. By comparing them with Greek language and literature, Jones is seeking to fashion a palatable version of Hinduism. It is the study of classics which provides the benchmark for measuring, analyzing, and explaining non-Western cultures and religions.

The kind of orientalism at work in Jones' poetical works is different to the one we see in his recodification of Hindu laws. Being a product of both classical learning and the romanticism of the eighteenth century, Jones straddles two worlds. When he deals with Hindu laws, he functions as a Protestant hermeneut, subjecting them to a rigorous textual analysis and making them conform to the Justinian model of law. In his poetry, however, Jones yearns for the romantic past. In the former (Hindu laws) he appeals to rules, whereas in the latter (poetry), imagination comes before rules. He seeks for the uncommon and unconventional aspects in the poetical sphere. He turns to oriental poetry where he discovers the primeval state of innocence and freshness from which Europe has evolved, and which is now needed to revitalize and reinvigorate Europan poetic imagination which has become sterile. In oriental thought and literature, Jones finds the unspoilt simplicity of pagan Europe. It is mostly in his literary pursuits that he seeks to recapture the lost innocence. The world of Hindu mythology takes him on a journey to the uncontaminated pastoral past. As we have seen, Jones reconstructs the "pagan" or primitive past of Europe in his translated works such as Jayadeva's lyrical poem *Gītā-Govinda* and Kālidāsa's pastoral play *Śakuntalā*. He yearns for the unadorned simplicity and tranquillity of sage Kanva's hermitage in the forest. For Jones, India becomes a convenient hermeneutical location for nostalgic fantasies. In a way, Jones recreates his romantic longing for a "lost harmony" – the pastoral and idyllic life – by choosing to live in such an environment at Krishnanagar in Calcutta. Jones' discovery of the Hindu ancient past is simultaneously a nostalgic return to his own distant European (possibly Welsh) past – the lost primordial innocence.[60] In describing Hindus as "pagans," Jones is not distancing Hindus but rather affirming their closeness with Europeans, yet only in so far as they relate to the classical past of Europe. That which appears strange is in fact a part of Europe's own distant or forgotten past. What is exotic is intertwined with Europe's own classical past.

The "Other" loses its strangeness and assumes a familiar tone and character yet remains the Other for it is still anchored in its past. In portraying Hindus as trapped in their own infancy, Jones renders the Other as dependent. In other words, Jones appropriates the Other in terms of his own prior knowledge and pre-existing Western conceptual categories.

Palimpsest

One of the tasks of postcolonial critique is to bring to the fore the underlying assumptions and intentions at work in an orientalist engagement with Sanskrit texts. The idea of palimpsest is a helpful tool for interrogating Jones' attitude to Hindu laws. The term "palimpsest" was originally used "for a parchment on which several inscriptions had been made after earlier ones had been erased. The characteristic of the palimpsest is that, despite such erasures, there are always traces of previous inscriptions that have been 'overwritten'" (Ashcroft *et al.* 1998: 174). The term is particularly suggestive for it demonstrates how physical and textual spaces of the colonized are constantly reinscribed yet despite such deletions "the traces of earlier 'inscriptions' remain as a continual feature of the 'text'" (ibid.: 174–5). The sheer volume of textual production in the form of dictionaries, grammars and translations of oriental literature in eighteenth- and nineteenth-century colonial India is indicative of such an exercise. Jones' recodification of Hindu laws (although undertaken for the benefit of colonial subjects) is a clear instance of invasion and manipulation of the textual space of the colonized, denying them their own agency. In recasting Hindu law in Justinian terms, Jones is displacing the indigenous text and creating a new form of colonial and textual authority. In seeking to cleanse the text and recover its original meaning, Jones is blotting out earlier inscriptions and reinscribing his own version. As we saw, he dismisses the existing Halhed translation of Hindu laws from Persian, on grounds of its being far removed from the original, and he embarks on constructing an authoritative text – translating from Sanskrit to English, thus delegitimizing the original. As with other orientalists, Jones is interested in restoring to Hindu texts what he sees as their original meaning. By undertaking translation of *The Laws of Manu*, Jones seeks to purify and recover its "original" status. "It is of the utmost importance," Jones states in his letter to Charles Wilkins, "that the stream of Hindu law should be pure; for we are entirely at the devotion of the native lawyers, through our ignorance of Shanscrit" (Cannon 1990: 666). As we have seen in his letter to Earl Cornwallis, Jones speaks of bringing clarity to Hindu laws by translating them and thus replacing the existing unsatisfactory code. Although Jones seeks the assistance of brahmin pundits for his task, he regards them as unreliable hermeneuts. He sees himself as an authoritative spokesperson for Hindus who are too politically naive to understand or interpret their own laws, and therefore in need of being educated in them. Although Jones acknowledges that Hindus had a great civilization and excelled in certain arts, they are still in a primitive state as far as rationality is concerned. Jones' privileging and canonizing of the Sanskrit law illustrates how orientalism functions as a corporate body exercizing its authority over the orient.

For all his positive appreciation of India's achievements, Jones' representation of India is not free from Eurocentric bias. In his view, oriental cultures, however great, are still in their infancy, needing the assistance of progressive European culture. As for rational thinking, the East is still stuck in its primitive state whereas the West has made undisputed scientific progress. Affirming the superiority of European expertise and progress "in all kinds of useful knowledge," Jones asks his people not to condemn the people of Asia from whom Europe can learn for their own improvement and advantage. But at the same time, for Jones, Asia has nothing much to contribute to what he considers "useful knowledge." In his Second Anniversary Discourse to the Asiatic Society, delivered in 1785, Jones confirms this:

> Whoever travels in *Asia,* especially if he be conversant with the literature of the countries through which he passes, must naturally remark the superiority of *European* talents: the observation, indeed, is at least as old as ALEXANDER; and, though we cannot agree with the sage preceptor of that ambitious Prince; and that 'the *Asiaticks* are born to be slaves,' yet the *Athenian* poet seems perfectly in the right, when he represents *Europe* as a *sovereign Princess*, and *Asia* as her *Handmaid*: but, if the mistress be transcendently majestick, it cannot be denied that the attendant has many beauties, and some advantages peculiar to herself ... Although we must be conscious of our superior advancement in all kinds of useful knowledge, yet we ought not therefore to condemn the people of *Asia*, from whose researches into nature, works of art, and inventions of fancy, many valuable hints may be derived for our own improvement and advantage.
>
> (Jones 1799a: 10)

Chapter 2

Max Müller

Mobilizing texts and managing Hinduism

> Fantasy is beautiful and truth is more beautiful, but half-truth is terrible .... I was no enigma. The mystery is your creation. You love the fantastic and unreal.
>
> (Devi 1994: 255)

This chapter investigates the kind of India and Hinduism Friedrich Max Müller (1823–1900) represents, both in his public discourses and in his personal letters. Müller is mainly known for the series of volumes he edited, *Sacred Books of the East*. I will be drawing upon various works from among the voluminous literature he produced, but will be focusing primarily on his well-known Cambridge lectures published under the title, *India: what can it teach us?* Müller was invited by Cambridge University in 1882 to give a set of lectures on "some Indian subject, with special view to Indian Civil Service students" (Müller 1902b: 107). They were intended to challenge and rectify prejudices about India as a strange country, about its people being morally depraved, and its ancient Sanskrit literature and language having little relevance for Europeans.

Müller was born on 6 December 1823 in the town of Dessau in Germany.[1] His romantic interest in India went back to his school days. When he was ten years old he came across a majestic picture of the sacred city of Benares in one of his school textbooks, which made a deep impact on him. Realizing that he would have little luck in the field of European classical studies, Müller turned to Indic studies (although he never made it to India) in order to enhance his financial prospects. He studied Sanskrit in Leipzig, Berlin, and Paris, before making his way to Oxford in 1848 where he was to undertake the editing and translating of the text of the *Ṛg Veda*. He spent the rest of his life with his English wife in Oxford, where he was initially Professor of Modern European languages. He was utterly disappointed when he was not appointed to the Boden Professorship of Sanskrit when the position fell vacant in 1860 and went to his fellow contender, Monier-Williams. Müller eventually came to occupy the newly created chair in comparative philology, which was a sort of compensation for his failure to get the much coveted Boden Professorship – a privately endowed chair to promote Christianity through translating the Bible into Sanskrit. Although Müller affirmed a non-dogmatic Christianity, he had the evangelical ardor that was required of the candidate for the Boden Professorship. He delivered a lecture on "Missions" in Westminister Abbey in December 1873 (Müller 1875: 251–80). He was keen that the members of the Brahmo Samāj, a nineteenth-century socio-religious movement, should declare themselves as "Christian Brahmos, or Christian Aryas" (Müller 1902b: 397) and become members of the Church of England (ibid.: 391). More importantly, he was interested in the usefulness of the *Sacred Books of the East* to missionaries, although he was the subject of trenchant missionary criticism.

Territorial and intellectual conquest

Western orientalists such as William Jones and Max Müller eulogized India's Sanskrit past, for in the East they found glimpses of Europe's own distant past. Jones' discovery of the common origins and an Indo-European family of languages brought India closer to Europe, and Müller went further than Jones in equating linguistic affinity with racial affinity (although he later rejected this thesis). In eighteenth-century India, British administrator-scholars undertook a study of oriental languages and literature to meet the administrative needs of the empire in the making. In the nineteenth century, oriental studies came to be undermined by Anglicists who privileged European science and arts, but intellectual curiosity about India's classical past became the object of academic study, leading to the emergence of the study of comparative philology, religion, and mythology in Western universities (Thapar 1993: 2–3).

By the early nineteenth-century most of the Indian subcontinent came under the purview of the British East India Company, and by the the middle of the nineteenth century British rule had been firmly established. Most orientalists, as well as others including some Indians, saw British rule as Divine Providence and therefore beneficial both for the colonizer and the colonized. For instance, Keshub Chunder Sen regarded British rule not as "man's work, but a work which God is doing with His own hand, using the British nation as His instrument" (Sen 1980: 84). Max Müller was no exception. Although German by birth, he was a naturalized Briton, and believed in the benevolence of Britain's colonial rule, deeming it as good for both ruler and ruled. Reflecting the mood of the time, Müller not only spoke approvingly of the establishment of British rule but also of the need to colonize India's minds. In other words, Müller did not stop with endorsing the territorial and political colonization of India; he went even further and advocated intellectual and cultural colonization, including that of the minds of Indians. Urging young British civil servants to undertake the study of Sanskrit, Müller declared that "the material conquest of India" alone will not suffice and that Britain ought not to leave "the intellectual conquest" of India to other countries. In his letter to Cowell to whom the book *India: what can it teach us?* is dedicated, Müller remarks: "You know that at present and for sometime to come *Sanskrit scholarship means discovery and conquest*" (Müller 1892: vi, emphasis mine). He states that it is important to

> show to the world that Englishmen who have been able to achieve by pluck, by perseverance, and by real political genius the material conquest of India, do not mean to leave the laurels of its intellectual conquest entirely to other countries, then I shall indeed rejoice, and feel that I have paid back, in however small a degree, the larger debt of gratitude which I owe to my adopted country ....
>
> (Müller 1892: viii)

Müller has a clear agenda which is not only to discover but also to master and control the knowledge gained from the study of the Sanskrit language and the Sanskrit text, the Veda.

As with Jones, Müller's interest in oriental texts is not simply that of a scholar interested in pure knowledge. A close link between knowledge and power is noticeable even in his use of the language. Müller freely uses the language of conquest in his lecture on the Veda:

> When the two last volumes of the *Veda* are published we shall have saved from destruction a work older than the *Iliad*, older than any other literary document of that noble race of mankind to which the greatest nations in the world's history have belonged – a race which after receiving from a Semitic race, from the Jews, its best treasure, its religion, the religion of the Old and New Testaments, is now, with the English in the van, carrying on slowly but irresistibly the conquest of the world by means of commerce, colonization, education, and conversion.
>
> (1902a: 289)

Similarly, in his address on the *Importance of Oriental Studies*, delivered at the International Congress of Orientalists in London in 1874, Müller speaks of the need to conquer oriental knowledge. He remarks: "We have not only conquered and annexed new worlds to the ancient empire of learning, but we have leavened the old world with ideas that are already fermenting even in the daily bread of our schools and universities" (Müller 1875: 338). His quest for oriental knowledge goes hand in hand with the desire to exercise power over the Orient. It is not some form of disinterested or objective knowledge that Müller is seeking, but knowledge that will empower European hegemony over the Orient.

Domesticating the Veda

The Veda as an Aryan testament

Müller is mainly interested in the historical importance of the ancient Sanskrit text, the Veda, and the lessons it can teach Europeans and Hindus about their own past. For Müller, the Veda is significant not so much for its own worth as for the light it is seen to shed on a supposed common ancestry, that is, the Aryan race to which he sees Indians and Europeans as belonging. He draws attention to this new discovery in his address to the young British civil servants. The Veda, he states,

> can teach us lessons which nothing else can teach, as to the origin of our own language, the first formations of our own concept, and the true natural germs of all that is comprehended under the name of civilization, at least the civilization of the Aryan race, that race to which we and all the greatest nations of the world, – the Hindus, the Persians, the Greeks, the Romans, the Slaves, the Celts, and last, not least, the Teutons, belong.
> (Müller 1892: 116)

The Veda, in Müller's reckoning, bears testimony to all that has gone into the making of the European race. It is an antiquated document giving a valuable insight into the earliest phase of the Aryan people, and without which the history of the world is incomplete. It is historically important for it unfolds the lost childhood of the European race (ibid.: 254), or, to use his own words, "the first chapter in the life of Aryan humanity" (Müller 1878: 145). He tells young British men that there is in the Veda "something that concerns ourselves, something of our own intellectual growth, some recollections as it were, of our own childhood, or at least of the childhood of our race" (Müller 1892: 254). It is this innocent past that Müller is keen to resurrect or rather construct – an uncontaminated past free from any "foreign influence" (ibid.: 140). In other words, Müller constructs a romanticized past which he desires to preserve.

In his letter to the Duke of Albany dated 13 December 1875, Müller highlights the importance of the Veda for the entire human race, and its significance for the study of the origin and evolution of religious ideas.[2] He asserts that the Veda "alone can help us to solve many of the most critical problems in the Science of Religion" (Müller 1902a: 501). He sets himself the momentous task of recovering the *Ṛg Veda*, which he calls Europe's "oldest inheritance" and making it accessible to the European world (Müller 1902b: 74).

Extolling and caricaturing the Veda

Before proceeding to the next section, I would like to take a critical look at Müller's hermeneutical attitude to the Veda. Müller views the Veda from a nineteenth-century Western evolutionary perspective. He fixes the historical value and meaning of the Veda by placing it at the lowest end of the evolutionary scale (starting not with the beast as in Darwin's theory but with the child).[3] For him, the Ṛg Vedic "hymns represent the lowest stratum in the growth of the human mind that can be reached anywhere by means of contemporaneous literature" (Müller 1902a: 271). Therefore it is important "to dig, to collect, to classify, and to decipher them, in order to lay free once more the lowest chambers of that most ancient of all labyrinths, the human mind" (Müller 1878: 144). He cautions that the Veda should not be treated as anything more than a primitive document of tremendous historical worth. For Müller, the Veda is primitive not in the anthropological sense but in the sense that it contains "the utterances of beings who have just broken their shells and were wonderingly looking out for the first time upon this strange world" (Müller 1892: 118). In other words, for Müller the Veda embodies thoughts which are still in their infancy. He represents the Veda as a product of a not fully enlightened mind. In his view, the Veda in itself does not offer any room for the development of ideas for its true worth lies in its being the first sigh of a newborn child. Therefore one should not look for a well-developed monotheistic conception of God in the Veda. To put it another way, one should not even try to look for anything other than natural revelation in the Veda. Müller explains:

> What is beneath, and above, and beyond this life is dimly perceived, and expressed in a thousand words and ways, all mere stammerings, all aiming to express what cannot be expressed, yet all full of a belief in the real presence of the Divine in Nature, of the Infinite in the Finite. Here is the childhood of our race unfolded before our eyes, at least so much of it as we shall ever know on Aryan ground – and there are lessons to be read in those hymns, aye, in every word that is used by those ancient poets, which will occupy and delight generations to come.
>
> (1901a: 248–9)

Müller establishes an evolutionary link between the Veda and Kant's *Critique of Pure Reason*: the former representing the first "stammerings" of a child and the latter the mature thinking of a human being. For him, the Vedic sage is but a child – a noble savage, or to use his terminology, a "*progressive*" savage (Müller 1901a: 156) He states that "while in the Veda, we may study the childhood, we may study in Kant's *Critique of Pure Reason* the perfect manhood of the Aryan mind" (ibid.: 249). To put it another way, the Veda lacks the rationality of Kant's treatise; it cannot offer us the hermeneutical tools that we find in Kant's *Critique*. In his view, it is but natural that the Veda is devoid of reason or logic. He remarks: "In the Veda we see how the Divine appears in the fire, and in the earthquake .... In Kant's *Critique* the

Divine is heard in the still small voice – the Categorical Imperative – the I Ought – which Nature does not know and cannot teach" (ibid.: 249).

In his approach to the Veda, Müller employs both the rhetoric of affirmation and negation at one and at the same time. As we have seen, Müller's affirmation has more to do with the Veda's historical importance as a primitive document than for its spiritual or theological significance. He acknowledges that the Veda contains noble thoughts, but much in them appears to his Protestant and Eurocentric perspective as "childish in the extreme: tedious, low, commonplace" (Müller 1868: 27). He remarks that there is "much that is elevated and elevating, and much that is beautiful and sublime;" but at the same time there is much in them that is immature and repugnant, that it can be of little interest to anyone except a historian (Müller 1902b: 10–11). For Müller, even from an esthetic point of view the Veda has nothing much to offer. He reckons that "those who have vague ideas of primeval wisdom and the splendour of Eastern poetry will soon find themselves grievously disappointed" (ibid.: 10–11). He emphasizes that "there is little that is beautiful, in our sense of the word, to be found in the hymns of the *Rig-veda*" (Müller 1875: 369). In his view, "the intrinsic merit, and particularly the beauty or elevation of its sentiments, have by many been rated far too high." Nevertheless, the hymns are seen as valuable for "hidden in this rubbish there are precious stones ... " (Müller 1868: 27). Müller reckons that, in spite of the *Upaniṣads* containing some marks of "poetical eloquence" and philosophical worth, they are at the same time "utterly meaningless and irrational" and "utter rubbish." He goes on to say that "there will always remain in the Upanishads a vast amount of what we can only call meaningless jargon" (Müller 1884: xix–xx). In the same breath Müller praises the Bible as being far ahead of other sacred books (ibid.: xx).

What I have tried to demonstrate is that Müller's affirmation of the Veda has more to do with its significance as a historical document than with its spiritual content. He constructs a textualized Hinduism which is informed by nineteenth-century ideas of evolution, historicism, and comparative philology.

Fragile monotheism

Ever since orientalists, Christian missionaries and colonialists encountered Hindu religious practices, they were confronted with the question of whether Hindus believed in one God or many gods – a question that continues to vex the European mind. Faced with an array of Hindu gods and goddesses, European scholars grappled with it by using biblical monotheism as the yardstick to examine Hindu understanding of the relation between the One and the many. Müller is struck by the fact that the *Ṛg Veda* affirms many gods whilst at the same time each god is given supreme importance in their respective hymns and becomes the sole object of devotion at given time while at another time another god is given similar attention. Neither the multiplicity of gods nor the affirmation of a particular god at a particular time diminishes the unique importance of other gods, even if the same attributes are ascribed to them. Müller finds such an understanding and treatment cumbersome, and characterizes it as "chaotic theogony" (Müller 1892: 168). That is to say, the gods, in Müller's view, are not organized in any systematic manner but seemed to emerge with ease and occupy a supreme position. Müller coins two terms to describe what he considers the true nature of Vedic religion: *Henotheism,* which is "the worship of single gods," and *Kathenothesim*, which is "the worship of one god after another." He thus distinguishes it from Greek and Roman polytheism, and from Semitic monotheism. Preferring the term *Henotheism,* Müller draws a distinction between Semitic and Vedic monotheism: "This shorter name of *Henotheism* has found more general acceptance, as conveying more definitely the opposition between *Monotheism*, the worship of one only God, and *henotheism*, the worship of single gods" (Müller 1892: 147). Müller goes to great lengths to highlight this distinction in order to show that if at all there is any form of monotheism in the Veda, it is rather fragile and "defenceless," degenerating into polytheism. In his letter to the Duke of Argyll, Müller speaks of Vedic religion being closer to untainted monotheism – a monotheism that is still in its infant state:

> The earliest known religious form of the Aryan race is, as nearly as possible, a pure monotheism – yes, that is perfectly true. But it was an undoubting monotheism, in one sense perhaps the happiest monotheism – not yet safe against doubts and negation. Doubt and negation followed, it may be by necessity, and the unconscious defenceless monotheism gave way to polytheism.
>
> (Müller 1902b: 289–90)

In brief, Müller locates in the Veda a "primitive monotheism" but not a distorted version of biblical monotheism, as Jones does. For Müller, the Veda, being an archaic document, can only offer an insecure and vulnerable monotheism. What he fails to see is that there is no contradiction between Oneness and multiplicity in the *Ṛg Veda*. For Hindus, each Vedic deity is a symbol or expression of the One which is also known by other names. The Ṛg-Vedic hymn which declares: "That which is one, sages name it in various ways – they call it Agni, Yama, Matrisvan" (1: 164: 46) indicates that these are different names, symbols, powers, and forms of the One which in itself transcends all these. The text draws attention to the limitations of human language in defining the One that exceeds all descriptions. What we find in the Veda is not a rigid but an inclusive monotheism which sees oneness as the basis of multiplicity. As Sri Aurobindo, the freedom-fighter turned philosopher and mystic, remarks: "The monotheism of the Veda includes in itself also the monistic, pantheistic and even polytheistic views of the cosmos and is by no means the trenchant and simple creed of modern Theism" (1971: 30).

Restoring, fixing and privileging the Veda

The nineteenth-century European search for "origins" is reflected in Müller's approach to the Veda. Müller sets himself the task of recovering or rather reconstructing its true or original meaning. In his introduction to the *Upaniṣads* which he translated, Müller is concerned with recovering the original meaning of the text:

> But I know full well how much still remains to be done, both in restoring a correct text, and in discovering the original meaning of the Upanishads; and I have again and again had to translate certain passages tentatively only, or following the commentators, though conscious all the time that the meaning which they extract from the text cannot be the right one.
>
> (1884: xii)

He employs what was known at that time in biblical circles as higher criticism (which later came to be called historical criticism) in order to discern the "original" meaning of the Veda. He uses his philological skills to reinforce a narrow or a fixed meaning rather than uncover the spiritual sense of the text. As we have seen, Müller constructs the Veda as an archaic document and warns that tampering with its meaning would result in the loss of its real worth. In his reckoning such a discovery will unsettle the foundations on which Hinduism is based. In Müller's view, to look for a rational religion is contrary to the spirit of the Veda. He sees himself as having the hermeneutical key to unlock the original meaning of the Veda. He cautions Hindus not to look in it for modern Western scientific, philosophical, and rational categories or moral values. He claims that he has the right clues to make an historical assessment of the Veda, and urges Hindus to accept his verdict. He is saying, in effect, that one should not look for signs of modernity in the Veda.[4] He remarks in a letter to his Parsee friend Malabari:

> Accept the *Veda* as an ancient *historical* document, containing thoughts in accordance with the character of an ancient and simple-minded race of men, and you will be able to admire it, and to retain some of it, particularly the teaching of the *Upanishads*, even in these modern days. But discover in it "steam-engines and electricity, and European philosophy and morality," and you deprive it of its true character, you destroy its real value, and you break the historical continuity that ought to bind the

> present to the past. Accept the past as a reality, study it and try to understand it, and you will then have less difficulty in finding the right way towards the future.
>
> (Müller 1902b: 111)

In his approach to the Veda, Müller reflects the dominant biblical thinking of the time by going back to an "Ur text" and recovering the "true Gospel" in it. Müller fashions himself in the tradition of the Protestant reformer and wants to rescue the Veda and recover its original meaning for Hindus. In other words, he engages in a textual cleansing mission – he wants to restore Hinduism to its pristine form.[5] Like Jones and other orientalists, Müller, too, constructs a picture of a magnificent age of Hindus which he locates in the Vedas. Hindus need to go back to the Veda to recover the lost purity of their tradition. He tells Malabari (a member of the Brahmo Samāj) that "it is the fate of all religions to form these thick crusts of superstition around them"; the important thing is to seek for the true meaning "below the surface." The point is that Hindus need to be enlightened about the true value of the Veda. He wants Malabari to be the transmitter of what he, Müller, has discovered and has done with the Veda: "If you could tell your countrymen something of what I have written in these lectures, it might bear some good fruit" (Müller 1902b: 59). Similarly, in his letter to Colonel Olcott, Müller takes upon himself the role of a moral reformer, urging the Colonel "to persuade [his] friends in India to make a new start, i.e., to return to their ancient philosophy in all its purity" (Müller 1901b: 294). He adds that it would do a great deal of good if the Colonel would "help the people in India to discover and recover the treasure of truth in their old Brahma-Sophy" (Müller 1902b: 295).

As we have seen, Müller brings his Protestant presuppositions about the written word to his study of the Veda. But for Hindus, the meaning of a text is not confined to nor firmly entrenched in the written word. It is important to take a brief look at the meaning and significance of sacred texts within the Hindu tradition. Hindu texts are traditionally classified into *śruti* ("that which is heard") and *smṛti* ("that which is remembered"). The Veda belongs to the *śruti* tradition – one that has its genesis in hearing and has been transmitted orally for generations before it came to be written down. In the oral transmission the meaning of the text is conveyed through an accurate rendering of the sound. As Sri Aurobindo puts it: "The language of the Veda is itself a *śruti*, a rhythm not composed by the intellect but heard, a divine Word that came vibrating out of the Infinite to the inner audience of the man who had previously made himself fit for the impersonal knowledge" (1971: 8). The Vedic seers are seen as channels through whom the divine *Vāk* (word) manifests itself. In other words, the Vedic revelation offers us the experience of Divine as *śabda* (sound), hence the notion of *śabda-brahman*. Of all sounds, Aum (OM) is the most sacred sound of all others; it is the primordial sound from which all others are seen to originate. The *ṛṣi* (seer) is also a *kavi* (poet) who renders the deep spiritual meaning and significance of the experience in a poetic language. *Śruti* is primary for this reason. It is a direct mode of experience whereas *smṛti* is a recollection or remembrance of that experience. Although *smṛti* is secondary, it has had a greater impact on Hindus and it continues to be transmitted orally through story-telling, dance music, drama, and chanting portions or entire texts such as Tulsīdās' *Rāmcaritmānas.*

European orientalists, for whom the written word is paramount, tended to view oral transmission of sacred knowledge not only as an inferior mode of communication but as a sign of backwardness. For Hindus, however, the orality of their texts (both *śruti* and *smṛti)* signified a highly developed spiritual culture. In fact, the act of writing was regarded as polluting. As we have seen, the sacrality of the Veda was retained in oral form before it was committed to writing, and even to this day oral recitation of the Veda and even *smṛti* texts such as the *Rāmāyaṇa* is highly preferred and valued. However, faced with the orientalist critique that Hindu textual tradition lacked any discernible, coherent structure, Indian scholars embarked on bringing together varied oral and textual versions of epics such as the *Mahābhārata* and the *Rāmāyaṇa* in order to construct a unified tradition. Given that there are diverse written and oral traditions and contextual variations, "the attempt to produce a critical edition of these traditions is almost against their very nature" (van der Veer 2001: 121). Being preoccupied with the Hindu textual tradition, Western orientalists located what they perceived as "true" or "real" India and Hinduism, in texts and they sought to textualize India.

Müller is the first European to edit and bring out the six-volume edition of the *Ṛg Veda* together with the commentary of Sāyaṇa. In Sri Aurobindo's view, both nineteenth-century European scholarship and traditional Hindu scholarship have tended to rely heavily on the ritualistic interpretation of the Veda given by the fourteenth-century commentator Sāyaṇa, thereby overlooking the inner symbolic import of the Veda. The main drawback of Sāyaṇa's ritualistic interpretation, according to Aurobindo, is that it "seeks continually to force the sense of the Veda into that narrow mould," thus obscuring the inner significance implicit in the hymns and rendering it in its minimalist sense (Aurobindo 1971: 18). He draws attention to how European scholars like Müller have made skillful use of traditional aspects of Sāyaṇa's commentary by subjecting the commentary to a comparative approach based on nineteenth-century Western notions of philology, mythology, history, and myth, thus constructing an elaborate body of Vedic mythology, history, and culture. In Sri Aurobindo's reckoning, Sāyaṇa is largely responsible for the modern theory of the Veda as a primitive document. He remarks: "The ritualism which Sayana accepted as part of a divine knowledge and as endowed with a mysterious efficacy, European scholarship accepted as an elaboration of the old savage propitiatory sacrifices" (1971: 23). Müller sees the Veda as repository of natural revelation and the Vedic deities as no more than mere personifications of the natural phenomena rather than as potent symbols or expressions of the One. The ritualistic and mythological sense predominates in Müller's approach to the Veda. In trying to discover and fix the original meaning the Veda, Europeans scholars like Müller have thus rendered the meaning of the Veda in its minimalist sense.

European scholars have placed an undue emphasis on the written word. It has been of utmost significance for Europeans since the seventeenth century, signifying a certitude of meaning, stability, and security that orality was lacking. As Bernard Cohn states:

> Meaning for the English was something attributed to a word, a phrase, or an object, which could be determined and translated, at best with a synonym that had a direct referent to something in what the English thought of as a "natural world." Everything had a more or less specific referent for the English. With Indians, meaning was not necessarily constructed in the same fashion. The effect and affect of hearing a brahman chant in Sanskrit at a sacrifice did not entail meaning in the European sense; it was to have one's substance literally affected by the sound.
>
> (1996: 18–19)

There is a tendency to apply modern ideas about language to the Veda. In other words, the word is not seen as a living thing, a potent symbol or power. In early language the root meanings of a word were important as they brought out the complex nuances and senses of it. Both a ritualistic and a naturalistic interpretation of the Veda tend to undermine the potentiality of language, which Vedic seers were aware of. Both traditional Hindu and Western scholarship tended to downplay the spiritual importance of the Veda. Sri Aurobindo remarks:

> Neither Western scholarship nor ritualistic learning has succeeded in eliminating the psychological and ethical value of hymns, but they have both tended in different degrees to minimize it. Western scholars minimize because they feel uneasy whenever ideas that are not primitive seem to insist on their presence in these primeval utterances; they do not hesitate openly to abandon in certain passages interpretations which they adopt in others and which are admittedly necessitated by their own philological and critical reasoning … Sayana minimizes because his theory of Vedic discipline was not ethical righteousness with a moral and spiritual result but mechanical performance of ritual with a material reward.
>
> (1915 (1984: 17–18))

In brief, what comes through clearly is that Müller divests the Veda and other sacred texts of any spiritual, moral or ethical import. In his preface to *The Sacred Books of the East*, Müller warns that these texts should not be treated as "books full of primeval wisdom and religious enthusiasm, or ... of sound and simple moral teaching." He states that it is "high time to dispel such illusions, and to place the study of the ancient religion of the world on a more real and sound, on a more truly historical basis" (Müller 1879: ix). Müller's approach leaves little room for any recovery of the religious and ethical value of the Veda. Such a hermeneutical stance allows no room for any other meaning or significance the Veda might have for Hindus.

Müller privileges the Veda, thus delegitimizing other textual and oral forms of knowledge. He undermines any Sanskrit text that is not part of the *śruti* tradition. He regards Sanskrit works such as *Śakuntalā* and *Hitopadeśa* as "excellent specimens of what story-telling ought to be. But all this literature is modern, secondary" (Müller 1878: 142). For Müller, these works are no more than mere "literary curiosities" undertaken by men like William Jones and Colebrooke, and can "never become the object of a life-study" (ibid.). Müller shows utter disregard for Sanskrit literature other than the Veda. "The only original, the only important period of Sanskrit literature," he remarks, "which deserves to become the subject of earnest study ... is that period which preceded the rise of Buddhism, when Sanskrit was still the spoken language of India" (ibid.: 145). Although the Veda is seen as the ultimate source of authority and has been drawn upon by various schools of Hindu philosophy and religious groups, its pre-eminent role has not been unanimously accepted by all Hindus, especially by *bhakti* sects. This in no way undermines its sanctity or significance for other Hindus. Furthermore, its authority has little to do with whether Hindus are conversant with it or not. As much as it is important as an authoritative source of knowledge in theological and philosophical schools of thought, for ordinary Hindus its significance may vary or may not matter all that much. Given that it was not previously accessible to those outside brahminical circles, its authority has been affirmed by only a minority of Hindus.

For Müller only the Sanskrit Veda matters. What Müller fails to take into account is that the term Veda is also extended to the Tamil devotional poems of *Āḻvārs*, particularly to *Tiruvāymoḻi* (meaning "word of sacred mouth"), one of the works of the eighth/ninth-century poet-saint Nammāḻvār. Orientalists like Müller who are so obsessed with the Sanskrit language fail to note that there is another Indian language, Tamil, which is as old as Sanskrit, and which has its own sacred text. The point is that the divine revelation is not confined to the Vedic seers but is also seen as manifesting itself through the twelve *Āḻvārs*. Therefore Tamil devotional literature "is seen as parallel to the Vedas" (Carman and Narayanan 1989: 4). It is held that *Tiruvāymoḻi* came to be called "the Tamil Veda" in the tenth century by the Śrīvaiṣṇava teacher, Nāthamuni. This designation is particularly significant given that the term

Veda was strictly used with reference to revelation through the medium of the Sanskrit language. It was in the tenth century CE that a vernacular language for the first time became the medium of revelation. Furthermore, the notion of the Tamil Veda did not conflict in any way with the Sanskrit Veda or result in its being treated as inferior. As Narayanan and Carman point out: "For the first time in Hindu consciousness, hymns in a language other than Sanskrit were considered to be revealed. The claim was also unique in that none of the teachers in the Śrīvaiṣṇava community felt that they were rebelling against the Sanskrit tradition; nor did they hold either Veda to be inferior to the other. In the Śrīvaiṣṇava tradition, we see ... the coming together of Sanskrit and Tamil cultural traditions and religious literatures" (Carman and Narayanan 1989: 4). In fact, some of the secondary texts such as the *Mahābhārata* and the *Bhagavadgītā* have been elevated to the status of *śruti*. The epic, the *Mahābhārata*, is designated "the fifth Veda."

Aryanizing Hindus

Sanskrit, self-definition, and spiritual kith and kin

For European orientalists, the discovery of Sanskrit meant the discovery of the common origins of both Europe and India, and therefore it was important to investigate this past. Müller, in his address to a young British audience, draws attention to the lessons that India can teach Europe. One of the most important lessons is that Sanskrit is not an alien tongue but one that is closely related to Greek and Latin. "To speak the same language," he states, "constitutes a closer union than to have drunk the same milk; and Sanskrit, the ancient language of India, is substantially the same as Greek, Latin, and Anglo-Saxon" (Müller 1892: 27). Müller goes a step further than Jones in equating linguistic similarity with racial affinity. He states: "As the language of the Veda, the Sanskrit, is the most ancient type of English of the present day, (Sanskrit and English are but varieties of one and the same language,) so its thoughts and feelings contain in reality the first roots and germs of that intellectual growth which by an unbroken chain connects our own generation with the ancestors of the Aryan race" (Müller 1868: 4). This new discovery indicates that Europeans and Indians are not strangers but related; they belong to the Aryan stock. He states: "We are by nature Aryan, Indo-European, not Semitic: our spiritual kith and kin are to be found in India, Persia, Greece, Italy, Germany ..." (ibid.). For Müller, India is necessary for Europe's own self definition. India is not the Other but it is Europe's own distant self. To put it in another way, Europe's origins lie in the East. The discovery of Sanskrit and the Veda unfolds a new chapter in the history of Europe. Speaking about why a knowledge of India is "an essential portion of a liberal or an historical education," Müller draws attention to the implications of Europe's contact with India, especially its discovery of Sanskrit: "The concept of the European man has been changed and widely extended by our acquaintance with India, and we know now that we are something different from what we thought we were … the discovery of Sanskrit … has added a new period to our historical consciousness, and revived the recollections of our childhood, which seemed to have vanished for ever" (Müller 1892: 29–30). Thus, with the discovery of Sanskrit, the so-called theory of the Aryan race came to be constructed. India's distant past came to acquire a new and extraordinary historical significance – it had to be preserved, for it told the story of European childhood. Müller draws attention to this significant discovery in his address to the British audience, in order to allay fears that India is a strange country. For Müller, unlike Jones, India is the ancestral home of Europeans. He states: "We all come from the East – all that we value most has come to us from the East, and in going to the East, not only those who have received a special oriental training, but everybody who has enjoyed the advantages of a liberal, that is, of a truly historical education, ought to feel that he is going to his 'old home', full of memories, if only he can read them" (ibid.: 31–2). He considers a knowledge of Sanskrit essential in order to feel at home in India (although it is spoken only by a minority). Like Jones, he rates Sanskrit literature higher than Greek literature, and recommends it to British civil servants as a subject worthy of leisurely and serious study (ibid.: 5–6). Müller's concept of the Aryan race, which came to be employed by Hindus to combat negative portrayals of India and its traditions, will be dealt below in the next section.

Although Müller very much desired to visit India, he never made it, but from his Oxford study imagined a romanticized Indian past. Müller urged civil servants to search for India's past, for it was only there that one could locate the early beginnings of the European race. "I am thinking chiefly of India, such as it was a thousand, two thousand, it may be three thousand years ago … I look to the India of the village communities, the true India of the Indians" (Müller 1892: 7). By constructing a fixed, static and timeless India, immune to the progress and change that characterizes a passing phase in Western history, Müller makes the Other a less daunting experience for his audience. He appropriates the Other by making the strange familiar, but only as a relic of the Aryan past – a past that does not unsettle Europe's sovereign status.

Aryan theory: implications and appropriations

The Sanskrit term ārya[6] which occurs in the *Ṛg Veda* means an honorable or noble person. Müller was the one to invest this term with a racial connotation. In other words, Müller's use of the term Aryan has little do with the meaning the Sanskrit word *ārya* implies. He interpreted the linguistic similarity between Sanskrit and European languages such as Greek and Latin as evidence of racial affinity. He equated the Sanskrit language with race, thus constructing the theory of Aryan race and invasion. Although he later realized the mistake he had made, the damage had already been done. He disassociated the link between language and race but retained the idea of linguistic affinity. The Ṛg Vedic text mentions the animosity between two groups, *āryas* and *dāsas*, and the reference to *varṇa*, or the color of these groups, was easily mistaken for the light-skinned Aryan conquering the dark-skinned inhabitants. The reference to color and conflict between the two groups neatly fitted with Müller's theory of Sanskrit-speaking Aryans, from Central Asia, invading northern India in the second millennium BCE, and subjugating the local dark-skinned inhabitants (Thapar 2000: 28–9). Most textbooks and even reference works on Hinduism attribute the beginnings of Hinduism to the Aryan invasion theory. Seen in the light of such a theory, the ancient Sanskrit text, the *Ṛg Veda* (which Müller spent the best part of his life editing), does not have an indigenous origin but an Indo-European one. Therefore it is not surprising that the text assumes an extraordinary historical significance for Müller for it contains the history of the lost European childhood.

The Aryan invasion theory is now being contested by many contemporary Indian scholars. In fact, as early as 1914, Sri Aurobindo rejected it, pointing out in his *The Secret of the Veda* that there is no reference to any such theory. He draws attention to the exaggerated claims made for philological and linguistic discovery in the nineteenth century: "The first error committed by the philologists after their momentous discovery of the Sanskrit tongue, was to exaggerate the importance of their first superficial discoveries. … Comparative Philology, guilty of this error, has seized a minor clue and mistaken it for a major or chief clue" (Aurobindo 1971: 553).

The term Aryan became a disputed category which both high-caste Hindus and *dalits* made use of to advance their own cause; the former to reclaim their equality with Europeans, and the latter to claim an authentic indigenous status. The upper-caste Hindus saw themselves as of Aryan descent and therefore superior to other indigenous castes. Caste came to be seen in racial categories, each caste conceived of as a separate race (Thapar 2000: 29). The invasion theory came to be employed by different social and political groups to affirm their own ideological agendas. Jyotiba Phule used the invasion theory to challenge "brahmin domination, arguing that they were alien Aryans and therefore not the rightful inheritors of the land" (Thapar 1999b: 20). In today's India, the Aryan invasion theory has "become an essential part of the Dalit version of history" (ibid.: 19). Müller's two-race theory resulted in an artificial distinction between Sanskrit-speaking Aryans and non-Sanskrit Dravidians, and this was exploited by the Protestant missionary, Robert Caldwell. Caldwell reconstructed the notion of Dravidian identity using the theme of Aryan brahminical domination of indigenous people in the south, thus sowing the seeds for a Dravidian movement in South India (Ravindran 1996: 83–110). Those who see the term Aryan as referring to the indigenous people tend to define Indian identity in Hindu terms – Aryan referring to Hindu and therefore Hindus being the rightful inhabitants of the land known as *Āryāvarta*. It has a become a powerful weapon in the hands of Hindutva politicians to reconstruct a Hindu India. All extraneous origins are ruled out and all Hindus are seen as indigenous – as Aryans – from *brahmin* to *Caṇḍāla*, thus encouraging reconversion to the ancestral faith.

Aryan masculinity

Nineteenth-century comparative philology was to have far reaching implications, as Chaudhuri remarks: "Comparative Philology came to their rescue by showing that not only in their language, even ethnically, they [Hindus] were related to Europeans" (Chaudhuri 1974: 316). This meant that Hindus were no more the barbarians they were once thought to be, but of Indo-European stock. Müller's construction of the Aryan theory of race and of the common origins of Europeans and Indians came to be employed by the upper strata of the colonized to affirm their dignity and self-worth and forge a national identity. For Hindus, this newly discovered racial identity with Europeans meant that they were not thought of as effeminate – as they had been portrayed by colonialists. It changed the character of Hindu identity in that Hindu nationalists such as Bankimchandra Chatterjee and others now began to affirm a vigorous masculine identity.[7] It was important to resurrect *kṣtariya* values of honor, chivalry, and conquest; the notion of valor and chivalry was already embodied in the concept of *kṣatriya* and it neatly fitted with the notion of Aryan invasion and conquest. In popular historical works masculine qualities came to be commended, paving the way for "a militant cultural nationalism" (Chakravarti 1993: 48). Bankimchandra Chatterjee played a significant part in the construction of a new Indian national identity which combined both the role of the warrior with the renunciant. In his historical work, *Krishnacharita*, Kṛṣṇa of the *Bhagavadgītā* became a role model – a man of contemplation and action. The Aryan theory resulted in the creation of further divisions in Bengali society between high and low castes, in that the former were associated with Aryan purity and the latter with impurity. In Chatterjee's reconfiguration of national identity both Muslims and *dalits* were written out. This kind of perception "was fairly representative of the nineteenth-century cultural nationalists" (ibid.: 50).

Dayānanda Saraswatī, the founder of the nineteenth-century socio-religious movement Ārya Samāj, rejected the term Hinduism in favor of *ārya* because the former was seen as imposed by foreigners. For Dayānanda, the term *ārya* signified a purified form of Hinduism. While for Müller, the Veda was a past relic, for Dayānanda Saraswatī it was potentially a relevant text for social and religious reformation. In his view, Hinduism had to be purged of image worship and other ritual and superstitious practices.[8] He rejected all other Hindu texts except the *Ṛg Veda*. He called for a revitalization of Hinduism based on a return to the Veda. He was prompted into action by his own guru, who urged him to go back to the Veda, the authoritative source of knowledge. The orientalist thesis that Hindus had fallen from past glory, symbolized in the Vedic religion, concurred with Dayānanda's claim that the Veda alone could function as the foundation for reformed Hinduism. He posited the Veda as constituting the true religion that Hindus need to recognize. Unlike for Müller, the Veda had more than a historical value for Dayānanda. He challenged the caste system which he saw as a fall from the idea of a four-fold *varṇa* found in the *Ṛg Veda*. Although he was a brahmin himself, Dayānanda delegitimized brahmin authority by allowing any Hindu, regardless of caste, to become a member of the Ārya Samāj, by declaring that the Vedic sacrificial ritual was no more the prerogative of brahmins. Dayānanda constructed a kind of pure Hinduism based on the Veda and at the same time challenged brahminical priesthood and authority, thus making it accessible to Hindus of different castes – a brahminical Hinduism without the constraints of brahminical authority. His teachings had a greater impact in the Punjab where power was not vested in the hands of the brahmins but with the followers. He reconstructed his own version of an immaculate age of Hindus, drawing on orientalist formulations, and, like Müller, he attributed the degeneration of Hinduism to Muslim rule. He called for a return to the Vedic religion in order to recover the "loss of masculinity and cultural regression of the Hindus." This loss "was due to the loss of Aryan qualities which they had shared with westerners" (Chakravarti 1993: 55). In Dayānanda's reconfigured Hinduism, women's role was to produce healthy sons for the continuation and regeneration of the Aryan race. Women's roles were confined to motherhood but with a difference in that "the sexuality of the women was transformed into a force which could be constructively channelized to serve the regeneration of the Aryas" (ibid.: 57).

Eulogizing the ancient past and Aryan character

Müller constructs an imagined and noble Hindu past in terms of which he evaluates Hindu character. He privileges and idealizes village India as the embodiment of virtues such as honesty, gentleness, truthfulness, purity, innocence, and passivity. His theory is that in order to arrive at a correct estimate of Hindu character and morality, one has to trace one's steps back to the ancient past – the village India – which is seen to be free from the blemishes of urban India. As we have seen, like other orientalists Müller locates India's greatness in its ancient past, and urges civil servants, officers, missionaries, and merchants "to search for the Indian past." Although he never visited India, Müller wrote with a sense of authority about what he envisioned to be "true India." For him, village India epitomizes real India, whereas urban India (metropolitan cities such as Bombay and Calcutta) lacks the benign qualities he associates with rural India. He remarks: "It is that village-life which in India has given its peculiar impress to Indian character, more so than in any other country" (Müller 1892: 47). He associates Hindu truthfulness with idyllic village life, where people are naturally gentle and of a peaceful nature. Müller's idealized account of the Hindu character is heavily dependent on Colonel Sleeman's *Rambles* (although written much earlier than its publication in 1844). Müller's remarks invoke a child-like innocence: "Take a man out of his village-community, and you remove him from all the restraints of society. He is out of his element, and under temptation, is more likely to go wrong than to remain true to the traditions of his home life" (ibid.: 49). It is the ruralized and rustic India of the European imagination which constitutes the true India, and which Müller uses as a yardstick to judge Hindus. Müller's contrast of village India with urban India throws light on Europe's own romantic longing for the idyllic village life community Europe lost in the wake of its own march towards modernity. As Inden points out:

> Indeed, throughout much of the nineteenth century the Indian village was even taken as typical of both Europe and Asia. Many of the early orientalists, envisioning an original Aryan religion and society that were more or less isomorphic with an original Aryan language, believed it to be the living descendant of the Aryan village ... They supposed the Indian village was analogous with the post-tribal, agricultural village of the Teutons or Germanic branches of the Aryans in ancient and medieval Western Europe ... That village in Europe had all but disappeared as it became a "modern" society, India, however, was still an "ancient" society. The ancient Aryan village still survived there.
>
> (1992: 132)

Müller sets Hindus fixed in their past because the Hindu past, in his view, reflects what Europe has lost in its transition from village to urban life. In other words, Müller's search for the real India is a search for lost European origins. As Thapar points out: "The village community was also seen as the root of Indo-European life and it was thought that in the Indian village community, Europe had rediscovered its origins" (1994b: 32). For Müller and Jones, village India is not an alien India but one that brings memories of their own European childhood – the state of innocence. To draw on Inden again:

> The village India was not an Other that in any way threatened the European Self. It did not exist in the same time as the Self, nor did it occupy the same political and economic space. On the contrary, the two

> occupied complementary, hierarchically related "spaces." The modern in the form of the British Indian State had the power to know and to govern not only itself but also the Indian villagers, embodiments of the ancient incapable of any action on their own even in their own time, never mind the "present" where they now found themselves.
>
> (1992: 148)

In the nineteenth-century Western discourse on Hindus we find a range of attitudes, from appreciation to denunciation to ambivalence. If some nineteenth-century Anglicists and missionaries portray Hindus as utterly corrupt and lacking in moral virtue, Müller goes to the other extreme of rectifying such caricatures and defending the truthfulness of Hindus.

But Müller's defence has much to do with a romantic notion of Hindus in an archaic past which he venerates. In his lecture entitled "The truthful character of Hindus," Müller challenges the European prejudice that Indians as a race are "so depraved morally, and more particularly devoid of any regard for truth, that they *must* always remain strangers to us, and that any real fellowship or friendship with them is quite out of the question" (Müller 1892: 76). He attributes this jaundiced view to Europeans looking upon Hindus as being totally different from Europeans. His defence of the Hindu character functions as a timely critique of the negative assessment of Hindus made by colonialist historians and missionaries. His appraisal of Hindu character stands in sharp contrast to that of early nineteenth-century figures – the Baptist missionaries such as William Ward and William Carey, and the Utilitarian James Mill, who paint Hindus as corrupt and morally decadent. William Ward goes to the extent of saying that Europeans would not want their children to have any contact with Hindus (Ward 1820a: 294–5). Müller criticizes Ward's denunciatory approach and regards him as an incompetent and biased judge of Hindu character (Müller 1892: 43). He is equally scathing about James Mill, whose three-volume *History of British India* was recommended reading for candidates for the Indian civil service. Drawing on the idealized representations of Hindus[9] by men like Warren Hastings, Bishop Heber, Sir John Malcolm, Sir Thomas Munro and Elphinstone, and on his own experience of meeting with Hindus[10] in England, Müller challenges Mill's presentation of "Hindus as such monstrous mass of all vices" (ibid.: 44). He cautions civil servants against having preconceived notions that Hindus are all liars and are to be distrusted. He remarks: "It has become almost an article of faith with every Indian Civil servant that all Indians are liars" (ibid.: 35–6). He also warns against collapsing different Indian identities into one: "There is a great difference between an Afghan, a Sikh, a Rajput, a Bengali, and a Dravidian than between an Englishman, a Frenchman, a German, and a Russian – yet all are classed as Hindus, all are supposed to fall under the same weeping condemnation" (Müller 1892: 37).

Müller represents Hindus as God-fearing people and as people who do not lie on oath. He remarks: "It was an excellent superstition, inculcated in the ancient law-books, that the ancestors watched the answers of a witness" (Müller 1892: 51). By contrast, William Jones, who in other instances affirms Hindus, says the opposite in this regard in his "Charge to the Grand Jury" – that Hindu witnesses need to be reminded "that false evidence even by their own *Shastras* is the most heinous of crimes ... such, after all, is the corrupt state even of their own erroneous religion ..." (Jones 1799b: 22). But both use texts as a yardstick to assess Hindu actions. Müller gives numerous textual examples of Hindus exemplifying Truth – from the Vedas to the epics: "The whole of their literature from one end to the other is pervaded by expressions of love and reverence for truth. Their very word for truth is full of meaning. It is sat or satya" (Müller 1892: 64). Müller's point is that, left to themselves, Hindus are truthful. As with other orientalists, Müller subscribes to the thesis that in ancient times Hindus were honest and truthful and that with Mohammedan rule Indian character came to be affected (ibid.: 54),[11] a common rhetoric used by orientalists and replicated later by nationalist Hindus. "I do not wish to represent the people of India," Müller remarks, "as 253 millions of angels, but I do wish it to be understood and to be accepted as a fact, that the damaging charge of untruthfulness brought against that people is utterly unfounded with regard to ancient times" (ibid.: 71–2).

What is often overlooked is that Müller's defence of Hindu character has more to do with his affirmation of the theory of the Aryan past than with Hinduism itself. As Thapar remarks: "Inevitably those who were sympathetic to Indian culture tended to romanticize the ancient Indian past. These interpretations carried the imagery and the preconceptions not only of the sources, but also of those interpreting them" (Thapar 1993: 3). Müller finds in Sanskrit language and literature the raw material to reconstruct an imagined Indian and the European past. Now that he has established the link between language and race, Indians and British are to be considered lost cousins. Therefore it is important to discover this European past – the lost innocence – and in the ancient Sanskrit text the *Ṛg Veda* Müller finds a clue to it.

Unlike orientalists, the Utilitarians and missionaries in the nineteenth-century found the Indian past and present stagnant, devoid of any enduring virtues. While orientalists constructed an India in terms of its supposed past glory, Utilitarians and missionaries constructed a decadent India. For all three, however, in different ways, India needed to be reformed in the light of the modern values of European Enlightenment.

Müller and James Mill had never been to India, but both represent India, and they do so in diametrically opposite ways. Mill, a Benthamite Utilitarian and a product of the Scottish Enlightenment, challenged British orientalists' claim that India, although now degraded, had once been a glorious civilization. Orientalists were fighting a losing battle because of the growing opposition to orientalist interest in and support for oriental learning in the early nineteenth century, from Anglicists such Thomas Babington Macaulay, and evangelical missionaries such as Alexander Duff. Orientalists, Anglicists, and evangelicals were engaged in a civilizing mission but with a purpose. While orientalists saw themselves as "discovering" India's ancient past and enlightening Hindus with their newly discovered knowledge, Anglicists and evangelicals saw Hindu society as primitive and decadent and in need of moral refining. Anglicists felt that Hindus had to be introduced to and educated in English manners and morals through the medium of English education. Macaulay's infamous *Minute* of 1835[12] is an example of this. In contrast, missionaries such as Carey preferred to use vernacular languages in order to convert Hindus. All three, in different ways, were engaged in modernizing Hindus and their tradition.

Fall from Aryan glory

As with other orientalists, Müller constructs an immaculate Hindu past and a defiled present. Although Hindus in their ancient past "had reached in the Upanishads the loftiest heights of philosophy," they "are now in many places sunk into a grovelling worship of cows and monkeys" (Müller 1878: 67). In other words, he regards the contemporary form of Hindu worship as a degeneration of the "pure monotheism" of the Veda into idolatry. Like his nineteenth-century missionary counterparts such as William Ward and William Carey, Müller subjects Hindu veneration of images to a Protestant appraisal. Although Müller critiques William Ward for his negative assessment of Hindu character, like Ward, Müller uses the language of negation when he speaks about Hindu worship of images. The worship of deities such as Śiva or Viṣṇu, and other popular deities, in Müller's view, is "of a more degraded and savage character than the worship of Jupiter, Apollo, and Minerva … " (Müller 1875: 263). He describes Śiva as "a monster with three eyes" (ibid.: 264) and uses terms such as "savage," "degraded," "hideous," to describe the nature of Hindu worship. He regards the images of gods as "hideous owing to their unrestrained symbolism and the entire disregard of harmony with nature" (Müller 1901b: 63). Müller is unable to appreciate the deeper levels of meaning these images may have for Hindus. His negative approach to their image worship is further reinforced in his private correspondence with Mozoomdar of the Brahmo Samāj, where Müller states: "You know for how many years I have watched your efforts to purify the popular religion of India, and thereby to bring it nearer to the purity and perfection of other religions, particularly of Christianity" (Müller 1902b: 389). He predicts that this mode of pietistic activity is something that has no place in the future. He remarks: "How long this living death of national religion in India may last, no one can tell: for our purposes, however, for gaining an idea of the issue of the religious struggle of the future, that religion too is dead and gone" (Müller

1875: 264). A religion which is in a state of decay "can't stand the light of day" (ibid.: 263). Clearly, the current vibrant and robust form of Hinduism is a living testimony that Müller's predictions haven't come true, and, as for his misperceptions, he is not without followers.

Müller seeks to fashion a purified form of Hinduism devoid of its images and idolatrous tendencies. His Protestant bias is clearly noticeable when he rates "the idolatry of prayer" higher than that of "the idolatry of temple worship." While he denounces Hindu temple worship, he values prayers addressed to the deities. He distinguishes between earnest prayers addressed to Hindu gods and the actual rituals that take place in the temple. He states: "Yet the prayers addressed to Siva and Durga are almost entirely free from these blemishes, and often show a concept of Deity of which we ourselves need not be ashamed" (Müller 1901b: 63). He desires a rational monotheistic faith resting on pure contemplation rather than on the worship of images. It is the Vedāntic Hinduism that attracts the attention of Müller.

As with Jones, Müller attributes the worship of images to the notion of Hindus being still in a state of noble savagery. Jones differs from Müller in that he shows a sympathetic attitude to temple worship and in his hymns, a lively sense of engagement with Hindu deities. Where both Müller and Jones concur is that they see Europeans as having progressed from idolatry to Protestant monotheism, whilst Hindus are seen as still lagging behind. In their view, the cure for such "idolatrous" practices lies in the civilizing influence of European ideas of the Enlightenment. Once such a form of worship comes into contact with the ideas of the enlightened West, it will be snuffed out. Müller remarks: "It belongs to a stratum of thought which is long buried beneath our feet; it may live on, like the lion and the tiger, but the mere air of free thought and civilized life will extinguish it" (Müller 1875: 263). While he acknowledges that there have been attempts to reform Hinduism from within, he regards them as far from adequate. He considers the formation of Brahmo Samāj, a nineteenth-century Hindu socio-religious movement, as a step in the right direction in that its founder, Rammohan Roy, sought to purify and restore Hinduism to its original character. Müller attributes the emergence of the Brahmo Samāj, which rejected the use of images, to the impact of modernity and to Christian influence. Müller's intentions do not simply end with reforming Hinduism; they go even further. He calls for a radical transformation of Hinduism along Christian lines. Although Müller locates a "sanitized" form of worship in the Veda, he points out the futility of establishing reformed Hinduism on the basis of the divine origin of the Veda (ibid.: 271–4). His counsel is that the Brahmo Samāj should seek its basis in Christ – a position that, as we shall see later, came to be espoused by John Farquhar. For Müller, the Veda is pure but its purity is of a primitive kind and therefore it cannot serve as a foundation for the Brahmo Samāj. Since Müller regards the Veda as belonging to the lowest stratum of the human mind, or the lower end of the evolutionary scale, it cannot provide a sound basis for reformed Hinduism.

Müller takes upon himself the role of reforming and refining Hindus who are seen as still indulging in what Müller regards as idolatrous practices. In a letter to Bunsen, Müller speaks of his desire to go to India, to overturn Hindu priestcraft and to make room for the spread of Christian teaching (Müller 1902a: 182) – a clear indication of the reforming role that he attributes to Christianity. His hermeneutical intentions become demonstrably clear in his letter to Henry Acland, where he expresses his wish to see India and Hinduism Christianized. "If we get such men again in India as Rammohun Roy, or Keshub Chunder Sen," Müller remarks, "India will be christianized in all that is essential in the twinkling of an eye" (Müller 1902b: 378). He urges Mozoomdar and other members of the Brahmo Samāj who had directed their efforts at "reforming" Hinduism, to look for guidance in the New Testament. Müller assumes the role of a moral reformer, instructing them, and at times goading them, to make a firm decision as to how much of their old religion they are willing to abandon: "*if not utterly false, still antiquated*" (ibid.: 390, emphasis mine). Müller urges them to take a serious look at the New Testament: "Take then the New Testament and read it for yourselves, and judge for yourselves whether the words of Christ, as contained in it, satisfy you or not (ibid.). For Müller, the fact that the members of Brahmo Samāj had given up idolatrous practices and even "the claim to a divine revelation,"[13] meant that educated Hindus too were responding to modernity and Christianity and thereby making their religion acceptable and appealing. What is apparent is that for Müller, Hindu worship is of no value; the only way it could be made palatable is by Christianizing it.

It is against an idealized construct of Christianity that Müller evaluates Hinduism. He calls Hindus to return to a purer form of faith located in Christ. Declaring that "India, at least the best part of it, is already converted to Christianity," Müller exhorts Mozoomdar: "You want no persuasion to become a follower of Christ. Then make up your minds to act for yourselves. Unite your flock, and put up a few folds to hold them together, and to prevent them from straying" (Müller 1902b: 394). Müller's proselytizing zeal becomes all the more apparent during his last days when he was recovering from illness. He makes every possible effort to persuade Mozoomdar and Brahmos to come clean and confess their faith in Christ. In fact, Müller goes as far as suggesting an appropriate name for the Samāj – "Christian Brahmos or Christian Aryas" – and compels Brahmo members to accept one of two names since their movement would not have come into being without Christ. Müller considers Brahmos as "Christians, without being Roman Catholics, or Anglicans or Lutherans" (ibid.: 406). He does not act merely as a colonial reformer, he pressurizes the colonized to demonstrate their gratitude to Christianity:

> But surely you owe much to Christ and Christianity, your very movement would not exist without Christianity. One must be above public opinion in these matters, and truth which is stronger than public opinion ... Only I thought the truth and gratitude would declare in favour of Christian Brahmos, or Christian Aryas.
>
> (Müller 1902b: 397)

Although Müller had given up his Aryan race theory by this time, his use of such a title is not only indicative of the supposed superiority of Aryan culture but also indicative of his willingness to appropriate such a contentious term for proselyting purposes. In his view, Brahmos should be proud to consider themselves as "Christian Aryas." In his last letter written to Mozoomdar, Müller urges Brahmo members "to speak out and declare *their real faith*, and their entire separation from modern Hinduism" (Müller 1902b: 405). He strongly emphasizes the futility of Hindu practices and instructs Mozoomdar not to tolerate what the Brahmos consider to be false. Popular Hindu practices, in Müller's view, are not suitable for the civilized Brahmos, but only for those in the savage state:

> When you think of the popular Hinduism of the present day, with its idol-worship, its Pujahs, its temple-service, its caste, its mendicants, surely you do not approve, you rather shrink from them. It is easy enough to come to an understanding with you individually, and with Brahmos who have a philosophical culture. You would admit at once that all these things are not essentials, though they may have some kind of exercise in their historical origin. You want something of that kind for the great masses of uneducated people. All that is true; but what you know to be false and dangerous should be distinctly condemned, and should not be tolerated as part of your religion.
>
> (Müller 1902b: 406)

Comparing religions

Hinduism in relation to Christianity

The hermeneutical intention of what Müller terms "the Science of Religion" (or the comparative study of religions) is to demonstrate that all religions contain some truth, and that the difference between religions is a matter of degree, and that Christianity contains the truth in fuller measure than other religions. But to discover the truth of any religion one needs to go back to "religions in their ancient form" or their original source (Müller 1868a: 49). Unlike the Baptist missionaries of the time, Müller does not categorize religions as true or false. In one of his letters, he states: "There never was a false god, nor was there ever really a false religion, unless you call a child a false man" (Müller 1902b: 135). Nor does he see religions as distorted versions of some perfect "primeval revelation" or "primeval monotheism" (Müller 1878: 254) – a view held by conservative evangelical Christians in the early nineteenth century. On the contrary, he regards religions as expressions of our search for the Infinite. "I feel convinced," Müller remarks, "that all religions spring from the same sacred soil, the human heart; that all are quickened by the same divine spirit ... " (Müller 1875: 345). He applies the historical-critical method to the study of religions including Christianity, in order to show that we can come to understand the truth of religion by the exercise of reason alone and without the help of special revelation. He declares that he has "tried to prove this, not, as others have done, by reasoning a priori only, but by historical investigation" (Müller 1902b: 276–7). To put it another way, Müller holds that without natural religion "revealed religion itself would have no firm foundation" (Müller 1868: xxxiii). On this view, the differences between religions is one of degree, as is the difference between the child and adult. In a letter to Dean Stanley, he remarks on the link between "so-called heathen" or natural religions and Christianity. He states:

> There is no distinction in kind between them and our own religion. The artificial distinction which *we* have made has not only degraded the old revelation, but has given to our own almost a spectral character. No doubt the man is different from the child, but the child is the man and the man is the child, aye, even the very suckling. We can hardly believe it, yet the fact is there, and so it is in the growth of religion. God does not date from 754 AUC; that is what I want to teach ...
>
> (Müller 1902b: 54–5)

But this does not mean that for Müller all religions are equal. He has no difficulty in acknowledging truth in all religions but is keen to demonstrate Christianity as a universal religion. While conceding that all other religions are true, Müller regards Christianity as superior. In his interview with the *Christian World*, Müller accepts that all religions have something in common but that Christianity ranks higher than the others:

> My interest in all religions is chiefly historical; I want to see what has been, in order to understand what is. Our religion is certainly better and purer than others, but in the essential points all religions have something in common. They all start with the belief that there is something beyond, and they are all attempts to reach out to it.
>
> (Müller 1902b: 363)

In his letter to Lady Welby, Müller's underlying reasons for undertaking the translation of the *Sacred Books of the East* become apparent. He assures her that his translation of monumental sacred texts "will do a great deal towards lifting Christianity into its high historical position" (Müller 1902b: 67). It follows, then, that for Müller the main aim of a comparative study of religions is to identify the differences between religions as well as confirm which one of them is of higher value. In the first volume of his *Chips from a German Workshop*, Müller's chief motive for engaging in a comparative study of religions is unambiguously clear – to establish the superiority of Christianity as a historical and revealed religion. "The Science of Religion," Müller states, "will for the first time assign to Christianity its right place among the religions of the world; ... it will restore to the whole of history of the world, in its unconscious progress towards Christianity, its true and sacred character" (Müller 1868: xx). In other words, such a study will lay bare both similarities and differences between religions yet at the same time establish the unique position of Christianity. Müller states:

> Nor it should be forgotten that while a comparison of ancient religions will certainly show that some of the most vital articles of faith are the common property of the whole mankind ... the same comparison alone can possibly teach us what is peculiar to Christianity, and what secured to it that pre-eminent position which now it holds in spite of all obloquy.
>
> (1868: xxvii-viii)

Müller reiterates the specialness of Christianity when he speaks of the value to missionaries of a comparative approach. He points out that there is a greater need to look for common ground than for differences, but at the same time holds that such a study will reveal the true content of Christianity. To put it differently, it is not the historical Christianity – not the Christianity of the nineteenth century, or that of the Middle Ages or the early Church – but the "the overpowering love of God and man, that conquered the world and superseded religions and philosophies, more difficult to conquer than the religious and philosophical systems of Hindus and Buddhists" (Müller 1868: xxvi).

Müller, it is also to be noted, introduces a system of classification that privileges Christianity over other religions. He classifies religions into missionary and non-missionary religions and rates the missionary higher than the non-missionary. He views Judaism, Brahmanism, and Zoroastrianism as belonging to the latter, and Buddhism, Mohammedanism, and Christianity to the former. He remarks that the old religion may persist longer but without the vitality and dynamism of missionary religions. He states: "But when a religion has ceased to produce defenders of the faith, prophets, champions, martyrs, it has ceased to live, in the true sense of the word" (Müller 1875: 263–4). Like most missionaries of his and a later time, Müller regards non-missionary religions as lacking the force and magnetism of missionary religions, which are seen as being "progressive, world-embracing," and he contends that it is missionary zeal that joins them together and "lifts them to a higher sphere" (Müller.: 258–9). Müller remarks:

> From the very earliest dawn of their existence these three religions were missionary: their very founders, or their first apostles, recognized the new duty of spreading the truth, of refuting error, of bringing the whole world to acknowledge the paramount, if not the divine, authority of their doctrines. This is what gives to them all a common expression, and lifts them high above the level of other religions of the world.
>
> (ibid.: 255)

Müller's theory of religion is based on the Protestant notion of progressive revelation that sees a continuity between natural and special revelation. For Müller, natural revelation is the starting point or the first step in the evolutionary progression towards a religion's culmination in Christianity; not, as we noted earlier, the historical Christianity but "the religion of Christ." He sees the link between Hinduism and Christianity in terms of an evolutionary progression from child to adult, from lower to higher. In his view, it is but natural that Hinduism should progress towards Christianity. On the face of it, it may seem that Müller is taking a sympathetic view of other religions but on closer analysis it turns out to be less sympathetic. At a time when Hinduism was being demonized by Protestant missionaries and colonialists, Müller challenged the exclusive claims made for Christianity, by subjecting all religions including Christianity to comparative and historical critical scrutiny, but it must not be forgotten that his eventual aim was to demonstrate that such a scrutiny would not endanger Christianity, but would place it higher in the evolutionary scheme.

Müller applies an adapted version of Darwin's evolutionary hypothesis to the study of religions. His evolutionary hypothesis begins not with the beast, as in Darwin's *The Origin of Species,* but with the child, but for both Müller and Darwin the pinnacle of modern European civilization is represented by Europe. Müller regards Hinduism, when compared with Christianity, as a less developed expression of a universal or transcendental truth. He perceives religions as being in various stages of development, with Hinduism at the lowest end of the evolutionary ladder and Christianity at the top. Stated differently, he regards Christianity as the repository of universal truth; Hinduism contains some truth but Christianity alone possesses the universal truth in fuller measure.

Müller's science of religion, which he regards as an objective study, turns out to be a blatant form of spiritual colonialism. In an address to young civil servants, Müller points out that the material conquest of India by the British should go hand in hand with an intellectual conquest, and to this he now adds spiritual conquest. Müller remarks in his letter to Bunsen: "After the last annexation the territorial conquest of India ceases – what follows next is the struggle in the realm of religion and of spirit, in which, of course, centres the interests of the nations. India is much riper for Christianity than Rome or Greece were at the time of St. Paul" (Müller 1902a: 182). Müller locates a purified form of Christianity in biblical texts and considers this to be the religion of humanity and the fulfillment of religions. Müller declares that "if Christianity were not only preached, but lived in that spirit, it would then prove itself what it is – the religion of humanity at large, large enough itself to take in all shades and diversities of character and race" (Müller 1875: 276). In his estimation, Hinduism and other religions lack something that Christianity has, which is the special revelation of the love of God for humanity. It is this "Gospel which will conquer all other religions" (ibid.: 278). There is a two-fold implication in Müller's approach: one is a reiteration of the deficiencies of Hinduism and the other is the presentation of a gentler and less masculine form of Christianity that would appeal to Hindus. He states that Christianity must shed its aggressive form in order to conquer the hearts of people:

> If Christianity is to retain its hold on Europe and America, if it is to conquer in the Holy War of the Future, it must throw off its heavy armour … and face the world like David, with his staff, his stones and his sling. We want … less of doctrine, but more of love. There is a faith, as small as a grain of mustard-seed but that grain alone can move mountains, and more than that, it can move hearts.
>
> (Müller 1875: 280)

Classifying sacred texts

Müller classifies the sacred texts of different religions in a hierarchical order. Christian texts – the Old and the New Testaments – are placed at the top, and the Veda is assigned the second lowest position, followed by the Zoroastrian Avesta. He applies a modified version of the nineteenth-century evolutionary hypothesis in order to grade religious texts, and in doing so, Müller introduces a single universal standard of truth in terms of which the value of other texts are assessed. As noted earlier, the primary aim of his comparative study of religions is to establish the superior position of Christianity. This comes out clearly in his response to the question posed by the Christian Commonwealth, the question of whether he would consider any one sacred book superior to all others in the world. He replies: "It may sound prejudiced, but, taking all in all, I say the New Testament. After that, I should place the Koran, which in its moral teaching is hardly more than a later edition of the New Testament. Then would follow, according to my opinion, the Old Testament, the Southern Buddhist Tripitaka … the Veda, and the Avesta" (Müller 1902b: 322). Commenting that such a classification may not be acceptable to others, he goes on to point out that in terms of ethical teaching Christian scriptures score higher than other sacred texts, and that this is what makes the Bible distinctive (ibid.: 203). In his letter to the Revd Cox, Müller states that the *Old Testament* stands on a higher ethical stage than other sacred books – "it certainly does not lose by a comparison with them" (ibid.: 174). He uses the prevailing pietistic theology of the time (the Fall, punishment and redemption) as a hermeneutical key to compare the Christian texts with others, thereby establishing the primacy of the Christian texts. While other sacred texts have only a nominal value, Christian texts are seen as having a real value. In Müller's view, "other sacred books are generally collections of whatever was remembered of ancient times. For instance, in the Veda you get a description of the Flood simply as a deluge; in the Old Testament it takes an ethical meaning, it is a punishment and a reward; there is a difference between the two; and that distinction runs through the whole of sacred books" (ibid.: 323).

For Müller the Veda is not like any other document; it is different from the Psalms or Pindar or the *Bhagavadgītā*. The Vedic hymns, he states, "are Aryan, the Psalms Semitic; they belong to a primitive and rude state of society, the Psalms, at least most of them, are contemporaneous with or even later than the heydays of the Jewish monarchy" (Müller 1875: 369). For Müller, the Veda is unique in the sense that it is the earliest document which unfolds "the earliest gems of religious thought" in a language more primitive than any that was known before. Its poetry for this reason is, Müller declares, "savage, uncouth, rude, horrible" and therefore it is important to dig deep to unravel and recover the buried past in order to know "what we were, before we had reached the level of David, the level of Homer, the level of Zoroaster, showing us the very cradle of our thoughts, or words, and our deeds" (ibid.: 370). What is clear is that it is only by denying or negating the intrinsic value of other sacred texts that Müller is able to make tall claims for Christian texts. Clearly, such an approach suggests of theological arrogance.

Redacting the sacred books of the East

Müller's translating activities are neither innocent nor altruistic. First, let me briefly spell out Müller's own attitude to the *Sacred Books of the East* to which he devoted most of his working life. As we have seen, Müller values the Veda not so much for its spiritual import as for its archival/historical worth. He states that "these Sacred Books of the East will become in future the foundation of a short but universal religion, they will become the most interesting archives of the past, studied or consulted when thousands of books of the day are forgotten" (Müller 1902b: 141). In his view, most of the material is unintelligible, that it is of no use except to an historian. "It cannot be too strongly stated," Müller remarks, "that the chief, and, in many cases ... the only interest of the Sacred Books of the East is historical; that much in them is extremely childish, tedious, if not repulsive; and that no one but the historian will be able to understand the most important lessons which they teach" (ibid.: 11). In his letter to Moncure Conway, Müller makes clear that he prefers to use the expression "Sacred Books" to "Bibles of the World": "Strictly speaking, 'Sacred Books' are such only as have received some canonical sanction, and form a body of writings to which nothing could be added. They need not be considered of Divine origin or revealed, but they must have been formally recognized as authoritative by a religious body or their representatives" (ibid.: 129). It is ironical that Müller should have spent all his time and his energies on studying, translating and editing the *Sacred Books of the East* which he felt were worthless except as antiquarian documents. While speaking of his gratitude to the East India Company for the publication of the Ṛg Veda, Müller remarks that "such a publication would have ruined any bookseller, for it must be confessed, that there is little that is attractive in the Veda, nothing that could cite general interest. From an esthetic point of view, no one would care for the hymns of the Rig-veda" (Müller 1875: 367). He firms up his view quoting Colebrooke who saw the Veda as being "too voluminous for a complete translation, and what they contain would hardly reward the labour of the reader, much less that of the translator" (ibid.).

Clearly, there is an ulterior motive behind Müller's massive translation enterprise. His aim is evidently to expose the deficiencies of the *Sacred Books of the East* and make Christian proselytization easier for missionaries. In fact, he makes clear that one of the principal aims of translating the *Sacred Books of the East* is to assist the missionaries (Müller 1902b: 455–6). As noted earlier, Müller assures Lady Welby that the translation will enhance and firm up the exalted position of Christianity. In his letter to the Dean of St Paul's, Müller remarks: "I myself have the strongest belief in the growth of Christianity in India (Müller 1902a: 332).

Concluding remarks

In summing up Müller from a postcolonial perspective, I would like to draw on theoretical categories such as the trope of the child, representation, classification, and colonial patronage.

Trope of the child

As we have seen, one of the significant features of oriental and colonial discourse is that it uses the trope of the child to represent the "Other." The trope of the child functions as a useful hermenutical device in that it establishes a link between the invader and invaded, but at the same time situates the former in a position of superiority. As Ashcroft remarks:

> The child, at once both other and same, holds in balance the contradictory tendencies of imperial rhetoric: authority is held in balance with nurture; domination with enlightenment; debasement with idealization; negation with affirmation; exploitation with education; filiation with affiliation. This ability to absorb contradiction gives the binary parent/child an inordinate hegemonic potency.
>
> (Ashcroft 2001: 36–7)

The trope of the child serves a number of purposes useful to the colonizer: it allows the colonizer to exercise his benevolent parental authority over colonial subjects. For the colonial parent the child symbolizes a state of innocence, unspoiled purity or a natural state, and therefore the child cannot exercise its rational faculties. The colonial parent now becomes the guardian into whose care colonial subjects are entrusted. In other words, the colonial parent takes upon himself/herself the responsibility of looking after the physical, mental, moral, and spiritual welfare of colonial children. The problem is that the child is never allowed to grow; its identity is permanently fixed and frozen. As we have seen, for Müller the Veda embodies thoughts which are still in their infancy. He affirms the Veda but only as a product of an infantile mind which lacks the rationality of a mature adult. Critiquing the anthropological significance attached to the term "savage," meaning primitive or "uncivilized," Müller introduces two classes of savages – "*progressive*" and "*retrogressive*" – signifying "a hopeful and hopeless barbarism"; "a growing and a decaying civilization" (Müller 1901a: 156). In his view, "Man certainly began as a savage, but as a progressive savage" (ibid.: 178), regressing now and then, only to rise again. A "retrogressive savage" is one who has descended from a higher state but has the possibility of ascending again (ibid.: 156). Müller puts forward the much favored orientalist thesis – that Hindus had once reached a higher stage of civilization, but had regressed into a state of barbarism. They could regain their ancient purity with the help of the evolved European culture. Hindus in their present state had lost touch with their archaic purity, which Müller sought to recover for them, but his thesis does not end here. Once the lost childhood is regained, Hindus need nurturing in order to grow into full maturity. For Müller, the religious journey begins with the Veda – symbolizing childhood innocence – and attains the "perfect manhood of the Aryan mind" in Kant's *Critique of Pure Reason*. The Vedic child is always a child; it needs the nurturing parent to facilitate its growth. The child lacks the necessary stimuli (reason and logic), which can be offered only by the European colonial parent. Müller constructs the Veda as the product of the newborn child's first attempts to unravel the mystery of the Infinite. Whether the colonized cultures are thought of in terms of "primitive savage" or "progressive savage," it (the very concept "savage") legitimizes colonial intervention and the exercise of authority over the colonized in the interests of the colonized subjects. Müller's idea of "a progressive savage" implies the possibilities of evolution and fulfillment in a higher and universal truth, which, in his view, is no other than Christianity in its non-ecclesiastical form. Such a concept authorizes the colonizer to inscribe his particular vision, thus negating the intellectual space of the colonized. In construing Hindus as locked in their infancy, Müller renders them powerless, needing the help of enlightened cultures. The trope of the child enables Müller and other orientalists to romanticize about their own (Europe's) lost innocence. As Ashcroft *et al.* remark:

> The concept ["noble savage"] arises in the eighteenth century as a European nostalgia for a simple, pure, idyllic state of the natural, posed against rising industrialism ... It creates images of the savage that serve primarily to redefine the European. The crucial fact about the construction is that it produces an ostensibly positive oversimplification of the "savage" figure, rendering it in this particular form as an idealized rather than a debased stereotype.
>
> (ibid. 1998: 210)

Representation

Representation functions as an important hermeneutical tool in orientalist and colonial discourses. It has to do with power dynamics, between the one who represents and the one who is represented: it is about power over the "Other." Representation is largely informed by the interpreter's own historical location, together with socio-economic, political, religious, and other factors. No representation is a neutral or innocent activity; it functions as an interpretative act at the same time. As we have seen, Müller's representations of India and Hinduism are largely constructed images – images that reflect Müller's own nostalgic search for the supposed lost origins of European culture. Müller regards his own conception of India as being an authentic representation of actual India. He sees himself as a spokesperson for Hindus who are regarded as being oblivious of their own glorious past. There is a long line of orientalists engaged in the task of discovering the "real" or "true" Hinduism for Hindus; in their view, Hindus, being in a state of degeneration, have lost touch with their pristine past. Müller tells Hindus where to look for the "real" India and Hinduism: as with other orientalists, he invents an India of his own imagination. A closer look at his representation reveals more about what India means to Müller than what India is. As David Richard remarks: "[t]he representation of other cultures invariably entails the presentation of self-portraits, in that those people who are observed are overshadowed or eclipsed by the observer" (quoted in McLeod 2000: 41). In Müller's discourse India becomes the site of the West's search for, and discovery of, its own self. It is the constructed glorious past of Hindus that is vital for

Europe's own self-definition and self-representation. The theme of venerable past and degenerate present is a common rhetoric employed by orientalists, the ancient past of Hindus signifying the lost pristine purity of Europe, and the Hindu present, negation of European modernity. Whereas the Hindu present is totally the Other, the Hindu past has affinities with Europe's past. Müller is interested in Hinduism as a relic of the past – a past that confirms Europe's superiority. Hinduism has only an archival significance. To put it differently, the ancient past is made harmless by representing it as static and timeless, thus rendering it familiar and accessible to Europe. There is nothing to fear or dread about it, for it is Europe's own distant Other in its primitive state. For Müller, as we have seen, the Veda, to the exclusion of other Hindu texts, contains a pristine form of Hinduism, and Hindus, in his view, need to wake up to the truth of this fact – the truth that orientalists like Müller have discovered for Hindus. Hindus do not know the truth about their own religion. What often goes unnoticed is that for Müller, the purity of the Veda is of a primitive kind. In other words, he regards the Veda as a less refined version of truth. The Veda is not the product of a spiritually enlightened person but that of a child attempting to unravel the mysterious Infinite. A reading such as this is far removed from any objectivity, as claimed by Müller. He fashions a Hinduism that suits his Protestant taste and evolutionary hypothesis. He offers a non-dogmatic Protestant interpretation and imposes his own views of what the Veda is or should be. Müller claims objectivity for his theory of the science of religion which places the Veda at the beginning of the evolutionary paradigm. He considers his theory of religion as a scientific study of the history of the evolution of religious ideas, but his evolutionary hypothesis allows him "a positional superiority." He adopts a convenient hermeneutical strategy that affirms Hindus and Europeans as cousins but which at the same time maintains the West's superiority by placing Hindus in a permanent state of infancy. As Said remarks, "In a quite constant way, orientalism depends for its strategy on this flexible *positional* superiority, which puts the Westerner in a whole series of possible relationships with the Orient without ever losing him ever the relative upper hand" (1985: 7). Müller takes for granted the superiority of the West in its relationship with the East. Although he regards the East as "the ancestral home of Europeans," that in no way diminishes the superior status of the evolved West. Müller does not resort to binarisms but he treats the "Other" as less developed compared to the rational West.

Classification

Another example of the link between knowledge and power is markedly visible in the way the colonizer classified the colonized and their cultures. In nineteenth century colonial discourse, classification was a way of domesticating and appropriating the Other on terms congenial to the colonizer.

Classification meant reordering and restructuring in terms of the modernist norms and values of the European Enlightenment. The collecting and cataloguing of texts, artifacts, trees, plants, seeds, and animals of non-Western peoples were clear markers of colonial dominance in nineteenth-century India. Classification, naming, and mapping the Other, was a way of asserting European supremacy. The invader worked on the assumption that the cultures of the invaded were "chaotic," needing reordering and categorizing. Müller's theory of the science of religion resonates with the nineteenth-century discourse of colonial science. Gyan Prakash demonstrates that colonial science worked on the premise that the natives' knowledge of their agricultural products was muddled and requiring reorganization, and that the natives needed to be educated in the science of classification. He explains: "If one aim of colonial pedagogy was to instruct peasants by exhibiting their own products and knowledge organized and authorized by the science of classification, its other aim was to render manifest the principle of function so that it could be applied to improve production" (Prakash 1999: 23). A similar exercise is evident in Müller's classification of religions along evolutionary lines. Müller's aim is to demonstrate that such a classification would give a clear insight into the origin and evolution of the religious ideas of humankind. Müller's evolutionary hypothesis legitimizes a hierarchical view of religions, with Hinduism occupying the lowest position and Christianity the highest. Implicit in Müller's evolutionary paradigm is the modernist notion of a single universal standard of truth applicable to all cultures – a standard by which they can be evaluated; the modernist paradigm imposes a monolithic vision of truth on all cultures. Müller finds in non-ecclesiastical Christianity the universal criterion for grading religions and determining their place in the evolutionary ladder. While Müller's inclusivist approach to Hinduism and other religions challenges exclusivist attitudes, it denies Hinduism any independent agency.

After the publication of Said's *Orientalism* the connection between knowledge and power could not be ignored. Drawing on the Foucaultian thesis that knowledge is inextricably linked with power, Said shows that the production of knowledge about the Orient by the West is not an innocent activity. A significant number of textual projects (from editing to the translation of Sanskrit texts) were initiated, approved, and authorized by the colonial government from the eighteenth century onwards. In the first place, it is the West's power over the East that facilitated the production of knowledge about the East, and this in turn fortified the power of the West over the East. As Said remarks:

> Under the general heading of the knowledge of the Orient, and within the umbrella of Western hegemony over the Orient, during the period from the end of the eighteenth century, there emerged a complex Orient suitable for study in the academy, for display in the museum, for

> reconstruction in the colonial office, for theoretical illustration in anthropological, biological, linguistic, racial, and historical theses about mankind and the universe, for instances of economic and sociological theories of development, revolution, cultural personality, national or religious character.
>
> (1985: 7–8)

Colonial patronage

Müller's undertaking of the textual production of *Sacred Books of the East* falls into the category of what is termed colonial patronage in postcolonial discourse. The term patronage

> refers to the economic or social power that allows cultural institutions and cultural forms to come into existence and be valued and promoted. Patronage can take the form of a simple and direct transaction, such as the purchase or commissioning of works of art by wealthy people, or it can take the form of the support and recognition of social institutions that influence the production of culture.
>
> (Ashcroft *et al.* 1995: 43)

For example, Charles Wilkins' translation of the *Bhagavadgītā,* and Müller's translation and edition of the six-volume *Ṛg Veda*, which had the financial backing of the East India Company, were not totally apolitical ventures. Müller's project had royal patronage as well; in a colonial reversal of roles, the then Prince of Wales took with him numerous copies of Müller's *Sacred Books of the East* to give as gifts to Indian kings during the Durbar.[14] They were partly undertaken with a specific political objective.[15] True, early orientalist-administrators such as Warren Hastings and Sir William Jones were more appreciative of India and its culture, but they believed that the sound knowledge of Hindu beliefs and practices gained from their texts would be politically beneficial, inasmuch as that it would enable them to exercise effective control over the natives. Müller's translation projects not only legitimized British colonial rule but also justified intellectual and spiritual conquest. In other words, the orientalist pursuit of knowledge was inextricably bound up with the desire for colonial expansion and domination. As Eric Sharpe remarks: "The reason why East India Company in London had been prepared to fund the first translation of the Gita was partly that they had allowed themselves to be persuaded that it might prove politically expedient for them to do so. … Max Müller's text of the *Rig-Veda* was funded by the same commercial company on the same grounds" (1985: 45).

Postcolonialism draws attention to the Eurocentric assumptions underpinning the textual projects undertaken during the colonial era, which regarded literary culture as superior to orality. What Müller's *Sacred Books of the East* project did was to privilege the written word. In other words, the printed page became the means of revelation. The written text was seen as a mark of modernity and progress, while the oral text was primitive. For missionaries, the written word was not merely a mark of civilization; salvation was to be mediated through the word. Both orientalists and missionaries aimed at bringing about a separation between the written and the oral, privileging the written. The outcome of such an exercise resulted in the production of textual knowledge about Hinduism that had little relevance to the vast majority of Hindus whose lives were not directly informed by written texts. As pointed out elsewhere, the link between the written and oral cultures has always been fluid in the Hindu tradition – one impacting on the other to varying degrees. Hindus already had a highly developed literary culture, but they wanted to demonstrate that their traditions were on a par with European cultures. As van der Veer states: "The colonial, textualizing project of modernity, however, elicited a strange reaction. It provided a sufficient motivation to prepare a critical edition of the Mahābhārata and, later, the Rāmāyaṇa and the Purāṇas, since Indian scholars wanted to represent their tradition in a manner equal to how other civilizations represented her traditions" (2001: 119).

To conclude, for Müller Hinduism in its archaic form signifies an eternal state of childhood and it is this discovery that matters to him. Müller's Hinduism reflects his own romantic quest for the lost origins of European culture, and India becomes a fertile hermeneutical location for his nostalgic ruminations.

Chapter 3

William Ward's "virtuous Christians, vicious Hindus"

> It is not so much the material as the moral and spiritual subjugation of Indian civilization that in the end impoverishes humanity.
>
> (Coomaraswamy 1909: i)

This chapter concerns the nineteenth-century Protestant missionary William Ward's *A View of the History, Literature, and Mythology of the Hindoos.*[1] This four-volume text went through several editions both in India and England (the first edition, titled *Account of the Writings, Religion and Manners of the Hindoos*, was published in 1811). It came to be seen as an important text providing reliable and authoritative information on Hindu religion and society. It also became a convenient tool in the hands of Protestant evangelicals in Britain such as William Wilberforce and Charles Grant, who used it to enlist the support of the British parliament for the renewal of the East India Company's Charter in 1813, allowing missionaries (who until then were not welcome) to enter India.

Born in Derby to a carpenter and builder, William Ward (1769–1823) was one of the trio of Baptist missionaries associated with the Serampore Mission, a pioneering mission station in nineteenth-century Bengal. Serampore, a town north of Calcutta, was at that time a Danish colony.[2] The other two were William Carey and Joshua Marshman. Ward was initially a printer, a bookseller, and a journalist before becoming a Baptist. It seems that he offered himself as a Baptist missionary to help William Carey, who needed a printer for his mission work in India. Though Ward mainly spent his time supervising the printing of scriptures into Indian vernacular languages, it was for his four-volume text on *Hindoos* that he was best known. These volumes, which were a mixture of observation of everyday Hinduism and an evangelical critique of popular practices, opened up to the British and the American public a complex tradition which hitherto had remained mysterious. While orientalists such as Jones and Müller were trying to recover a textual and a pristine form of Hinduism, Ward was largely engaged with Hinduism at the ground level, and in denouncing most of what he witnessed.

To examine Ward's Hinduism, I draw on the rhetorical strategies identified by David Spurr, in terms of which Western writing interprets and represents non-Western cultures. He identifies "twelve rhetorical modes, or ways of writing about non-Western peoples" (Spurr 1993: 3), such as surveillance, appropriation, estheticization, classification, debasement, negation, affirmation, and so forth. These categories are not discrete; they impinge on one another. Of the twelve categories, I will employ the rhetorical strategies or themes of negation and debasement which are particularly relevant to my examination of William Ward's construction of Hinduism. In using these categories, my intention is to bring to light some of the hermeneutical factors at work in Ward's representation of Hinduism.

Negating a tradition

In colonial discourse, negations serve to undermine the cultures of the colonized; they allow the "civilized" race to take on the role of moral and social reformers of what they see as a corrupt religion and society. David Spurr draws attention to the rhetorical device of negation by which Western discourse conceptualizes the Other "as absence, emptiness, nothingness, or death." He remarks:

> First, negation serves to reject the ambiguous object for which language and experience provide no adequate framework of interpretation; second … negation acts as a kind of provisional erasure, clearing a space for the expansion of the colonial imagination and for the pursuit of desire. In this way, the structures of discourse, in which language is divided, subordinated, and made into a working system, recapitulate the historical process of establishing and maintaining colonial rule.
>
> (Spurr 1993: 92–3)

Ward's text is replete with a series of negations in terms of which Hinduism is represented. Hinduism is made to signify nothing; its texts, beliefs, and practices are all stripped of their meanings. For Ward and his Baptist colleagues (Carey and Marshman), Hinduism is to be purged of what they see as its numerous evils such as idol worship, caste, *satī*, polygamy, child-marriage, infanticide, and so on. Hindu beliefs and practices belong to a different order of reality and the source of these practices is to be found in their texts. Hinduism needs to be exorcised of its demonic powers and this can only be done by introducing the Gospel to the heathens. Ward constructs the notion of an eternally "degraded India" which requires the moral and virtuous influence of Britain. As with orientalists and missionaries of the time, Ward, too, considers British rule as a sign of divine providence:

> It must have been to accomplish some very important moral change in the Eastern world, that so vast an empire as is comprized in British India, containing nearly One Hundred Millions of people, should have been placed under the dominion of one of the smallest portions of the civilized world ... This opinion, which is entertained unquestionably by every enlightened philanthropist, is greatly strengthened when we consider the long-degraded state of India ... the moral enterprise of the age in which these countries have been given to us, and that Great Britain is the only country upon earth, from which the intellectual and moral improvement of India could have been expected. All these combined circumstances surely carry us to the persuasion, that Divine Providence has, at this period of the world, some great good to confer on the East.
>
> (Ward 1820a: xvii–xviii)

Hindu texts: corrupted and corrupting

Ward debases and trivializes Hindu sacred texts. He considers them impure, defiled, and disgusting. He describes the *Purāṇas* as "filth" (1817a: xcv) and sees *The Laws of Manu* as encouraging all possible vices such as adultery, stealing, perjury, and lying (1817a: xciii). "The modern Hindoos," states Ward, "believe, that the Vedus [Veda] is the source of all shastrus, just as an illiterate Englishman might suppose, that every part of English learning came from the Encyclopedia" (1820b: iii). It is interesting to note that *The Laws of Manu* which Ward denounces, Jones translated and codified in the belief that it would benefit both Hindus and the colonial government (see Juridical Jones). While for Ward Hindu texts are inconsequential, for Jones and Müller, Hindu texts are important only insofar as they validate their own theological presuppositions. For Jones, Hindu texts such as the *Purāṇas*, which Ward ridicules, confirm the historical authenticity and primacy of the biblical religion. For Müller, the Veda, which Ward dismisses, is of immense historical value; in it he finds the genesis and growth of religious ideas. If Ward regards Hindu texts as utterly corrupt, Jones and Muller view them as infantile. Despite approaching Hindu texts in different ways, all three nevertheless affirm the superiority of the Christian text.

Ward reads Hindu beliefs and daily practices largely through a restricted textual lens. For him and his Baptist colleagues, products of the Enlightenment and eighteenth-century Protestant pietism, the text is of paramount importance. They believe in the sufficiency of scripture and in its intrinsic authoritative value. Moreover, they subscribe to a literal meaning of the text. Ward is applying this criterion to scrutinize Hindu texts, totally overlooking the fact that Hindus have a different approach to their own scriptures. He is looking at Hindu texts from a literal point of view, and the passage below indicates the hermeneutical difficulties he was unaware of.

> In translating some parts of the Hindoo writings with a learned bramhun who assisted the author, this bramhun was himself almost covered with shame: he hesitated, faultered, and, while giving the meaning of various passages of his own shastrus, was thrown into great agitation. Multitudes of fables and scenes are found in the most chaste of the Hindoo writings, belonging to the histories of their gods and ancient sages, that are disgusting beyond all utterance; but the passages here more particularly referred to, describe acts of impurity daily practised by large bodies of Hindoos ...
>
> (Ward 1820a: xxxvii–xxxviii)

The brahmin's faltering or hesitation is seen as signifying his embarrassment at having to explain "obscene" passages. What Ward fails to register is that for most Hindus, the metaphorical meaning is more important than the reading of the text at a redacted level. Ward projects not only his puritanical view but also his literal understanding of text on to the brahmin's difficulty. What he fails to note is that the Hindu attitude to scriptures is rather less formal, and that one is not bound by them in all their complex details. Ward operates on the Protestant assumption that the written word plays a central role in the lives of Hindus.

Although the Baptist missionaries were interested in the classical and vernacular languages of India, and especially Sanskrit and Bengali, their main aim was to use language as a tool for conversion. They translated Hindu sacred texts in Sanskrit into various indigenous and European languages in order to draw attention to what they saw as their "sacred nothings" (in Young 1981: 349), and they contrasted Hindu texts with the Gospel to demonstrate the former's insufficiency. They saw their knowledge of Hindu texts as being superior to that of the brahmin pundits, and therefore considered they were in a fit position to denounce them as being useless. The Baptist missionaries, coming from a background of being dissenters at home, found in brahmins a priestly hegemony which they sought to undermine. They were seen as an obstacle to their missionary enterprise. Although the missionaries sought the assistance of the native interpreters, they did not trust them entirely. Carey's preface to *A Grammar of the Bengalee Language* affirms this mistrust: "The advantage of being able to communicate useful knowledge to the heathens, with whom we have a daily intercourse; to point out their mistakes; and to impress upon them sentiments of morality and religion, are confessedly very important" (1818: vi). The brahmin pundits were perceived as lacking the hermeneutical skills of a Protestant exegete. They were denied the power to speak their own language and interpret their own texts in their own way, and when one denies a voice to the native, the language is rendered powerless and almost silent.

Anglicists such as Thomas Macaulay who knew no Sanskrit affirmed the superiority of Western knowledge by stating that "a single shelf of a good

European library was worth the whole native literature of India and Arabia" (Young 1935: 349), while missionaries such as Carey and Ward translated Hindu texts with a view to undermining their influence and sanctity. The superior truth of Christianity and the wisdom of European literature and knowledge were to be conveyed through India's indigenous languages.

> But let Hindoost'han receive that higher civilization she needs, that cultivation of which she is so capable, let European literature be transfused into all her languages, and then the ocean, from the ports of Britain to India, will be covered with our merchant vessels; and from the centre of India moral culture and science will be extended all over Asia.
>
> (Ward 1820a: liii)

Christian monotheism and Hindu gods and goddesses

Ward constructs contrasting pairs to devalue and deprive Hinduism of any positive trait. Christian monotheism becomes the yardstick in terms of which Hinduism is evaluated and contrasted. He represents Hindu gods as lacking in morality and speaks of the disastrous effects these gods can have on Hindus. Such Hindu gods are not worthy of devotion or worship. In his view, Christians worship "the one living and true God" (Ward 1817a: xiv), whereas Hindus worship images that do not represent God but are "formed by the fancies of men" (ibid.). Christians have been given "the highest knowledge of the Divine Nature" whereas Hindus have gods who are unruly.

> The mysterious subject, which has confounded the human capacity in every age, the Divine Nature, is so plainly unfolded in the Gospel, that most unlettered Christian is able to reap all the fruits of the highest knowledge, that is, to worship God in spirit and in truth; but in the Hindoo system, we have innumerable gods, all of them subject to the discordant passions.
>
> (Ward 1820a: 295–6)

While Hinduism "has no one principle which can pacify the conscience," the Gospel offers hope and redemption from guilt (Ward 1820a: 296). Hinduism lacks a living monotheistic personal god who demands of the individual not only personal commitment but also moral responsibility:

> The doctrine of a plurality of gods, with their consequent intrigues, criminal amours, quarrels, and stratagems to counteract each other, has produced the most fatal effects on the minds of men. Can we expect a people to be better than their gods? … It is worthy of enquiry, how the

> world is governed by these gods more wicked than men, that we may be able to judge how far they can be objects of faith, hope and affection.
> (Ward 1817a: lxxxviii–lxxxix)

Ward projects his evangelical and puritanical attitude on to the lively Bengali popular culture which treated its gods and goddesses "as ordinary mortals with human feelings like love and jealousy, gratitude and vengeance, lust and selfishness" and freely indulged in oral "desecration of high-falutin and mystical theories ... or the coupling of serious myths with their earthy, abusive parodies of gods ... They offered a sort of non-official, extra-ecclesiastical version of the world, as seen by the lower orders of the society" (Banerjee 1989: 82–3).

The missionaries looked on in horror at the Hindu veneration of deities and at popular devotional practices which did not conform to their Protestant notion of a monotheistic god. Hindu devotion to the god Kṛṣṇa was ridiculed; it was divested of its meaning and made to signify nothing. The language of debasement is at work in Ward's description of Hindu devotional worship:

> During the celebration of worship in the house, the crowd out of doors sing, dance, and make a horrid discord with barbarous instruments of music, connecting with the whole every kind of indecency ... After eating and drinking, they literally "rise up to play:" youths, dressed so as to represent Krishnu and his mistress Radha, dance together ...
> (1817a: 196–7)

Ward's puritanical distaste for such harmless fun makes him ridicule Hindus. Cross-dressing, to which he refers, is not peculiar to any one culture; it was common in Shakespeare's plays, where young men played the part of women. Hindu *bhakti* (devotional) tradition has many examples of male devotees expressing their mystical longing for Kṛṣṇa; this requires a male devotee to suspend his masculinity so that he can approach Kṛṣṇa as his beloved. Sumanta Banerjee gives an insightful account of the impact of the Bengali popular culture on Europeans. He writes: "It was not only the contents of the songs of Bengali folk literature that shocked the sentiments of the Victorian Englishman, but it was the gay abandon, the playful musical laughter, the uninhibited prancing and rhythmic surprises which were a part of folk singing and dancing that disturbed him most" (1989: 157). David Spurr's comment on a Western description of a native African dance is equally applicable to Ward's account of Hindu ecstatic devotional singing and dancing:

> [T]his is the projection of a uniquely Western problematic onto the rituals of a non-Western people and that, as the working through of a modernist aesthetic, it conforms precisely to the deployment of a discourse

> in which colonized peoples are systematically represented in terms of negation and absence – absence of order, of limits, of light, of spirit.
>
> (1993: 96)

Similarly, the worship of the goddess Durgā, accompanied by dance and music, was seen as "a crime of high treason against the God of heaven" (Ward 1817a: 118). Religion to the Protestant missionaries such as Ward was a somber, pietistic and serious affair, and was to be free from any lively religious devotion. "A poor-ballad singer in England," Ward remarks, "would be sent to the house of correction, and flogged, for performing the *meritorious actions* [italics in original] of these wretched idolaters" (ibid.: 119).

Contrasting a particular version of nineteenth-century Protestant Christianity with Hinduism, Ward declares that Hinduism lacks any visible coherent system of beliefs and practices promoting moral behavior. The rhetorical strategy of negation is manifest in Ward's definition of Hinduism. He interprets and represents Hinduism in terms of his own understanding of Christianity and the West. Hinduism is deprived of its complexity and variety. It is seen as a total negation of his notion of religion. It does not conform to his Protestant concept of religion with its prescribed set of beliefs and its emphasis on history, centrality of scriptures, adherence to doctrine, and questions of truth and falsity. In other words, Hinduism lacks what Protestant Christianity affirms. Such negations, implicit in Ward's binarisms, highlight missionary colonialism; the differences are decisive to justify his high moral ground:

> The reader will perceive, that in all these religious ceremonies not a particle is found to interest or amend the heart; no family bible, "profitable for doctrine, for reproof, for instruction in righteousness, that men may be thoroughly furnished unto all good works;" no domestic worship, no pious assembly … No standard of morals … Here everything that assumes the appearance of religion, ends … in an unmeaning ceremony, and leaves the heart cold as death to every moral principle.
>
> (Ward 1817a: lxxxiii)

Feminized Hinduism and muscular Christianity

One of the hermeneutical devices employed by Ward to describe Hinduism is to see it in effeminate terms. Hindus are portrayed as effeminate people, and their effeminacy is attributed to the worship of deities who are perceived as encouraging immoral behavior. Qualities such as "deception" and "falsehood" are associated with Hindu effeminacy and all effeminate nations (Ward 1820a: 289), whereas these vices are scorned by manly nations. An effeminate society can only produce effeminate people. Ward uses the rhetorical strategy of debasement to undermine Hindus:

> Perhaps this is the vice of all effeminate nations, while blunt honesty, and stern integrity, are most common in climates where men are more robust. It is likewise certain, that people in a state of mental bondage are most deceitful: and that falsehood is most detested by men in a state of manly independence. An English sailor, however vicious in other respects, scorns to take refuge in a falsehood: but the Hindoos, imitating the gods, and encouraged by the shastru, which admits of prevarication in cases of necessity, are notoriously addicted to falsehood, whenever their fears, their cupidity, or their pride, present the temptation.
>
> (1820a: 289–90)

In Ward's view, Hindu effeminacy lacks any sense of the order or the rationality that characterizes Protestant Christianity. The implication is that Hindus need a male savior to free them from their effeminacy. The Hindu gods are seen as too effeminate to serve any useful purpose. Kṛṣṇa is represented as an effeminate deity and his effeminacy is equated with lasciviousness. By contrast, Jones, as a poet, speaks fondly of Kṛṣṇa and does not always associate effeminacy with moral depravity, although he sees it as indicative of a primitive state. Ward shows a total lack of any sensitivity in his treatment of Hindus and their gods who are represented as coarse and vulgar in every respect:

> [T]he characters of the gods, and the licentiousness which prevails at their festivals, and abounds in their popular works, with the enervating nature of the climate, have made the Hindoos the most effeminate and corrupt people on earth ... Suffice to say, that fidelity to marriage vows is almost unknown among the Hindoos; the intercourse of the sexes approaches very near to that of the irrational animals.
>
> (1817a: xciv–xcv)

Kṛṣṇa's "lascivious character" can only make Hindus all the more licentious. Ward even brings in a Sanskrit pundit from the College of Fort William to legitimize his claim that Hindus are more morally degraded. For Ward, the fact that most Hindu homes contain an image of Kṛṣṇa "exhibits pretty plainly the state of the public morals" (1820a: 288). He goes on to say: "The number of houses of ill-fame in Calcutta is almost incredible. Indeed, such is the licentious character of this people, that, notwithstanding all terrors of the cast, thousands of bramhuns live with parier and Musulman women" (ibid.).

Colonialists constructed a feminized India, inhabited by effeminate men who were incapable of ruling their country or looking after their women. In depriving the Indian male of his masculinity, the British assumed the role of civilizing and transforming the natives and their religion which was replete with feminine imagery and which allowed free expression of emotion in worship. The British construction of an effeminate India was largely based on their experience of Bengal; it acquired various shades of meaning and emphases at particular periods. As Mrinalini Sinha points out, "Whether effeminacy was explained in terms of social or economic factors or such supposedly scientific factors as climate, biology … the emphasis was inevitably on decline and degeneracy" (1995: 20–21).

"Corrupt Hindus"

Colonial constructions of the Other, which revolve round "themes of debasement," often assign to the colonized qualities such as "dishonesty, suspicion, superstition, lack of self-discipline" (Spurr 1993: 76). In Western discourse, as David Spurr points out, "the debasement of the Other often suggests a prohibition designed to protect the boundaries of Western cultural value against forces of this destructive desire" (ibid.: 79). Ward's text contains numerous examples of debasement. While for orientalists such as Jones and Müller, the Hindu past is untainted although the present is depraved, for Ward and other missionaries both the past and present are equally corrupt. In other words, Ward frames a morally decadent Hindu society which is beyond redemption. He sees Hindus as effeminate, superstitious, idolatrous, deceitful, corrupt, and lacking in morality. Any contact with them is not good for European children. Ward debases Hindus to such an extent that there can be no meeting point between Hindus and Europeans. He emphasizes the Otherness so that the distance between the two is maintained – too wide to be bridged. The idea is to protect Western virtue from Hindu decadence. There is a fear of being infected with vices which the West has shed as a result of becoming Christian. Hindus, however, remain in their savage state which Ward, as an evangelical Christian, loathes. He expresses his own fear and disgust:

> [I]f the vices of lying, deceit, dishonesty, and impurity, can degrade a people, then the Hindoos have sunk to the utmost depths of human depravity … The impurity of the conversation and manners of the Hindoos is so much dreaded by Europeans, that they tremble for the morals of their children, and consider their removal to Europe, however painful such a separation may be to the mind of a parent, as absolutely necessary to prevent their ruin.
>
> (Ward 1820a: 294–6)

Such negative images have their roots in one's "own fear and loathing" which are then projected on to the Other. David Spurr draws attention to the underlying motives of this rhetorical devaluation of the Other:

> [M]odern colonial discourse has produced a respatialization of the savage, or that it at least maintains, on the level of ideology, a projection of anxiety onto the racial and cultural Other that has always been part of the human imagination. The contributions of psychoanalytic theory, moreover, suggest that the interiorization of savagery does not simply replace a concept of the savage *out there,* [italics in original] but rather takes place simultaneously with a process of symbolic elaboration that objectifies savagery, wildness and animality in other human beings.
>
> (1993: 77)

Colonial discourse often constructs differences between the "savage" and the "civilized" in order to justify the superiority of the colonizer's culture over the colonized, and also to maintain a hold over them. Such a distinction, as we have noted, is also present in oriental discourse, but the difference is that while Jones and Müller regard the savage state as a mark of infancy or immaturity, Ward considers it as a negation of all civilized norms and values. Ward himself poses the question and answers it by remarking on the difference between the two states:

> What is the precise boundary which marks the distinction between the civilized and the savage state. Is it not, that in the former the improvement of the mind is recognized as the highest end of existence, but not in the later? The Hindoo manners strongly remind us of this distinction.
>
> (Ward 1820a: xvii)

In order to reinforce his negative picture of Hindus, Ward employs an indirect form of native speech to undergird his own claim. His text contains reported speeches of anonymous Hindus who discredit their own tradition. He records that he had heard from "Hindoos of all ranks" that strict adherence to truth in business transactions was not possible. Having said that, they also admitted that dishonesty was not approved by their scriptures (Ward 1820a: 290). Ward makes the colonized speak the language the colonizer wants to hear: namely, that Hindus are prone to such vices. Furthermore, deceit and lying are seen by Ward as having scriptural sanction. By contrast, Müller, as we have seen, defends Hindu character but his defense has to do with a mythical past. He gives textual examples in order to demonstrate that Hindus were truthful in the past, although they are now in a state of utter degradation. In fact, as have seen, Müller severely critiques Ward's negative representation of Hindus.[3] What we find in Ward is a total negation of any trace of civilized behavior on the part of Hindus. In other words, they are almost rendered incapable of any decent behavior. Although Ward acknowledges that Hindus are "mild, communicative and polite," he is quick to add, "we are not to look among them for the solid virtues, such as integrity, humanity, truth or generosity" (ibid.: 286–7). His acknowledgment of politeness in Hindus is immediately followed by a negative assessment of them:

> The politeness of the Hindoos, even of many of the poorest, has been generally noticed, though the effect of this is greatly counterbalanced by their proneness to flattery and deception ... Nor does their politeness arise so much from urbanity of disposition, as from early discipline and example; and, we must add, that in many respects, according to European ideas, the Hindoos, are guilty of the grossest infraction of good manners.
> (1820a: xxiv)

Ward employs a series of dualistic polarizations to debase Hinduism and affirm the moral and civilizing influence of Christianity over Hinduism. While "Hindooism has never made a single votary more useful, more moral, or more happy ... The Christian Religion, on the contrary, has turned millions upon millions from vice to virtue ... " (ibid.: 296–7). Ward goes on to say that Christianity's benign influence has "raised many to that exalted state of moral excellence" (ibid.: 297), whereas if Hinduism were to prevail, the world would be steeped in darkness and sin:

> Finally, let it be further considered, that it is only necessary for Hindooism to prevail universally, and the world becomes immediately covered with darkness, without a single ray of light; with vice, without a vestige of genuine morality ... Let Christianity, on the contrary, be universally embraced, its spirit imbibed, and its precepts obeyed, and wars will cease to the ends of the earth – ignorance and superstition will be banished – injustice and oppression removed – jails, chains, and gibbets, rendered unnecessary – pure morality, flowing from the religion of the heart, will diffuse universal happiness, and earth become the vestibule of heaven.
> (1820a: 297)

Ward constructs the notion of the Other as deceitful and corrupt and this is attributed to the idolatrous practices which are seen as having their basis in Hindu scriptures (ibid.: 290). Hindu beliefs and practices are perceived as rooted in idolatry, hence can serve no moral purpose. Hindu deities are seen as "monsters of vice" and therefore can only encourage immoral behavior. Ward writes:

> It has been common too to represent the idols as personifications of the *virtues*, [italics in original] as teaching, by hieroglyphics, a theory of morals. As it respects the Hindoos, however, the fact is, that they have still, for popular use, a system of morals to seek: some of their idols are actually personifications of *vice*; [italics in original] and the formularies used before the images, so far from conveying any moral sentiment, have

> the greatest possible tendency to corrupt the mind with the love of riches and pleasure.
>
> (1817a: xv)

Lost in darkness with no sense of history, time, or place

Ward paints a picture of India lost in darkness without any history. In denying Hindus any intellectual and moral qualities, Ward denies the possibility of Hindus making any meaningful progress, or being creators of their own history. He represents them as incapable of creating anything new and not equipped for valiant and heroic undertakings. Ward employs binarisms to establish the superiority of the European mind. If for Jones and Müller, Hindus are still in their childhood, for William Ward they are totally lost in darkness. Hindus, in Ward's view,

> [M]ay not be capable of forming plans which require great and original powers, nor fitted for bold and daring enterprises ... The European mind ... has attained its present vigour and expansion ... after the illumination of centuries; while we find the Hindoo still walking amidst the thick darkness of a long night, uncheered by the twinkling of a single star, a single Bacou.
>
> (1820a: xxvi–xxvii)

To borrow the terminology of David Spurr, Ward "denies history as well as place, constituting the past as absence, but also designating that absence as a negative presence: a people without history is one which exists only in a negative sense; like the bare earth, they can be transformed by history, but they cannot make history their own" (Spurr 1993: 98).

For nineteenth-century European colonialists and missionaries, "The absence of history is in fact a double absence – of history as written text and of history as movement toward a destiny" (ibid.: 98). Ward applies the Western notion of linear history to Hinduism to show how meaningless the Hindu notion of chronology is. Jones, too, takes a linear approach but his aim is to demonstrate that Hindu chronology begins with Genesis. In other words, for Jones Hindu history is meaningful in so far as it validates biblical revelation, whereas Ward is totally dismissive of Hindu chronology. Although Hindus have written texts, they are seen to have no sense of coherent history or historical destiny. If they have any history at all, it can be referred to only in a negative sense. Anything that "resists adequate representation" is ridiculed and rejected. Ward writes:

> Such is the Hindoo History, as given by themselves, or rather an imperfect gleaning from a great and confused mass of materials which they

> have thrown together in the pooranus, to arrange and settle which, so as to select what is true, and reject which is false, requires a mind more than human. It appears to be conceded on all hands, that, except in a few particular periods, the Hindu chronology is inexplicable; it does not admit being traced, ... even for a single century, a course of historical facts.
>
> (1820a: 39–40)

If written texts signify the absence of any meaningful history, oral histories can have no significance for Ward who was steeped in Protestant notions of history. It is with such restricted vision that Ward interprets Hindu history.

In Ward's view, Hindus not only lack a sense of history but also a proper sense of topography. "The Hindoos," writes Ward, "have no idea of regular streets, of spacious roads, or of forming open square for markets: the benefits of order, regularity, and cleanliness, seem never to have attracted their attention, and the beauties of architecture or of a landscape they are utterly incapable of perceiving" (ibid.: xxv). Ward's negative description "defines precisely the dilemma of the Western writer who, recognizing none of the familiar constructions of social reality, falls back upon the discourse of negation in writing of the non-Western world" (Spurr 1994: 96). Ward's denunciatory remarks form part of his thesis that Hindus may have attained some degree of civilization if one looks at their towns, markets, and shops, but "there is not a single bookseller's shop in any town in India, Calcutta excepted, and these are for the sale of English books ..." (1820a: xxv).

Hindu women as hapless victims

The rhetorical strategies of negation and debasement are also evident in Ward's construction of Hindu women. British colonial attitudes to Hindu women ranged from admiration or ambivalence to utter contempt and horror. The Baptist missionaries portrayed Hindu women as pathetic victims of a barbaric faith that burned its women alive. Although a minority practice, *satī*[4] (which means a "good" or "virtuous woman"), the rite of self-immolation of a Hindu woman on the funeral pyre of her dead husband, came to be sensationalized by the missionaries to emphasize what they saw as the degraded state of Hindu society. The missionary papers publicized the "horrors" of a cruel religion. *Satī* became a useful tool in their hands to win support in Britain for their evangelical campaign.[5] Ward presents a dramatic picture of *satī* in one of his farewell letters: "O that I could collect all the shrieks of these affrighted victims, all the innocent blood thus drunk up by the devouring element, and all the wailings of thirteen thousand orphans" (Marshman 1859: 246). In the second volume of his text, Ward paints a horrific picture of *satī*: "The funeral pile devours more than war itself! How truly shocking! Nothing equal to it exists in the whole work of human cruelty! What a tragic history would a complete detail of these burnings make!" (Ward 1817b: 114–15). In Ward's view, Hindus do not attempt to conceal the murder of the helpless victims, "but rather glory in them as proofs of the divine nature of their religion" (ibid.: 101), and consider them as "an act of great piety" (1817a: lxx). Hindus are seen as either murdering their women or condemning them to a life of perpetual widowhood, and this is seen as being endorsed by religion: "The Hindoos," Ward writes, "not only seize many of their widows, and burn them alive: but the perpetual degradation and starvation to which those widows are reduced whom they permit to live, sinks them below many of the most savage tribes" (1820a: 280–1). Hindu texts are seen as recommending *satī*, and Hindu women are perceived as being used to this long-standing custom which would deliver them from "the disgrace of widowhood" and from being at the mercy of their relatives (Ward 1817b: 112–13). Ward appears to assume that Hindus are scripture-oriented, that is, they conduct their lives in terms of scriptural prescriptions. In other words, *satī* is established as a religious act sanctioned by scriptures, and Hindu women are required to conform to it. It is ironic that the Baptist missionaries also use scriptural warrants for the abolition of *satī* (it was abolished in 1829). Although they are dismissive of Hindu texts as "sacred nothings," the missionaries summon them to argue that *satī* has no scriptural basis.

The Baptist missionaries saw themselves as moral reformers of Hindu society, while at the same time their own women in Britain were denied rights. *Satī* became a convenient hermeneutical battleground for colonialists, missionaries, Hindu reformers, and traditionalists to contest and justify their political, theological, and personal agendas. While the missionaries highlighted what they saw as the low position of women in Hindu society in order to justify their civilizing and Christianizing mission, Hindu reformers constructed images of the ideal Hindu woman of the golden past, to counteract negative perceptions of Hindu tradition and its women. Ward resorts to "oppositional essentialisms" to devalue Hindu women and extol European women. Hindu women are perceived as lacking the womanly graces and the education of European women. This is seen as hindering them from becoming suitable companions to their husbands, or good mothers to their children. Ward states:

> The deficiency in the education and information of females not only prevents their becoming agreeable companions to their husbands, but renders them incapable of forming the minds of their children, and of giving them that instruction which lays the foundation of future excellence: by which tender offices, European mothers become greater benefactors to the age in which they live, than all the learned men with which a country can be blessed.
>
> (1820a: 279)

Furthermore, European women are regarded as pure and chaste whereas Hindu women are seen as corrupt – degraded by their men and by a tradition which keeps them in seclusion. Ward legitimizes his negative construction of Hindu women by seeking the approval of the native:

> It is a fact which greatly perplexes many of the well informed Hindoos, that notwithstanding the wives of Europeans are seen in so many mixed companies, they remain chaste; while their wives, though continually secluded, watched, and veiled, are so notoriously corrupt. I recollect the observation of a gentleman who had lived nearly twenty years in Bengal, and whose opinions on such a subject demand the highest regard, *that the infidelity of the Hindoo women was so great, that he scarcely thought that there was a single instance of a wife who had been always faithful to her husband.* [Italics in original].
>
> (1820a: 288)

Such comparisons not only emphasize the superiority of European women but also erase Hindu women out of existence. They become non-entities – signifying nothing. Ward evaluates Hindu women's roles in terms of Victorian patriarchal notions of an ideal wife and mother. Hindu women are to be modeled on the modernist and liberal ideology of the colonizer. As Rajeswari Sunder Rajan points out: "The perception that Hindu women were victims was the basis for the establishment of satī as a woman's issue ... it provoked an implicit comparison of their devalued social position with the freedom and privileges of the British women – thus offering further proof of the superiority of British civilization" (1993: 45–6).

Concluding remarks

Ward and his Baptist colleagues are products of the eighteenth-century evangelical revival in Britain, with its emphasis on the fallen state of humankind and the need for salvation from a state of sin through the atonement of Jesus Christ. Informed by such an exclusive and aggressive evangelical theology, Ward finds Hinduism failing to measure up to Protestant standards. His concept of religion leaves little room for any meaningful understanding of the complex nature of Hinduism with its heterogeneous elements and varied indigenous religious beliefs and practices. Hinduism does not fall within his exclusive Protestant evangelical understanding of what a religion is. It is forced to fit within the narrow confines of a monotheistic understanding of God, and the demands of a historical religion are imposed on it. It is defined in Christian categories, and is judged in terms of what it lacks in comparison with Christianity – no founder, no one holy book or a prescribed set of beliefs.

Ward constructs dualistic oppositions to emphasize the differences between Christianity and Hinduism. The differences are essentialized, reduced to fixed categories in terms of which Hinduism is interpreted and represented. Such essentialist reductions of the Other "do not exist on their own" but reflect what James Carrier calls "occidentalisms, essentializing simplifications" (1995: 3). Ward's construction of Hinduism reflects both oriental and occidental essentialisms, the difference being that the former is denounced and the latter is exalted. In other words, Ward over-valorizes the West and undermines India. Such essentialist understandings are used both by the West and the East to define and represent each other. It is through such partial constructs or even biased constructs of one's own culture that one defines and makes authoritative statements about the Other. Ward's Hinduism is informed by a particular brand of eighteenth-century Protestant evangelical Christianity. He constructs an exalted and idealized image of Christianity, contrasting it with his negative image of Hinduism. Christianity's involvement with slavery, the burning of witches, and oppressive patriarchal traditions are conveniently overlooked. The differences between Hinduism and Christianity, as Ward perceives them, are essentialized, dramatized, and manipulated in such a way that Christianity's moral and absolute superiority is maintained.

The Baptist missionaries considered themselves pioneers in rescuing the hapless Indians, and took upon themselves the role of reforming and civilizing Bengali society – a society that had already been through social and religious changes long before the arrival of the missionaries. Bengal had witnessed the rise of *Vaiṣṇava bhakti* (devotional) and *Sufi* (mystical Islam) sects which affirmed *bhakti* or devotion as a valid path to reach God, and they challenged the worship of images, caste rigidity, and brahminic hegemony. Furthermore, the eighteenth-century was a period of cultural revival despite economic and political instability.[6] The popular tradition in eighteenth-century Bengal produced poets, musicians and artists who offered a sound and lively critique of their contemporary society. The hermeneutical tools employed by Protestant evangelicals such as Ward lacked the sophistication and rigor needed to understand and interpret the varied nuances of a complex and vibrant tradition. Ward constructs a fixed and decadent India – its diverse traditions, its sacred texts, beliefs and practices are discredited and frozen so that future generations can marvel at what he calls, "the most splendid trophies of the glory of the British name in India" (1820b: xlvii).

(This chapter is a revised version of an article originally published in *Studies in World Christianity* 1999; 5 (2): 196–212.)

Chapter 4

Decrowning Farquhar's Hinduism

> I do not expect the India of my dream to devlop one religion, i.e., to be wholly Hindu or wholly Christian, or wholly Mussulman; but I want it to be wholly tolerant, with its religions working side by side with one another.
>
> (Gandhi, in Ellsberg 1991: 59)

This chapter looks at a seminal nineteenth-century missionary text, *The Crown of Hinduism* (1913) by a Protestant Scottish missionary, John Nichol Farquhar (1861–1929), a text that propounded a thesis that came to be known as "inclusivism."[1] His other important works include *A Primer of Hinduism* (1912), *Modern Religious Movements in India* (1929), and *An Outline of the Religious Literature of India* (1920). Farquhar arrived in India at a time of rising national consciousness and Hindu awakening in the face of intense missionary proselytization. Seen in the light of the then prevailing missionary attitudes, the inclusivist stance does not dismiss Hinduism but sees it as finding enrichment and fulfillment in Jesus Christ. The chapter will provide some significant examples of Farquhar's notion of fulfillment from a postcolonial perspective. In examining Farquhar's construction of Hinduism, I will draw on David Spurr's rhetorical strategies of classification and appropriation – strategies worked out by the West to manage non-Western cultures and textual practices.

John Nichol Farquhar[2] went to India in 1891 as an education missionary for the London Missionary Society. Like most missionaries of this time, he had had an evangelical and pietistic upbringing and a zeal for preaching the gospel. His parents belonged to the Evangelical Union, a branch of Scottish independent Protestantism. After spending his formative years in Aberdeen, he went to Oxford. Two things were uppermost in his mind before he set out for India: the importance of the person and teachings of Christ, and the comparative study of religions. This was the time when Müller and Monier-Williams were articulating a Christian understanding of other faiths, especially Hinduism. Farquhar was influenced by these two orientalists who stood within the Christian evangelical tradition, although he was not always in agreement with their position.

His initial assignment in India was to teach in a Calcutta school of which he later became the principal. His talents blossomed when he became the literature secretary of the National Christian Council of India. During his tenure, he produced seventeen volumes and initiated three important series: *The Religious Quest of India*, *The Heritage of India* and *The Religious Life of India*. This was a time when missionaries were keen to converse with those whom they called intelligent Hindus, and Farquhar played a vital part in this endeavor. In 1923 he returned to England and became Professor of Comparative Religion at the University of Manchester. He died in 1929.

Classifying the Other

David Spurr sees classification itself as an ideologically charged rhetorical strategy devised by the West to investigate non-Western cultures.

> Every discourse orders itself both externally and internally: it marks itself off against the kind of language it excludes, while it establishes within its own limits a system of classification, arrangement, and distribution … Within the realm of discourse, classification performs this policing function, assigning positions, regulating groups, and enforcing boundaries.
> (Spurr 1993: 62–3).

There are different kinds of classification and "the nature of classification itself changes with the evolution of discourse" (ibid.: 63). In Christian missionary discourse one finds both exclusivist and inclusivist approaches to Hinduism. The exclusivist paradigm is characterized by binary oppositions – heathen and Christian, darkness and light, falsehood and truth. This kind of classification does not allow any negotiating space between the two; rather it requires the conversion of one into another, in this case, a heathen into a Christian. These polarizing distinctions tend to be rather fixed categories, allowing no room for any meaningful interaction. They rest or operate on the assumption that Christianity is the only true religion. In other words, if Christianity is true, other religions cannot possibly be true. If others possess truth, then it undermines the uniqueness of the Christian faith. In the exclusivist paradigm there is a complete dominance of one world-view over others (see William Ward).

In the inclusivist paradigm, the binary categories are slightly adjusted or modified to allow some space for negotiation but on terms set by the missionary. Hinduism is not rejected but is seen as a toddler steadying its steps, whereas Christianity is the adult into which a Hindu needs to grow. Hinduism is not outrightly dismissed; it is seen as containing a modicum of truth which needs to be refined in the light of Jesus' teaching.

Inclusivism itself is not monolithic. There are different kinds of inclusivism but one factor that holds them together is Jesus Christ who becomes the center and the final goal of all religious quests. A quick glance at some of the titles gives some indication of the nature of Christian inclusivism: Panikkar's *The Unknown Christ of Hinduism* (1964), Samartha's *The Hindu Response to the Unbound Christ* (1974), Thomas' *The Acknowledged Christ of the Indian Renaissance* (1969), Farquhar's *The Crown of Hinduism* (1913). It is explicit that the authors of these texts are keen too show that Christ is already present in Hinduism. This involves excavating or extricating what they see as the hidden, veiled, and shrouded Christ in Hinduism. They see the salvific process at work in Hinduism and other faiths, but this is seen as being effected by Jesus Christ. Hindus are included in God's scheme of salvation, not because of their faith but despite it. In other words, what is offered is a form of salvation predetermined by Christian conceptual categories. It is the hidden or the "unknown," or universal, Christ who is at work in Hinduism. Both in the exclusivist and inclusivist models, the center is the Christian God, the difference being that in the former there is no other truth besides the revelation of God in Jesus Christ, whereas in the latter, there are flickerings of truth in other religions but they are proleptic.

While in the nineteenth century one set of missionaries (Baptists) denounced Hinduism, there were others such as Thomas Ebenezer Slater (1840–1912) and John Nichol Farquhar who came to see Hinduism in inclusivist terms. As we saw earlier, the latter part of the nineteenth century saw the emergence of what came to be variously termed the "Science of Religion," "History of Religion," or "Comparative Religion," and the rise of historical criticism. Charles Darwin's (1809–82) evolutionary notion of progress came to be applied to religion and other disciplines. On this evolutionary view of development, Christianity was ranked higher than other religions; it was seen as having reached the highest degree of ethical perfection. Hinduism was at the lower stage of evolution and would eventually find its completion or fulfillment in Christianity. Jesus became the single and universal savior, and the supreme example of absolute moral and ethical perfection, the only valid criterion for assessing the moral value of other religions. This evolutionary model of development was popularized by Max Müller and Monier-Williams, although Monier-Williams later rejected the notion of fulfillment (Sharpe 1965: 52), and came to be profitably appropriated by Farquhar and others.

While for the nineteenth-century Serampore Baptist missionaries, Hinduism is morally corrupt and theologically suspect, Farquhar grants some moral credibility to Hinduism but it is by no means perfect. Farquhar's main thesis is that Hinduism is defective – its scriptures, philosophies, beliefs, religious practices, iconography, family, social structures, are all imperfect, needing to be cleansed. In other words, whatever truth is embedded in Hinduism, it has no inherent validity; it has no power to be energized from within; it needs the activating power of Jesus Christ. Farquhar does not totally reject Hindu religious aspirations but sees them as being fulfilled in Christianity. He writes: "Christ provides the fulfillment of each of the highest aspirations and aims of Hinduism ... In Him is focused every ray of light that shines in Hinduism. He is the Crown of the faith of India" (1913: 457–8). Furthermore, he makes an explicit affirmation of the supremacy of Christianity: "The Christian sees as distinctly the superiority of Christianity to the rest of the great religions; and he believes the evidence can be set forth with overwhelming force" (1913: 31).

At the Missionary Conference in Calcutta in May 1905, Farquhar called for a sympathetic approach to Hinduism,[3] but his work, especially *The Crown of Hinduism* undermines all that Hindus value about their tradition. Farquhar's inclusivist approach to Hinduism is not free from Eurocentric presuppositions. In applying Darwin's evolutionary hypothesis to religions and classifying them as being in various stages of growth, finally culminating in Christ, Farquhar legitimizes Christian superiority. As Spurr notes:

> The notion that societies can be classified according to their degree of advancement along the same path works, paradoxically, to support the notion of inherent ethical differences among races, that is, differences in *character*. The nineteenth century debate over human race and evolution reflects this tension between an essentialist and an historical view, yet the two views tend to reinforce one another when it comes to a system of classification for the actual state of peoples.
>
> (Spurr 1993: 65)

The classification of religions along evolutionary lines proved to be a convenient tool in justifying the Christianizing and civilizing mission – namely that of improving the moral state of the natives. It provided an important ideology for the missionary enterprise. As Spurr points out, "the order that classifies non-Western peoples according to the paradigm of modernization contains within it, already as a given, the judgment of their character" (1993: 71). Implicit in this evolutionary hypothesis is "the basic assumption of the modernist paradigm which posits a single standard of value according to which all societies may be measured" (ibid.: 73). Farquhar's evolutionary model introduced a single universal standard of truth in terms of which religions are evaluated. This modernist approach ignores the complexity and diversity within cultures and sees development, whether it be political, economic or religious, in terms of a set of Western categories and norms. Despite his first-hand experience and knowledge of religious diversity within Hinduism, Farquhar ends up constructing a monolithic and homogenized Hinduism.[4]

Trivializing texts

As with the Baptist missionaries, Farquhar takes a literal view of Hindu texts, overlooking the fact that Hindus relate to their textual traditions in a less formal manner. He attributes the moral inadequacy of Hindus to religious laws and rules formulated in their texts, which are seen as degenerate and dehumanizing. If Hindus, as people, are steeped in superstition, it is because their sacred texts are defective. In his view, a religion should be judged by its principles and not by those who fail to abide by them (1913: 119). He attributes the inhumanity of certain customs and practices, such as *satī* and child marriage, to Hindu texts. It is not Hindus but their laws which need transformation. For example, Farquhar sees the Hindu family through the textual lens of Manu, the Hindu law-giver, and adheres to a literal interpretation of Hindu laws. That Hindu women are accorded a subservient role and are subject to men, is, in Farquhar's view, "no mere popular prejudice, but a doctrine of Hinduism" (ibid.: 91). Hindus need to be liberated from their own textual traditions if they are to make any progress: "It is not that Hindus are hard-hearted: it is the beliefs and laws that are at fault" (ibid.: 101). Farquhar wrote:

> Thus the present weakness and unhealthiness of the Hindu family find their one remedy in the principles of Christ. The divine truths concerning man and woman which He revealed are needed to raise its best customs to their height, to universalize its highest laws, and to correct its glaring abuses. Christ will transfigure the Hindu family to glory.
>
> (1913: 133)

Farquhar seems to be following in the footsteps of his orientalist predecessors, such as William Jones, in treating certain texts as central to the tradition. Although Hindus have an ambivalent attitude to texts, Western orientalists privileged certain texts such as the laws of Manu, and these came to be treated as representative, authoritative, and universally applicable. As Romila Thapar points out:

> The selection of texts to be studied had its own purpose. The East India Company's interest in locating and codifying Hindu law gave legal form to what was essentially social observance and customary law. The concept of law required that it be defined as a cohesive ideological code. The Manu *Dharmaśāstra*, for example, which was basically part of Brahmanical *smṛti* was taken as the laws of the Hindus and presumed to apply universally.
>
> (1993: 72)

If the Baptist missionaries paid scant respect to Hindu texts, Farquhar regards Hindu texts as incapable of having a transforming effect on Hindus.

Although he is appreciative of the *Bhagavad-gītā*, he considers the text as basically inadequate. In other words, the *Gītā* is seen as incomplete without Christ. "The *Gītā*," Farquhar declares, "is the cry of the Hindu people for an incarnate Saviour" (1917: 32). In his view, Hindu texts such as the *Upaniṣads* and the *Bhagavad-gītā* pale into insignificance when compared with the Gospels for which he claims unrivalled universality, malleability, and adaptability:

> Where is there in all the world another book that shows this universal adaptability and simplicity? Imagine the *Gītā* and the *Chhāndogya Upanishad* translated and put into the hands of the cannibals of New Guinea, the savages of Terra del Fuego, or even the outcastes of India! But the Gospels are actually known and treasured by men of these races, men who through Christ have escaped savagery.
>
> (1913: 440–1)

With such Protestant textual conditioning, other ways of communicating with and receiving God's grace are silenced or, rather, negated. The Christian text is invested with power and authority that is denied to other sacred texts. Hindu texts do not seem to have any transforming power. There is no place for vernacular or oral forms of transmission of sacred wisdom. Farquhar does not grant any independent agency to Hindu sacred texts. Hindu scriptures contain truth but not of a salvific nature. For Farquhar, Kṛṣṇa in the *Gītā* is no more than an imaginary construction. He remarks:

> Let educated India look at the crucified once again, and let them realize that Jesus is the reality of which the Gītā gives an imaginative picture. The author of the Gītā would have been a Christian, had he known Jesus. The true Hindu, who accepts the great idea of the Gītā, will accept the incarnate Saviour, Jesus Christ, of whom the Gītā is really a marvellous prophecy.
>
> (1903: 31)

Christianity is the dominant partner in the inclusivist discourse in which the nature of engagement is already predetermined by theological presuppositions. Such an inclusivism is willing to grant only a secondary or lower status to Hinduism; it is not on a par with Christianity. For the universality of the Christian message to be affirmed, all other equally valid messages of the Buddha or Guru Nanak will have to take a secondary place. In his paper read at the Calcutta Missionary Conference in May 1905, Farquhar made his missionary intention clear, to woo Hindus to Christ, and he explained how to go about it. He believed that a sound knowledge of Hinduism would prove "to be an invaluable weapon," not only to bring to Hindus' attention their own ignorance about, and misrepresentations of, their tradition, but that this would also eventually make room for the spread of the Christian gospel (Sharpe 1963: 124).[5]

Hinduism through a Western Protestant lens

As with William Ward, Farquhar imposes his Western Protestant conception of religion on Hinduism. In his view, Hinduism as a religion lacks what Christianity has – Hinduism has no creative energy to transform itself into an organized religion. Farquhar draws a distinction between what he calls "religion" and "theory." For Farquhar, "religion is always found in a community, in an organized, historical form; and each individual receives it from the community in that shape. This is what distinguishes a religion from a mere theory" (1913: 445). Theories may generate interest for further speculation and may even have some impact on the individual, but unless they translate themselves into an organized system, they cannot possibly serve any useful or serious purpose (ibid.).

Employing these categories, Farquhar, in line with Western ethnographers, draws a neat distinction between philosophic and popular Hinduism. In his view, both are defective: the former lacks the vitality required to transform itself into a living religion, and the latter, although the living religion, is infested with idolatrous practices. Hindu, Buddhist and Jain systems of thought are seen as:

> lacking altogether that creative power which alone can produce a living religion. These theories attract the individual and influence him powerfully, but they do not succeed in creating that wonderful organism which seizes a community and forms it by producing for it a cult, a morality, a social and family system. No single one of all this mighty group of philosophies has succeeded in creating a religion, or in organizing itself as a religious system. In each case the cult is simply the idolatry of the traditional Hindu system appended to the philosophic theology, and justified in a crude or clumsy way. The impersonal pantheism of Śaṇkara, the atheistic metaphysic of Gautama and of Mahāvīra, and the personal theism of the great sects, have each, as the expression of their innermost reverence, a polytheistic idolatry.
>
> (1913: 453)

Having constructed this distinction between theory and religion, Farquhar concludes that "the Hindu system" has served a better purpose than Hindu philosophies. Hindu philosophies are seen to be too weak to challenge superstitious practices and therefore have "to acquiesce in all the folly and filth of Hindu worship and its accompaniments" (ibid.: 454). In other words, Hindu philosophy lacks the power to transform itself into a living religion despite its deep spirituality (ibid.: 455). In short, in Farquhar's evaluation, Hinduism is imperfect and lacks any real substance:

> It is the character of the Hindu system itself that is at fault. It is the very laws of Hindu family that require to be laid aside. It is karma itself that has weakened Hindu theology. The basal conceptions of the caste system must be repudiated, if Hindu society is to become healthy. The whole system of idolatry is essentially polytheistic and pagan. The gleams of light which stream from these things do not justify them.
>
> (ibid.: 456)

What we find in Farquhar is a dialectic process of differentiating Hinduism from Christianity and yet seeing it in terms of a particular Christian paradigm. Hinduism becomes meaningful only when it is cast in a Christian light. The differences become manageable as they are rendered in terms of the dominant partner in the discourse. In defining Hinduism in terms of Christian and Western presuppositions, Farquhar brings to the fore the differences between Christianity and Hinduism. It is a comparative exercise in which one's own conception serves to emphasize the differences. The Other is domesticated and molded to fit the theories of a particular Western conception of religion. As James Carrier points out: "In this process is the tendency to essentialize, to reduce the complex entities that are being compared to a set of core features that express the essence of each entity, but only as it stands in contrast to the other" (1995: 3). The following examples illustrate Farquhar's devaluation of Hinduism.

Hindu "idolatry" and Christian monotheism

Farquhar's work is replete with oppositional categories. He regards Hindu worship as idolatrous whereas Christian worship reflects "the richest devotional life and the most living worship ... without idols ... In Him [Christ] the purest spiritual monotheism rises to the highest joy and adoring veneration ..." (1913: 343). India is in need of "a pure spiritual worship, to set her free from the need of idols" (ibid.). The presence of images such as the *liṅga* is seen as a sign of a barbaric and crude religion. He writes: "It seems clear that the symbol does not stir impure thoughts or feelings in the average Hindu; yet here we have a survival of coarse, indecent, barbaric religion tolerated for centuries under a theistic philosophy" (ibid.: 397). Hindu practices such as taking a dip in the sacred Ganges river, bowing before a guru, repeating a *mantra* or offering *pūjā* or worship, are all seen as superstitious practices which need to be purified in Christ (ibid.: 454). Farquhar gives a detailed account of the meaning and significance the images have for Hindus, but does so in order to point out their futility. Hindus, in his view, need to be freed from idolatrous practices.

Farquhar considers "idolatry" as "one of the *chief hindrances to the progress of India* " (ibid.: 342); (emphasis is mine). First, his disparaging attitude to image-worship is not new; it fits in with the dominant missionary perception. Images are an anathema to the Protestant mind, which seeks God in the Word, whereas for most Hindus images enable them to connect with the unknown. Like Müller and William Ward, Farquhar expresses his utter disgust at what he calls "gross and grotesque images of the gods" (1912: 194). He is unable to appreciate their significance for Hindus. Even Gandhi, who had no personal interest in temple worship or images, was able to see that they had meaning for other Hindus. For Gandhi "idolatry" was not a problem as it had been for the earlier reformers like Rammohan Roy and Dayānanda Saraswatī. Gandhi was more concerned with Harijans (who now call themselves *Dalits*, "oppressed") not being allowed to enter the temple to worship. Speaking about Gandhi's attitude to images, Margaret Chatterjee states: "Idol worship is not a sin, but inability to see any virtue in any other form of worshipping the Deity save one's own, is a form of irreligion or untruth" (1983: 23). Although not a temple-goer himself, Gandhi felt that to "reject the necessity of images is to reject the necessity of God, religion and earthly existence" (ibid.: 23–4). An Indian novelist, Anantha Murthy, narrates a story illustrating a Hindu peasant's attitude to images. It is a story about a painter, a friend of the novelist who was interested in studying folk tradition. Seeing a stone anointed with the sacred red powder (*kunkum*) in the hut of a peasant, he wished to photograph it, with the peasant's permission. The stone was brought outside to be photographed in the sunlight. He soon realized that he had caused the dislocation of the stone from its ritual space and the image had been desacralized. But the peasant, taking a relaxed view of the event, assured him that he could always anoint another stone with the sacred powder. Anantha Murthy draws our attention to the profundity of the peasant's response. He states: "Any piece of stone on which he put *kunkum* became god for the peasant. What mattered was his faith, not the stone" (Murthy 1992: 109–10). This does not mean that the stone did not matter, but that the emphasis is on faith and attitude.

Second, Farquhar's ideology of progress is problematic. He affirms the moral and civilizing role of Western ideas and Christian principles in challenging Hindu beliefs and practices (1913: 19). He offers an idealized and universalized form of Christianity as the destination of all social and religious quests. Farquhar operates on an a priori assumption that the Western notion of linear history and evolutionary progress reaching its highest perfection in Christianity can function as a universal model. He homogenizes a particular notion of history and of progress current at that time. His fulfillment theory seeks to treat progress as being synonymous with improvement. From this viewpoint, Hindu veneration of images is a sign of backwardness and a hindrance to progress. What Jay Griffiths states in a different context is relevant: "Darwin disliked social applications of his theory, yet his ideas were widely used to maintain that progress was improvement, to equate later with better, to see succession as success" (Griffiths 1999: 186). Farquhar's notion of progress is a subtle form of colonialism for it seeks to dominate, not by rejection or exclusion as the Baptist missionaries did, but by the inclusion and domestication of Hinduism along Christian lines. In the hands of Farquhar and others Darwin's ideas become a convenient hermeneutic device to justify missionary colonialism. The worship of images has not stood in the way of what modernists call progress. Farquhar would be turning in his grave now if he were to know that diasporic Hindus in Britain, America, Australia, and other countries have not only brought in images of their deities, they have housed them in temples and have even take over redundant Christian churches in order to worship them. The newly constructed magnificent Swaminarayan Temple in London, the beautifully carved South Indian-style temples in Pittsburgh, New York, or in Melbourne, tell us yet more about the contribution that these image worshippers make to the economy of their respective adopted countries.

Hindu indifference and Christian engagement

As we have seen, Farquhar's inclusivism is not free from binary polarities. God in Christianity is seen as the embodiment of moral and ethical perfection, providing an impetus for social action and involvement. By contrast, God in Hinduism is seen as "non-moral." The Hindu Absolute or Supreme Being, Brahman, being actionless, is seen as leading to inaction and apathy (Farquhar 1913: 152). In other words, Brahmaṇ cannot possibly lead to the moral progress of the individual or society. Unlike Christianity which "stirs men and women to unselfish service" (ibid.: 277), Hinduism lacks the moral vigor to enthuse its adherents to get involved in social or humanitarian service. In Farquhar's view, since the Hindu conception of God lacks a moral dimension, it cannot possibly motivate Hindus to care for their fellow human beings. "The problem is," Farquhar states, "how are Hindus to be inspired to unselfish service?" He then goes on: "Clearly, it cannot be any form of Hindu philosophy; for that leads to inaction. Nor can there be any doubt that such inspiration can come only from religion. Where can we find a motive sufficient for the purpose?" (ibid.). The answer for Farquhar lies in Christ. If Hindus have discovered morality, it is due to Christian influence.

Farquhar does not see any virtue in the Hindu notion of renunciation. It can become a serviceable idea only when it is Christianized. In his estimation the Hindu *sannyāsi* "is not a servant of humanity" (1912: 197). The Hindu monastic ideal can become fruitful only if it is turned into self-surrender to Christ.

> Instead of the *world-surrender* Christ demands *self-surrender*. On the surface they seem to be opposed to each other; but self-surrender

> contains within itself world-surrender ... Christ's demand is infinitely deeper of the two; for it is inner, spiritual, real; and while it brings all that detachment from the world which is necessary for the moral and spiritual discipline of the soul, it leaves the man in the world to do his work there. Hindu world-surrender thus finds its spiritual consummation in self-surrender to Christ.
>
> (1913: 293–4)

Farquhar sees Hindu renunciation as "indifference" whereas Christian sacrifice is seen as service. The Hindu ascetic suppresses love whereas Christ stirs up a love which leads to unselfish action. In other words, the Hindu "inaction" springs from indifference whereas "Christ commands the *service* which springs from love" (ibid.: 294). The two are not opposed: "the inaction of the monk finds its true climax in the service which Christ demands" (ibid.: 293). The Hindu ascetic is thus de-Hinduized and fitted into the Christocentric framework. Christ is seen as completing and consummating the ideal of the Hindu *sannyāsi* (ibid.: 296). Farquhar states, "The convert from Hinduism to Christianity is the true modern *sannyāsi*. For the sake of the spiritual religion which he recognizes to be the truth he renounces the whole brahminical system" (ibid.: 295). What Farquhar calls fulfillment is no more than the Christianization of Hinduism, emptying it of its content.

For Farquhar, Christianity is the true religion towards which Hindus should move. He essentializes otherworldiness as the significant feature of Hinduism, failing to see that both world-denial and world-affirmation are found within the tradition, and that they are appropriated in many ways. The Indian historian Romila Thapar shows that the role of a renouncer has too many dimensions to be reduced to one single aspect. She draws on both normative texts and creative literature to substantiate her point. She notes: "The brahminical system insists on the fulfillment of the social obligations of a householder .... [It] reflects the fear that renunciation at an early age may upset the requirements of society and that the true value of renunciation comes after a socially fulfilled life." (1994: 12)

On the other hand, in the creative literature, a hermit lives in a forest, in harmony with nature. Although he renounces his social obligations, this does not mean that it totally rules out his role in society; rather he becomes a source of authority (ibid.: 13). The renouncer is not always a passive icon.

> [T]he renouncer often emerged as the symbol of dissent and protest and came to be regarded as an alternative source of power, a symbolism which has been respected in the Indian political movements of the twentieth century. The renouncer cannot be explained away in the simplistic formula of being a religious leader since he accumulates in himself a complex of inter-relation of social signals. As a source of alternative authority the renouncer is distinct from both priestly power and

> the coercive authority of the state. The socio-political role of the renouncer is, it seems to me, a characteristic feature of the Indian civilization and requires a more thorough analysis. This would question the notion that Indian society has always been other-worldly because of the attraction of renunciation. Instead, it requires that we examine more analytically the many dimensions to the role of the renouncer in society.
>
> (Thapar 1994: 13)

Hindu myth, Christian truth

Farquhar tends to see myth and history in dichotomous terms. For him history deals with actual facts whereas myths deal with facts or events which may not have any historical basis or may not have actually taken place. In other words, myths are mere fabrications and have no basis in reality. Farquhar relegates Hindu myths to a lower status and contrasts them with the Christian historical figures and events. Hindu *avatāras* such as Rāma and Kṛṣṇa are seen as belonging to the world of imagination. Farquhar states:

> The man who accepts Jesus as the incarnate Son of God certainly confesses that the Hindu mind has mistaken the Rama and Krishna myths for history; but he holds that the Hindu spirit was right in looking for God manifest in the flesh ... In loyalty to truth he cannot but confess the incarnation stories to be mythical; but, if he feels any confidence in the spiritual capacities of his people, he will expect to find in human history a real divine descent into human life. Thus Jesus, whose teaching so wonderfully crowns the ideas of Hinduism, is needed to give stability and reality, to the Hindu belief in incarnations. Without Him, *it must pass away like the baseless fabric of a vision.*
>
> (1913: 425; emphasis is mine)

For Farquhar, *Rāma* and *Kṛṣṇa* are not incarnations in the real sense of the term. In other words, the "humanity assumed by the god is unreal" (1913: 430), whereas Jesus "was truly a man. He was no actor, no sportive illusionist" (ibid.: 431). He seems to take a literal and a narrow view of the Hindu concept *līlā* or divine play and compares it with the seriousness of purpose and mission that Jesus embodied in his life. He writes: "Even at its best Hindu incarnation is no true incarnation; God only seems to become man" (ibid.: 433). Farquhar sees some virtue in the epic, the *Rāmāyaṇa*, but warns that it cannot possibly have any serious moral purpose. In his view, Rāma and his wife Sītā are no more than "beautiful and healthy examples of Hindu life." He remarks that "it would be unwise to think of them as likely to exercise any serious ethical influence on the world. They are good Hindus;

and there is much that is noble and helpful in their characters; but they do not lead the van of human life" (ibid.: 434).

Farquhar seems to assume that only historical events can have a moral purpose or address human dilemmas, and is dismissive of Hindu myths. For their part, Hindus see myths as having meaning and moral value; they have impacted on Hindu consciousness giving meaning, value and purpose to life. Myths are just as much concerned with change, continuity, decline, renewal, and progress. They have become very much a part of the historical consciousnes of Hindus and their reality. For example, Gandhi was profoundly influenced by the *Rāmāyaṇa*. He was not concerned with the historicity of Kṛṣṇa or Rāma, yet he was actively engaged in the political struggles of his time. He often spoke of *Rāmarājya*, a just society. As a person who was totally committed to the cause of Indian independence, he critically employed Hindu myths in order to change the course of India's history. The many tellings and retellings of the *Rāmāyaṇa* reflect varied social, political, gender, and ideological agendas. Most Hindus revel in the many retellings of the epic and are least worried about the Ur-text or for that matter about authenticity.[6] In a changed political and religious climate we find some Hindus claiming historicity for particular incarnations such as Rāmā, and decrying myth, thus replicating earlier Western approaches to myth and history.

Farquhar regards Hindu myths as being detrimental to social and economic progress. He reckons that no true Hindu would "desire that the poor of the people should be fed with mythology. A strong Indian nation can never be bred on such diet" (1913: 424). India is seen as needing "the historical Jesus" to enhance the nutritional value of its poor diet. In other words, what India lacks is a morally and ethically perfect historical God. "When we say that God is ethical, we mean that He himself conforms to the standard which He bids us live by; but no religion, except Judaism and Christianity, has had the courage to say this frankly" (ibid.: 437). Jesus is seen as being the most compassionate and loving God who stands above all others. Jesus is elevated to such Himalayan heights that Śiva's compassion is seen as paling into insignificance. Farquhar writes: "His [Jesus'] humility far surpasses anything told of Śiva. Compassion showed itself in daily toil for the sick and the suffering. Tulsī Dās and Māṇikka Vāchakar make their heroes endure suffering for the sake of men; but there is nothing in either poet to compare with the Cross of Christ" (ibid.).

Linear time, cyclic time

In keeping with orientalists and other missionary theologians of the period, Farquhar too perceives cyclic time as having no real significance or purpose. He regards it as a meaningless repetition of time which admits no change, whether it be progress or decline. In his reckoning, "Self-repetition is thus the characteristic of the process not evolution. The one end of the process is retribution: there is no world-purpose to be worked out" (1913: 140).

Since the eighteenth century linear time has been "associated with dialectical change;" cyclic time has been seen as "primitive and archaic", indicating lack of progress and change. Change was seen as progress, or rather "change was progress as defined in nineteenth century terms" (Thapar 1996: 5). Jay Griffiths' comments on how Western and other cultures perceive time and progress are worth citing here: "The Western idea of progress, straight as a Roman road running from the past to the future, is an idea which is so embedded in modernity's psyche that it seems the only possible model of time" (Griffiths 1999: 183).

In orientalist and missionary discourse, cyclic time is seen as leading to "a negative eschatology;" it is seen as repetitive, unchanging and therefore "amounts to a refusal of history, for no event can be particular or unique and all events are liable to be repeated in the next cycle" (Thapar 1996: 5–6). It is generally assumed that the cyclic view of time exemplified in the theory of the four *yugas* does not encourage responsible moral behavior and active participation in life in this world. Thapar offers a positive reading of the four *yugas*:

> But the four ages need not be perceived as enclosed units for it is said that king's conduct characterizes the identity of the age and this ties ethics and social behavior to time. Ultimately the possibility of the return of the cycle provides the necessary optimism for continuing human action and also gives a meaning to human action in the past: it makes history necessary.
>
> (ibid.: 24)

As we saw earlier, orientalist constructions of Hindu time were largely based on selective texts such as Manu's *Dharmaśāstra*, the *Purāṇas* and the *Mahābhārata*, while mathematical and astronomical views of time were ignored. Manu's *Dharmaśāstra* came to be used "as their exploratory text into concepts of time and history" (Thapar 1996: 4). Romila Thapar draws attention to the fact that there is more than one single category of time (both in the East and West), and therefore "categorizing societies as using either cyclic or linear time is an inadequate explanation for the centrality or otherwise of history" (ibid.: 44). The Hindu theory of four *yugas* or ages offers more than a simplistic notion of progress. Thapar explains it thus:

> Time, as conceived in cosmology or eschatalogy, does not exclude the use of other categories of time and these can be simultaneous in the same society. It seems more appropriate to enquire into how a society uses a particular category and what is being intended by that use ... The inclusion of cyclic time is not a characteristic of cultures which are historically stunted but an indication of *historical complexity*. This complexity is

> reflected in the perceptions of the past in premodern times, the premises of which were different from the writing of history today.
>
> (1996: 44; emphasis is mine)

Christianizing Hinduism

Farquhar's fulfillment theory reflects some of the characteristics of colonial discourse. What we see in his writings is a benign form of cultural colonialism, which does not condemn its subjects but feels responsible for educating, civilizing, appropriating, and modeling them after European modernist liberal values and Christian principles. Farquhar states:

> Thus Christianity, so far from being an intruder at this time, is most seriously required to sow the seeds of spiritual religion and healthy moral life. Thoughtful Indian leaders frankly recognize that the ethical and religious influence of missions is of extreme value in this time of trial; and every one who has been in close touch with the educated classes realizes that they need moral help most seriously.
>
> (1913: 43)

One of the devices of colonial discourse is to cite the speeches of the native(s) to reinforce the civilizing mission of the colonizer. The colonizer often makes the colonized participate in their discourse by making them express their gratitude to those who dispossessed them.

Although Farquhar is aware that most Hindus are averse to proselytization, he tries to show that educated Hindus acknowledge the impact of Christianity on Hindu thought and society. In order to legitimize his claim and justify the presence and propagation of Christianity, Farquhar quotes the then vice-chancellor of Bombay University: "The ideas that lie at the heart of the Gospel of Christ are slowly but surely permeating every part of Hindu society and modifying every phase of Hindu thought" (ibid.: 54). This is what any missionary longs to hear from a Hindu. The colonizer seeks to represent "colonized peoples as ultimately sympathetic to the colonizing mission and to see that mission itself as bringing together the peoples of the world in the name of a common humanity" (Spurr 1993: 32).

Farquhar, obviously, does not grant any independent status or identity to Hinduism. Hinduism is deemed to lack inner resources to meet the demands of the modernist project. In his reckoning, it is not Hindu religion that can rouse Hindus from their slumber but European ideas of scientific rationality, freedom, and humanism. He sees Hinduism as already disintegrating under Western influence and "great old religious ideas" as having no hold on the minds of educated Hindus. He remarks: "The thought of the West creates a new climate which is fatal to Hinduism. The air is too rarified. Its fundamental principles shrivel up in the new atmosphere. Those who have entered the world of Western culture simply cannot hold them." (1913: 42–3).

As with Müller, Farquhar wants Hindus to abandon their own religious foundations and embrace Western modernist and Christian ideas. "Thinking Indians," he states in his *A Primer of Hinduism*, "must inevitably form new conceptions of God, man, morality, religion, and the meaning of the world" (1912: 201). In other words, the answer, in Farquhar's view, lies in founding "a new religion" which will provide a truer and more solid basis, and this can only be provided by Christianity. He remarks: "Except Christianity, there is no religion in the whole world that is rich enough in theology, worship, emotion, literature to take the place of Hinduism" (ibid.: 202).

Central to Farquhar's thesis is his emphasis on the role of the West as the catalyst in activating and transforming Hinduism. In colonial discourse, non-Western peoples are often appropriated on terms formulated by the colonizer. The colonized are expected to assimilate the values of the colonizer and conform to their world-view. Spurr draws attention to this kind of manipulative hermeneutical exercise which makes the colonized believe that colonialism is beneficial to them:

> The rhetorical appropriation of non-Western peoples insists on their identification with the basic values of Western civilization and tends to interpret their acquiescence to the colonial system as approval of Western ideals. But this equation of simple collaboration with a deeper moral identification, far from being regarded as a weakness in the logic of colonial discourse, instead provides one of its fundamental principles: a colonized people is morally improved and edified by virtue of its participation in the colonial system.
>
> (1993: 32–3)

Farquhar's discourse on Hinduism operates on a similar basis. Hindus would morally and spiritually benefit from the values of Western civilization. It is not a reforming of Hinduism from within, but a reform based on terms formulated by missionary colonialists. While the Baptist missionaries are keen on converting Hindus, Farquhar (who was conscious of the rising nationalist spirit) calls for a cautious approach to Hinduism. It is not so much conversion from Hinduism to Christianity, but modernization and Christianization of Hinduism: the religion itself is "at fault" (Farquhar 1913: 456) and therefore requires transformation. As with Müller, Farquhar attributes the rise of the reform movement of Brahmo Samāj to Western and Christian influences. He sees Christ already at work in the movement, furnishing it with new ideas and thereby complementing and rectifying the deficiencies of Hinduism. Farquhar states:

> [T]he whole reform movement arises from the Western atmosphere now influencing India so deeply ... every principle that controls the movement springs from Christ Himself ... Christ has inspired the movement so completely, we shall do well to ask whether He does not also supply the ideas needed to provide the religious foundation for the new structure which we see taking shape before our eyes.
>
> (ibid.: 118)

Hindu religious ideas are seen as obstructing the progress of social reform and those "who have not had a modern education are still dominated by old beliefs. This is the gigantic barrier that stands in the way of the re-creation of the Hindu family" (ibid.: 109). Farquhar sees the traditional Hindu family crumbling under Western influence and the younger generation affirming their freedom and individuality (ibid.: 111–13). Commenting on the changed relationship between the older and younger Hindu generation within the family as the result of Western education, Farquhar comments: "That is the new spirit controlled by religion. The new wine of liberty needs new bottles to contain it" (ibid.: 117). Farquhar offers a far too simplistic analysis of a very complex situation. As Panikkar states: "Just as Western influences did not automatically lead to 'progressive' social and political consciousness, traditional influences did not inevitably create conservative attitudes" (1995: 69). He goes on to point out that nineteenth-century Hindus such as Radhakanta Deb and Narayana Guru who were "rooted in traditional knowledge and culture, held more advanced views on several social questions [such as female education and caste] than their Western educated contemporaries" (ibid.). Like Macaulay, Farquhar wants to create a new breed of Hindus modeled on European modernist values, who will leave behind their religious beliefs and customs, and affirm and act in conformity with Victorian norms of companionate marriage and family. Spurr highlights the danger of this kind of hermeneutical exercise, which makes the colonized validate the superiority of Western culture: "To see non-Western peoples as having themselves become the standard bearers of Western culture is in some ways a more profound form of colonization than that which treats them merely as sources of labour or religious conversion" (1993: 36).

The view that the emergence of the nineteenth-century reform movements largely testifies to the impact of Western education and European thought was prevalent among British colonial administrators, historians and Christian missionaries as well as among some Indian historians. I do not intend to make light of the influence of the West, but want to point out that such a perception was grounded in the assumption that the eighteenth century was a "dark age" for India. This offers a one-sided and restricted view of a highly complex nineteenth-century situation, and overlooks the voices of protest and dissent by heterodox sects in precolonial British India. As Pannikar states:

> Without belittling the importance of Western influence, it should be pointed out that such analyses not only ignore the complexities of the social and intellectual developments during the nineteenth century, but also overlook the elements of protest and dissent in the Indian intellectual tradition and the potentialities of social development in the eighteenth century before British intervention. Above all, they totally ignore the material conditions within which these developments occurred.
>
> (Panikkar 1995: 4)

Concluding remarks

Like his orientalist predecessors, Farquhar constructed a body of knowledge that has influenced Christian missionary thinking and inter-religious dialogue. Although he called for an empathetic approach to Hinduism, his notion of an evolutionary classification of religions itself defeats his purpose. *The Crown of Hinduism* is a classic example of orientalism at work. To use Saidian language, Farquhar deals with Hinduism "by making statements about it, authorizing views of it, describing it, by teaching it, ruling over it: in short orientalism as a Western style for dominating, restructuring, and having authority over the Orient" (Said 1985: 3). Farquhar's ostensibly liberal reading of Hinduism results in reactivating negative pictures of it. His fulfillment theory itself confirms his claim to a superior truth which Hindus do not as yet possess. He claims not only to represent Hinduism in a true light but to demonstrate "Christianity as the Crown of Hinduism" (1913: 64). What Farquhar's evolutionary/fulfillment paradigm does is to reduce all Hindus to a subaltern status – Western-educated Hindus are regarded as transformed subalterns, whereas those Hindus untouched by values of the European Enlightenment are seen as superstitious. The untransformed subalterns are steeped in idolatry and therefore cannot speak for themselves. In other words, "They cannot represent themselves; they need to be represented" (Said 1985: 272). As to the question "whether indeed there can be a true representation of anything" (ibid.), I share Edward Said's view that representations are "implicated, intertwined, embedded, interwoven with a great many other things besides the 'truth,' which is itself a representation" (ibid.). Like Müller, Farquhar offers a Christianized version of Hinduism – this is what he sees as a true representation. While one cannot avoid interpreting or representing one's own and other cultures, the danger lies in claiming to offer a better or a truer representation of them. For Farquhar, if there is any real Hinduism, it is Christianized Hinduism.

Chapter 5

Courtly text and courting *satī*

> It was colonialist discourse that, by assuming … the complete submission of all Hindus to the dictates of [brahminical] texts, defined the tradition that was to be criticized and reformed.
>
> (Chatterjee 1993: 119)

Preceding chapters have looked at the constructions of Hinduism in the works of European orientalists and missionaries. This chapter focuses on one particular aspect: the representation of *satī* in the work of a contemporary scholar, Julia Leslie. Compared with nineteenth-century Baptist missionaries, Jones and Müller themselves said little about *satī*.[1] It is perhaps in Henry Colebrooke's paper "On the duties of a faithful Hindu widow" that we find scriptural perspectives on it.[2] His account of the burning widow reflected both wonder and horror, and it came to have a profound effect on both lay and scholarly approaches to *satī*. It is with Colebrooke that orientalists turned their attention to issues concerning Hindu women (Chakravarti 1993: 30–31). The *satī* issue acquired a central focus in nineteenth-century colonial Bengal, and the debate about it has been extensively covered by the feminist Indian historian, Lata Mani, in her latest book *Contentious Traditions: The Debate on Sati in Colonial India*.

This chapter, although in some respects different from the preceding chapters, is linked to them in that Julia Leslie's treatment of *satī* has some resonances with the nineteenth-century Hindu-colonial discourse on *satī* where Hindu texts were summoned to argue for and against the practice. Leslie uses an archaic Sanskrit treatise on Hindu women to demonstrate the meaning and significance of it for Hindu women. As with orientalists, she turns to the classical past and privileges a heavily biased patriarchal text in order to discuss a *satī* incident in postcolonial India – namely, the death of Roop Kanwar on the funeral pyre of her husband. My main concern has to do with the hermeneutical implications of Leslie using such a text in order to posit women as active agents. Before I embark on that task, however, I need to say a few words about the Roop Kanwar incident and the *satī* terminology.

Satī continues to be a controversial topic in both academic and popular discourse on women's issues in India and the West. Since the highly publicized death of an eighteen-year-old woman, Roop Kanwar, in 1987, in the north-west Indian state of Rajasthan, there has been an explosion of literature on the subject. Roop Kanwar and her twenty-four-year-old husband had hardly been married for a year when Mal Singh was taken ill suddenly and died in hospital. His body was brought to his house in Deorala in Rajasthan, and the following day Roop Kanwar mounted the funeral pyre and died with him, an event witnessed by thousands of people. It is said that Roop Kanwar chose to become a *satī* and prepared herself for this momentous occasion. The photograph of Roop Kanwar in her wedding outfit, seated on the funeral pyre and holding her husband's head on her lap as the flames engulfed them both, was distributed widely. Whatever the reason, Roop Kanwar's death was glorified and she came to be seen as a true *satī*, exemplifying the noble ideal of Hindu womanhood. Given that between 1947 (when India attained Independence) and 1987 (the year of Roop Kanwar's death) there were more than forty incidents of *satī*, twenty-eight in and around Sikar district in Rajasthan, one wonders why Roop Kanwar's case received such extraordinary attention. As Veena Oldenburg points out: "What made the profound difference this time was the activism and concern of women. Arguably, the Roop Kanwar case has converted the idea that a woman can become (an alleged) sati – and be glorified for it – from a residual quasi-religious theme into a critical political issue on which women's voices were heard for the very first time" (Oldenburg 1994: 101). Even occasional instances of *satī* such as Roop Kanwar's seem to provoke varied responses ranging from ambivalence to endorsement and denunciation.

First, a brief word about *satī*. There is much debate surrounding the definition and interpretation of the term. In Sanskrit *satī* means "a virtuous woman;" it is derived from *sat* meaning "truth," "virtue" or "goodness." The term can refer to a person, to a practice (the self-immolation of a wife on her husband's funeral pyre), or to the goddess Satī, who is the wife of Śiva.[3] Some affirm the conceptual meaning of *satī*, while condemning the practice; others see a link between the two. Some see in the myth of the goddess Satī an example of wifely devotion, although the cause of Satī's death bore no relation to any belief in reunion with a dead husband in heaven, because her husband Śiva was still alive. Satī's self-sacrifice signified her deep hurt and strong protest against her father's refusal to invite Śiva to a sacrificial gathering.[4] Some are skeptical about *satī* being a religiously motivated act; they see it as being grounded in other ideological factors for which religious justification is sought. The term *satī* is highly complex, influenced and informed by geographical context, socio-economic and political factors, gender, and textual perspectives. *Satī* has never been a universal or an ongoing practice, nor has it been undergirded by a uniform scriptural view (Thapar 1988: 18–19). To construct a normative and definitive meaning would not serve any useful purpose.

There appears to be no straightforward explanation for the origin of the practice of widow immolation. It was practised by the early Greeks and Scythians, and within India it "was practised by variant social groups for different reasons at various points in time and where the controversy over whether or not it should be practiced was so clearly articulated over many centuries … it underwent changes of meaning as well as degrees of acceptance" (Thapar 1988: 15). Although numerically a minority practice, *satī* came to acquire a central focus in nineteenth-century colonial India. It was prevalent in certain parts of India, particularly in Bengal and Rajasthan, and it was largely confined to women of the higher castes, particularly *kṣatriyas* (the warrior class) and brahmins (the priestly class). *Satī* was abolished in 1829 (Kumar 1993: 9).[5]

This chapter looks at the representation of Roop Kanwar's *satī* by one Western woman scholar, Julia Leslie, and at the hermeneutical implications of using a heavily biased patriarchal text to see Hindu women "as the active agents of their own positive constructs" (Leslie 1992a: 1). In the first part of the chapter I intend to show that, although Leslie's empathetic approach to *satī* is commendable, it is also problematic in the sense that it reinforces stereotypical patriarchal definitions of feminine behavior and role. Her use of a single text to validate the relevance of *satī* tends to make other texts invisible. What Julia Leslie's reading of an eighteenth-century patriarchal Sanskrit text by Tryambaka, an orthodox pundit of the Thanjavur court in South India, seems to have done is to reposition women in the brahminical patriarchal paradigm, and to show how they cope with oppressive ideologies. It appears that in Leslie's hermeneutical landscape there is no room for women who try to disrupt or dismantle them. What appears on the surface to be a positive construct turns out in effect to be a conventional feminine role and identity, and in the process we are offered a picture of a fixed and unchanging tradition and a frozen Hindu patriarchy. Furthermore, in subtle ways Leslie's hermeneutical approach replicates to some extent the nineteenth-century Hindu-colonial discourse on *satī*, and appears to support the view of the present-day Hindu revitalizers who see it as the very essence of Hindu womanhood.

In the second part of the chapter, I draw attention to liberating texts and voices within the Hindu tradition that stand in striking contrast to Tryambaka's text. Some *Śrīvaiṣṇava* texts offer a far more liberating image of women. Despite their patriarchal orientation, these texts see women as "auspicious" and do not recommend *satī*. I also draw attention to the voice of a woman contemporary with Tryambaka: Muddupalani, also of the eighteenth-century Thanjavur court, who offers a lively and positive image of Hindu women – a sharp and challenging contrast to Tryambaka's subservient view. Finally, I take a brief look at women saints in the *bhakti* tradition, such as Mīrābaī who challenged conventional definitions of feminine roles and showed other valid ways of expressing the notion of the ideal Hindu woman. A tradition as diverse as Hinduism requires reliance on more than a single text to capture the diversity of feminine roles and images. A single brahminical text such as Tryambaka's has no room for other significant ways of being an ideal Hindu woman. In using a single text as the basis for understanding the notion of *satī* and its relevance to the twentieth century, other texts with humanizing and liberating voices tend to get overlooked or silenced. In the process, traditional models come to be seen as representing the ideal Hindu woman.

First, I begin my analysis by briefly outlining Julia Leslie's chapter "Suttee or *satī*: victim or victor?" in *Roles and Rituals for Hindu Women*, which was written soon after the death of Roop Kanwar. Her death was glorified, and she came to be seen as an example of true *satī*. Starting with a brief historical background, Julia Leslie goes on to focus on her main point: that some Hindu women may find practices such as dowry or *satī* empowering and may "see themselves not as victims of their culture but as active agents in the creation of their own identity and that of their daughter" (Leslie 1992a: 3). To buttress her case, Leslie summons "an unusual" (ibid. 1992b: 183) eighteenth-century Sanskrit text, the *Strīdharmapaddhati*, or *Guide to the Religious Status and Duties of Women*, by Tryambakayajvan, an orthodox south Indian Hindu pundit, as a hermeneutical platform to discuss the concept of *satī* and its relationship to the death of the young woman in the late twentieth century.

In her chapter Leslie juxtaposes two perspectives: "suttee as victim" and "*satī* as victor." Leslie sees the former as representing "the predominant view of the West," indicated by the Anglicized spelling of suttee which refers to the practice – the act of self-immolation of a woman on the funeral pyre of her husband – and has connotations of "widowhood and victimization." Leslie sees the latter as still representing "the predominant view of traditional India," exemplified by the Sanskrit word *satī* which means "a virtuous woman" – one who becomes *satī* by joining her husband in death. It has connotations of "great virtue, personal strength and religious autonomy." Leslie makes it clear that "while trying to understand the empowering aspects of sati, we must never forget the violent and degrading reality ... Understanding ... does not mean condoning it, or accepting the necessity for it, or even refusing to judge" (Leslie 1992b: 177). Then she goes on to challenge two Western representations of "suttee as victim" – one by an eighteenth-century American ship's captain, Benjamin Crowninshield, and the other by the radical feminist Mary Daly. I shall come back to Leslie's reading of Mary Daly a little later. The rest of her chapter is concerned with demonstrating that *satī* may seem oppressive to outsiders, but could be empowering and positive to Hindus. Now I intend to take a closer look at Julia Leslie's representation of *satī* and the hermeneutical questions it raises.

Satī as voluntary

Leslie's perception of Roop Kanwar's death as voluntary is based on early press accounts and the public response to her death (Leslie 1992b: 181–3). Leslie concedes that most cases of *satī* are not voluntary, yet goes on to ask: "Are we right to dismiss every case as murder? Are not some cases, most perhaps, in some sense 'voluntary'?" (ibid.: 180). There were some, no doubt, who saw her death as a voluntary act, demonstrating the ideal of devoted wife (*pativratā*), and who treated her as a true *satī*, a "virtuous woman." Yet, as we do not know for sure whether Roop Kanwar chose to become a *satī* or whether her death was forced on her, we cannot take for granted that it was voluntary. Leslie's reading of the event as a voluntary echoes the stance taken during the colonial period by the East India Company, which made a distinction between "voluntary" and "enforced" *satī*. Before finally banning *satī* in 1829, the East India Company legislated in favor of it, if it was a voluntary act chosen by women willingly (Kumar 1993: 9). Hindu traditionalists in nineteenth-century British India claimed that *satī* was always voluntary and used it as a ruse for attacking Western intervention. Lata Mani, an Indian feminist who investigated eyewitness accounts of *satī* in the nineteenth century and the testimonials of widows who escaped the funeral pyre, suggests that *satī* was not always voluntary and that "the testimonials of widows challenge the dominant presentation of *satī* as a religiously inspired act of devotion to the deceased husband" (Mani 1993a: 287). In other words, "The ideology of *satī*, as an act undertaken by a devoted wife with a view to future spiritual reward, is nowhere alluded to by the widow" (ibid.: 278). With regard to Roop Kanwar, how are we to know her true feelings and intentions? If, as Leslie points out in the concluding section of her chapter, "for most women choice itself is a fiction" (1992b: 190), then the question of *satī* being voluntary does not make sense.

Satī as a positive construct

Using *satī* as a template, Leslie attempts to show women as "the active agents of their own positive constructs" (Leslie 1992a: 1). She declares that she has "difficulty with a view of women that sees them only as victims" (ibid. 1992b: 177), and finds it necessary to challenge such a view. She agrees that women are victims to a large extent but is interested in exploring how, despite being oppressed, they emerge as victors. She writes: "But what is of significance for me – as a woman scholar interested in how women cope with oppressive ideologies – is how these same victims find a path through the maze of oppression, a path that to them spells dignity and power" (ibid.). This is the path that brings honor, glory, and power to the woman who chooses to become a *satī*. A true *satī* becomes "a goddess (*devī*), a deified eternal wife," showering her blessings on her family and relatives. This is what Leslie calls the "empowerment of sati: a strategy for dignity in a demeaning world" where for most Hindu women choice itself is an illusion (ibid.: 190).

As I have pointed out earlier, if "choice itself is a fiction," it does not make any sense to seek agency in the act of immolation. Surely we cannot claim to assume or know that Roop Kanwar found empowerment in the act of self-immolation. The idea of woman as a positive construct is encouraging and at the same time problematic. It is encouraging because women find a way of coping with oppressive ideologies and situations with dignity and strength, but problematic because the kind of empowerment that a woman may find in the act of immolation (encouraged by interested parties) has only a limited valence. Women are active agents to the extent that they make a virtue out of adversity – something negative has been transformed into a positive. Yet although this approach may help an individual cope with a given oppressive situation, it does not necessarily result in decentering or dismantling oppressive ideologies. *Satī* may be more empowering for those who witness it than for the person immolating herself. The portrayal of Roop Kanwar as an active agent of her own destiny, however remarkable, reinforces the image of women as heroic sufferers who affirm their dignity even in death. Roop Kanwar is projected as a heroic agent – not challenging dominant, oppressive ideologies and practices, but rather re-enacting the patriarchal image of women as long-suffering and enduring. In other words, Julia Leslie succeeds in showing women as spiritually strong in coping with patriarchal oppression but not in challenging it. The question remains: did Roop Kanwar see herself as an agent of her own destiny? The iconography of Roop Kanwar does not say anything about her being empowered, but what we know is that some witnesses glorified her death and perceived her act as an affirmation of *satī*. Kanwar emerges perhaps as a "victor" for those who glorify or romanticize her death. As Veena Oldenburg points out: "Witnesses affirm the nature of the event as religious; their gaze makes it sati ... the event also reinforces the base appetites of the male members of the audience to see women suffer, while in women sati confirms the ideology that women's strength lies in the act [of] sacrifice and the endurance of untold pain" (1994: 104–5).

The idea of women affirming their *śakti* – power – through self-immolation, or being active agents of their own destiny, can become a convenient tool – one that serves very well the ideology of Hindu fundamentalists who would want their women to affirm their *śakti* through their suffering and sacrifice for the good of others. It is a kind of empowerment that helps one to deal with conflicting situations, but at the same time recycles stereotypical images of women as long suffering. It is important to draw attention to Indian feminists' struggle with Hindu fundamentalists and other pro-*satī* groups, who saw Roop Kanwar's death as an affirmation of the *satī* ideal. For Indian feminists this was a crime against woman and they strongly protested against the glorification of her death. The feminists were seen as undermining the noble ideal of self-sacrifice exemplified by women who embraced *satī*, and thereby undermining Rajput honor and identity. The Rajput community deeply valued its royal traditions, social norms, and customs, and Rajput women were expected to defend and uphold the honor of their women. Furthermore, the pro-*satī* campaigners gained the support of a considerable number of women who propagated their cause, thereby making the feminists' anti-*satī* campaign appear as not being truly representative of the interests and views of Hindu women (Kumar 1993: 179). Feminists were seen as opposing tradition and affirming the values of the West. They stood accused "of being agents of modernity who were attempting to impose crass market-dominated views of equality and liberty on a society which once gave the noble, the self-sacrificing and the spiritual the respect they deserve, but which is now being rapidly destroyed by essentially selfish forces of the market" (ibid.: 174). Feminists who interrogated the construction and perpetuation of *satī* ideology were branded as "Westernists, colonialists, cultural imperialists, and – indirectly – supporters of capitalist ideology" (ibid.). On the contrary, it was the pro-*satī* campaigners who commercialized Roop Kanwar's death for their for their own profit.

Thus, a highly complex issue came to be seen in terms of tradition versus modernity. In the process, tradition came to be "defined so historically and so self-righteously that it obscured the fact that sati was being used to reinforce caste and communal identities along 'modern lines,' with modern methods of campaigning and organizing, modern arguments and modern ends, such as the reformation of electoral blocs and caste and communal representations within the state" (Kumar 1993: 179).[6] In Leslie's treatment, some features of the debate over *satī* in colonial India resurface. The controversy led both pro- and anti-*satī* Hindus to project an idealized Hindu womanhood in the face of Western condemnation of Hindu practices. Both constructed an essentialized image of the Hindu woman, the difference being that the former affirmed the practice and the latter denounced it.

Leslie does not investigate the witnesses' construction of voluntary *satī* but treats it as proof of *satī* being authentic for them. The fact that some feel inspired and honored by Roop Kanwar's death does not necessarily make it as authentic or as voluntary as Julia Leslie would want us to believe. Even if scriptures and biographical narratives of *satī* affirm its voluntary nature, it does not necessarily follow that *satī* incidents in history are of a voluntary nature. This is not to rule out exceptions wherein a wife may feel genuine and deep grief and a longing to join her husband in death. But as Romila Thapar points out, the act of self-immolation as "a form of sacrifice seems to be a more recent interpretation" (1988: 18).

Leslie does not address the question of women's agency in relation to other factors. Agency is located in the woman herself, as having an autonomous religious status or freedom. Indian feminists such as Sudesh Vaid and Kumkum Sangari show how the idea of voluntary *satī* is shaped by belief in the presence of *sat* ("a palpable force of virtue and truth"), and how it works in practice. They particularly draw attention to underlying complexities that are often ignored:

> The whole question of "voluntary" widow immolation hinges on the local acceptance of the presence of "sat." "Sat" structures the interrelated, mutually generative factors of community participation in widow immolation as well as its wider perception ... Once a woman is proclaimed to be possessed by "sat" an inexorable logic is set into motion and there seems to be barely any scope for her to protest or to change "her" mind or even to grasp the full implications of "her" decision, if that is, she ever made such a decision. *Once proclaimed, "sat" only creates a space for the woman's consent not for her resistance – for not only does the declaration of "sat" itself depend on others who can attest to the miracles, but it opens the way for wider community participation ... For the woman "sat" only provides the space for reflecting or accepting the will of others; she is swept on the wave of the gathered community's "religious feeling," compelled to die according to the dictates of "sat."* "Sat" makes the public burning of the woman possible by obliterating the horror of the act ... Crucially the concept of "sat" submerges the material and social basis of the event and gives a sense of religious euphoria to the mass witnessing of the immolation. At every stage, belief in "sat" becomes the religious equivalent of physical force.
>
> (Vaid and Sangari 1991: WS–5; emphasis is mine)

It is important to examine how "volition is constituted." Whether one speaks of *satī* in terms of choice made by the woman or facilitated by the presence of *sat*, both positions affirm *satī* to be voluntary, and the final outcome is that the woman who joins her husband in death becomes a true *satī* or a deified wife. Both versions treat *satī* as being extraordinary or exceptional in nature, and therefore it can only be voluntary. But in the absence of public participation in the event, its exceptional nature cannot be confirmed or established (Vaid and Sangari 1991: WS–10). Furthermore, as Veena Oldenburg points out, "even when agency can be forensically established, can the woman's act of self-immolation be judged to be a product of her own will, or must it be judged as a product of the very studious socialization and indoctrination of women (particularly for the role of wife) that shape her attitudes and actions from girlhood?" (Oldenberg 1994: 124). Women's agency or volition needs to be examined in relation to both particularities of each case and the social, religious, cultural factors specific to the given context (Vaid and Sangari 1991: WS–4).

Leslie's wish to recover the female agency, or the agency of Roop Kanwar, is problematic. Both Lata Mani and Spivak "deal with difficulty in recovering the agency, subjectivity and voice of the colonized woman, who is caught within indigenous and colonial male constructions of her, each parading as her liberator from the other" (Loomba 1993: 316). In the absence of any direct evidence of a woman's voice or subjectivity, to treat Roop Kanwar as an active agent is to blur the truth. As Gayatri Spivak says: "One never encounters the testimony of the women's voice-consciousness" (1993: 93) to confirm her autonomous choice, whether religious or otherwise. Leslie sees the female agency that is located in the conceptual and ideological meaning of *satī* ("good woman") and its practice (self-immolation), whether frequent or infrequent, as demonstrating *satī* as an ideal wife – a deified wife charged with *śakti* or divine feminine power.[7] Such a construct of woman, however impressive it may be, offers us not a liberating view of woman but one that would serve the patriarchal ideology of Hindu fundamentalists and those who have internalized such norms. If it is in this sense that Julia Leslie is seeing s*atī* as a positive construct, her vision has little relevance for women who do not feel empowered or enthused by her understanding or definition of a positive construct. In what sense does Roop Kanwar figure as an active agent of her destiny? What is the value of representing Roop Kanwar as a victor? Did she find meaning and value in becoming *satī*? The construction of an active agent is not necessary in order to demonstrate that women cope heroically with oppressive situations.

Leslie legitimizes her construction of *satī* as empowering by referring to witnesses' awe-struck reactions to Roop Kanwar's death. Witnesses often draw attention to the miraculous nature of the event, and this is seen as making it authentic and worthy of reverence. Leslie cites the responses of witnesses to show that *satī* is empowering for these people, even if it appears oppressive to others. Here are two examples:

> Sati is not possible for all women, only those who are very blessed. I have come here for the blessings of this holy place. …
>
> You cannot say when a woman will feel this way. People tried to prevent her, but she was very strong. She had faith. The people have come here to honor that faith.
>
> (Leslie 1992b: 182–3)

Leslie goes on to say that for these people, Roop Kanwar had the courage to become a *satī*:

> For these people, who perhaps knew Roop Kanwar best, the responsibility for her death was hers alone. They are inspired and honored by her example. For (according to this view) she had the courage to walk the sacred path extolled in so many teachings and myths: the path of sati.
>
> (ibid.: 183)

Not all can tread this noble path but those who do so feel no mental or physical pain or anguish, but "become endowed with stupendous powers" (ibid.: 190). Leslie does not question the construction of voluntary *satī* but takes witnesses' responses as confirmation of it. To treat witnesses' responses and their public participation in the ritual and the euphoria surrounding such a spectacle as a manifestation of a deeply held religious belief requires careful investigation. Beliefs do not exist in a vacuum; they are affected by socio-economic, cultural, political, and other factors, and are even sometimes manipulated for selfish interests. The decline of the social, economic, and political status of the hitherto dominant Rajput caste has probably led them to claim *satī* as a Rajput ritual and to demonstrate its relevance to present-day Rajput concerns by showing their solidarity in affirming "a ritual which is controversial and insist[ing] on supporting it" (Thapar 1988: 19). Romila Thapar points out that "*satī* memorials in the past were simple memorial stones, but the more recent temples are vast enterprises ... where the Marwari [wealthy business community] talent for finance has combined with Rajput notions of honour, to the material benefit of both" (ibid.: 17). If one looks at the construction of *satī* in Rajasthan's history, one can see how faith in *satī* has has been perpetuated by Rajput ideologues and nationalists who combine elements or aspects relating to the worship of immolated Rajput women in family shrines with contemporary incidents of immolation in order to demonstrate the unbroken continuity between the past and present (Vaid and Sangari 1991: WS–14). In the process, beliefs about *satī* come to be invested with authority. Sudesh Vaid and Kumkum Sangari show how beliefs are affected by ideologies and come to be institutionalized:

> Belief is inextricable from the social processes which generate it and has no autonomous origin; but once articulated in rituals and institutions it acquires a relative autonomy of the sort that other ideological formations have ... The divine miracle, among other things, also makes for an eminently commodifiable event. Belief in "sati" is partly fostered by the spectacular and systemic commodification of the event ... Without the glamour, recognition and institutionalisation of a palatial temple the meanings of immolation would neither "circulate" nor gather "value."
>
> (ibid.: WS–14)

Furthermore, belief in *sat* legitimizes the act of widow immolation and frees both the believers and onlookers from any guilt in preventing it from taking place. Sudesh Vaid and Kumkum Sangari show how belief in the power of *sat* sublimates the human agent:

> "[S]at" translates and sublimates human agency – the actual social agents involved in invoking "sat," family, villagers, other women – into something

> external or beyond control. "Sat" is manufactured and gains consent because it elides human participation then "benevolently" re-includes the participants who can express the pride of participation without feeling the guilt of collusion ... So by virtue of its exceptional character it gains consent in the form of religious belief from other women ... The "sat" which gains consent is at once legitimising the patriarchal and the supernatural, and more especially the former through the latter.
>
> (Vaid and Sangari 1991: WS–15–16)

That some see virtue in becoming a *satī* or feel empowered by the event, does not necessarily imply that it is intrinsic to the tradition, and that those who do not subscribe to it are not anti-Hindu or necessarily rejecting their tradition. For Leslie, Indian women who challenge conventional feminine roles in Hindu myths are "resisting not only aspects of Indian culture but, in a very real sense, parts of themselves" (Leslie 1989: 327). It appears that, for Leslie, Hindu notions of the feminine, as outlined in myths or in the classical Sanskrit texts, are fixed and resist new readings. In Leslie's hermeneutic framework there is hardly any room for reformulation and redefinition, as this would mean that Hindus who embark on such an exercise are not only being untrue to their tradition but also denying aspects of themselves. As Romila Thapar states:

> It is easy enough to take the stand that those who do not accept sati as part of the Hindu tradition are westernised Indians deracinated from the mainsprings of the Hindu ethos and therefore unable to understand either the Rajput concept of honour or to appreciate the idealised relationship between a Hindu husband and wife, such, that it is sought to be perpetuated to eternity through sati; or to see that sati is a pure act of the ultimate sacrifice (even if such an act is reduced to a public spectacle with a variety of entrepreneurs literally cashing in on it). Such arguments deny a discussion on the subject and the latter is necessary if we are to attempt an understanding of our traditions. Traditions in any case often arise out of contemporary needs but seek legitimation from the past. Therefore the past has to be brought into play where such legitimation is sought.
>
> (1988: 15)

One need not be an Indian or Western feminist to question or challenge certain accepted notions of wifely duty and behavior or how such notions are appropriated by women. History has examples of voices of dissent and protest but it appears that these voices are of little consequence for Julia Leslie. There are equally powerful counter-examples in terms of which one can see Roop Kanwar's death; she "chose" a path that many significant women in the epics did not choose, but they were nevertheless devoted to their husbands and continued to live a celibate life. The point is that the idea of a virtuous woman does not imply that she has to immolate herself to prove her devotion; there are other valid ways whereby her virtue may be demonstrated. There are examples of wifely devotion which show that women also subverted conventional norms. Epic figures such as Sāvitrī, Draupadī and Sītā were devoted to their husbands but also departed from traditional norms in some respects. For example, Sāvitrī chose to marry Satyavan knowing full well that he had only a short time to live. When he died she persuaded the god of death, Yama, to bring him back to life. Her wifely *dharma* or duty lay not in joining her husband in death but in bringing him back to life and living with him. (Sri Aurobindo, the twentieth-century philosopher and mystic, has transformed the legend of Sāvitrī into a powerful symbol or personification of *śakti* itself, in his monumental epic *Sāvitrī*. The birth of Sāvitrī indicates the birth and "descent of a new consciousness" into humanity (Mehta 1983: 3)). Sītā's devotion to her husband Rāmā in the epic *Rāmāyaṇa* does not necessarily make her a subservient wife. She refuses to go through the second ordeal of proving to his subjects that she is chaste. She declines Rāma's request to come and live with him, by choosing her own course of action (disappearing into Mother Earth). Although she fulfils the role of an ideal wife by following him into the forest, toward the end of the story, Sītā departs from conventional expectations and norms. Draupadī, who figures as a devoted wife in the epic the *Mahābhārata*, does not hesitate to show her rightful anger when one of her husbands, Yudhiṣṭhira, pawns her in a game of dice after he has forfeited all his possessions. She challenges all of her husbands and their first cousins in the presence of elders in the assembly. One could add to the list the princess Kaṇṇagi in the Tamil epic *Śilapaddikāram*, who does not immediately follow her husband into death but instead sets out to avenge him because he was falsely accused by the Pandyan king. She challenges the king, and her curse burns the city of Madurai to ashes. Here we see her *śakti* shaking the very foundations of the Pandyan kingdom because a terrible injustice was done to her husband. I do not intend to seek refuge in these classical images of women, but I want to point out these women show that devotion does not and need not mean subservience, although most tend to equate the two. Devotion can be expressed in different ways.

Textual warrant: resurrecting an eighteenth-century Sanskrit text

Leslie looks for a positive construct of Hindu woman in a strongly biased eighteenth-century patriarchal text produced by Tryambaka, who sets a high value on *satī*. This resurrected Sanskrit text reflects traditional views of the pundit "drawn from older and more authoritative religious and legal texts" (Leslie 1992b: 183). Such a text, like the *Dharmaśāstras* (legal texts), reflect to a great extent the views of the author on how women ought to behave.[8]

Tryambaka assigns a subservient role to women, who are seen as essentially wicked and in need of patriarchal monitoring and control; it is only through their *strīdharma* (devotion) and service to their husbands, that they can become good or virtuous. It is important to demonstrate this devotion by joining their husbands in death, as this brings enormous blessings to both husband and wife (Leslie 1992b: 183–90).

The Sanskrit pundit outlines two paths for women: *satī* and widowhood, recommending the former. Although both paths "enable her to demonstrate the essential power of the good woman for the salvation of her husband," the path of *satī* is easier and safer than the path of widowhood, as it brings merit not only to the woman but also to her husband and family. Julia Leslie writes:

> Tryambaka's point is simply this: sati is both easier in terms of gaining merit (for oneself and, most important, for one's husband and family), and also safer for all concerned, than the alternative path of the widow. The *sati* is thus seen as making a conscious choice, both for her own sake and for the sake of her family, a choice that is grounded in the soteriological power of the good woman.
>
> (1992b: 190)

Applying the views of an orthodox pundit to the montage photograph of Roop Kanwar seated amidst flames with her husband's head on her lap, Julia Leslie concludes that Roop Kanwar "has done precisely what Tryambaka might have told her to do" – she chose the path of *satī*.

> This is the iconography of a modern legend. As the legend spreads and the new sati myth takes shape, we shall probably never know the true circumstances surrounding her death. But what the iconography tells is important. It tells us that Roop Kanwar has made a conscious choice not to become a widow. It tells us that – as a *sati*, a "truly virtuous woman" – she ceases to be a woman at all. For she has become endowed with stupendous powers: she will bring salvation to her husband and to generations of their two families ... ; she will be worshipped in her own community for ever. According to the iconography, Roop Kanwar has chosen to become a goddess (*devī*), a deified eternal wife ... This is the empowerment of sati: a strategy for dignity in a demeaning world. The tragedy is that Roop Kanwar could find no other. For in such a world, for most women choice itself is a fiction.
>
> (ibid.)

I do see the point Julia Leslie is trying to make: that Hindu women find a way of affirming their dignity even when choice itself remains an illusion or myth for most of them. I agree that we need to see women as positive agents of their own destiny. However, there are two problems with Leslie's hermeneutic strategy.

First, the iconography itself is questionable in that it masks the real problem. It may give the impression that Roop Kanwar was a true *satī*, a victor who affirmed her *śakti*, power. It may be convenient to read the iconography as affirming the ideal of *pativratā*, devoted wife, but whether she made a conscious choice to become a *satī* will remain a speculation. We do not know for certain that Roop Kanwar found empowerment through *satī*, but what we do know is that some see her as a true *satī*, and worship her as a goddess, and will continue to venerate her. To use Julia Leslie's words again, if "for most women choice itself is a fiction," we must also treat the iconography with some skepticism, although it may give the impression of Roop Kanwar embodying the ideal Hindu woman.

Second, in privileging a particular text with a pronounced patriarchal bias towards women, other liberating texts and voices tend to get overlooked. The construction of women in brahminical texts, although not relevant to all Hindu women, is given preferential status. But texts do not play a central role in the lives of Hindus. There are innumerable texts within the tradition, both primary and secondary, that could be used to argue for or against *satī*. Moreover, local customs have influenced religious, cultural and social practices. In keeping with the logocentric approach of Western and Hindu scholars, however, Julia Leslie engages with the textual tradition, and examines Roop Kanwar's *satī* and Hindu responses to it in the light of a single text. Eighteenth-century British orientalists such as William Jones saw the *Dharmaśāstras* as representing the law of the Hindus and therefore applicable to all Hindus. Both British orientalists and brahmin pundits collaborated in conferring on the legal texts an authentic and authoritative status (see Juridical Jones). Just as during the colonial period a little used text, Manu's *Dharmaśāstra*, came to be invested with excessive authority, now Leslie in the postcolonial era retrieves Tryambaka's "unusual" text and accords it a privileged status over other liberating texts and voices. There is a danger in placing undue faith in the text; it prevents other ways of addressing the notion of ideal womanhood.

In according a special status to an eighteenth-century brahminical text, Julia Leslie seems to follow, to some extent, in the footsteps of nineteenth-century British colonialists and Hindu reformers who assigned a primary role to particular texts in order to use them for legislating against *satī*. In the nineteenth-century Hindu-colonial discourse on *satī*, there was an implicit assumption that Hindu scriptures played a central role in the lives of Hindus, and that they conducted their affairs in accordance with scriptural injunctions. In seeking scriptural sanction, the British not only introduced the Protestant principle of relying on texts but also imposed some kind of uniformity on a religion that was loosely structured, and which did not rest entirely on scriptural authority. In making brahminical scripture the basis of the religion, colonialists were inventing a tradition and legitimizing it on their own terms, and Hindu reformers collaborated in this colonial textual project, thus creating a new hermeneutic precedent. Relying on certain pundits as authoritative interpreters of the texts, colonialists and Hindu reformers were forging a tradition to suit their hermeneutic aim: to establish that the practice of *satī* had no scriptural warrant. In other words, the high-caste Hindu woman became a site for both colonialists and nationalists to argue whether *satī* had any scriptural sanction (Mani 1993b: 190–92). Likewise, Julia Leslie summons an eighteenth-century text to demonstrate the relevance of *satī*. She does not address crucial questions such as *satī*'s status as tradition and the perpetuation of *satī* ideology, which Indian women scholars such as Lata Mani investigate. Contemporary Indian historians and feminists who interrogate textual and popular constructions and perpetuation of *satī* are relegated to Leslie's footnotes.

Like Indian and Western orientalists Leslie searches the classical texts of the past to explore the "religious ideology" behind *satī* (1992b: 183). Concerning the ideology of the proper role of women, she declares in her introduction to an earlier work, *The Perfect Wife: The Orthodox Hindu Woman According to the Strīdharmapaddhati of Tryambakayajvan*:

> Where may we find its ideals, aims and arguments set out? An increasing number of books and articles are being written in English on the role of women both in India and elsewhere. But India is in the special position of having an ancient, complex and highly intellectual socio-religious tradition of its own. Scholars from all over the world have spent lifetimes studying the contributions of the pandits of this rich classical past. Where then are the great debates on the status and role of women? Is there not a Sanskrit text on the subject from within this orthodox Hindu tradition?
> (Leslie 1989: 2–3).

For Leslie, it appears that it is only the classical past that can possibly give answers to contemporary problems. We are taken on a trip back to the origins, the ancient and revered past, embodied in the Sanskrit text of the pundit. Although the text is not a social description of reality, Leslie summons it to demonstrate the significance of *satī* for Hindus in the postcolonial era.[9]

Although Julia Leslie's intentions may seem egalitarian, she uses the text to show that the ideology of *satī* is intrinsic to the Hindu tradition. Hindu women such as Roop Kanwar are seen as conforming to an ancient ideal that is eternal and central to the tradition. In so doing, Julia Leslie essentializes *satī* and Hindu womanhood, unintentionally reinforces the stance taken by Hindu fundamentalists and provides hermeneutical fodder for them. Whereas Hindu fundamentalists tend to spiritualize pain, Julia Leslie sees *satī* as empowering women to cope with oppressive ideologies. Although her

"Suttee or *satī*: victim or victor?" is about repositioning women in a positive light and the empowerment of *satī*, it is paradoxically also about tradition, which is seen as being static – not affected by social, historical or economic changes and political agendas. In choosing a heavily biased eighteenth-century patriarchal text and demonstrating its relevance to the twentieth century, what Julia Leslie does is to perpetuate the notion that Hindu society, religion, cultural customs are fixed, and that the role of women has to a great extent remained static and frozen:

> First, *satī* remains as an ideal. While the numbers of women who died in this way have always been statistically small, the ideal of such women and such a death is reverenced throughout traditional India today. *Satī* evidently needs to be practised sometimes in order to serve as a model, but it becomes irrelevant how many times it is actually practised because its social effect as a model of the good (that is, socially-valued) woman remains.
>
> (Leslie 1992b: 176)

It does not matter whether *satī* is practiced regularly or occasionally, by some or many; it remains an ideal – a timeless phenomenon. Given the complexity surrounding the terminology of *satī* and its usage, and given the varied intertwining historical, contextual, and other factors that contribute to the formation of *satī* ideology, to construct *satī* as integral to the tradition is to ignore not only these essential factors but also to erase alternative ways of being a good woman.

Leslie takes textual images or constructions of *satī* for granted; she does not attempt to question the construction and perpetuation of such an ideology. Moreover, she does not address political, economic, and social factors of *satī* ideology but sees it purely in religious categories. *Satī*, it appears, is not affected by any of these factors; if Leslie mentions them at all, she relegates them to the background. *Satī* is seen as "the indirect, impersonal – but none the less powerful – force of Hindu religious ideology concerning Hindu women" (Leslie 1992b: 182). In her reappropriation of *satī*, it seems to have more to do with Hindu religion than with other factors. As Veena Oldenburg points out, *satī* needs to be seen "as a social and historical construct with mythological resonances, and not a mythological one with social and historical distortions and corruptions" (1994: 169). It appears that Julia Leslie endows Roop Kanwar's *satī* with a timeless quality. In other words, *satī* is dehistoricized and given a timelessness which is immune to any kind of change or mutation.

Two voices framing *satī*: Julia Leslie and Mary Daly

I now turn to Leslie's critique of Mary Daly's representation of *satī*. Daly, a leading and controversial feminist, has mounted a formidable attack on received patriarchal structures. In her chapter "The Indian suttee" in *Gyn/Ecology*, Daly sees Hindu women as victims of their religion and patriarchy (1984: 113–33). Although Leslie is in agreement with Daly's main thesis that the act of *satī*, whether voluntary or forced, "is an act of violence against women," she challenges Daly's view of the woman who becomes a *satī*. Leslie remarks: "It is precisely this idea of the *satī* as the apparent agent of her own destruction that I believe we need to confront" (1992: 180).

Although Leslie is critical of Mary Daly's portrayal of Hindu women as victims of their religion, she overlooks particularly Daly's uncritical use of the views of Katherine Mayo (an American journalist) on Indian women. Daly resurrects the colonial views of Mayo expressed in her book *Mother India*, published in the halcyon days of colonialism.[10] Daly does not critique Mayo's Eurocentric attitudes to women, nor her portrayal of Hinduism and India as decadent and therefore not fit for self-government. In a footnote to the chapter, Daly draws a picture of a stagnant India in which the position of most women has not changed dramatically since the abolition of *satī* in 1829, "or since the publication of Katherine Mayo's book *Mother India* in 1927" (Daly 1984: 114n). Daly essentializes India and the role of women there; they remain fixed and are not affected by social, economic, historic, or political changes. It is ironic that a radical feminist such as Daly should consider Katherine Mayo an authority on Indian society and women. It is equally ironic that Julia Leslie has not raised any objections to Daly's reliance on Mayo's colonial approach to India and its women. Daly's reading of *satī* is not free from orientalist tendencies. Daly gives the impression that *satī* is a common practice among all Hindus. She universalizes *satī*, ignoring heterogeneous scriptural views on it, and the contextual and historical differences in its practices. As Uma Narayanan remarks: "Daly's account of *satī* not only erases its *temporal* context but blurs other important *contextual* features of the practice with respect to its variations across class, caste, religion and geographical location ... Daly completely fails to make clear that *satī* was not practised by *all* Hindu communitie ... in the Indian population" (1997: 49).[11]

It appears that Daly's critique of patriarchal oppression requires a portrayal of a religion and its beliefs, social and cultural practices as unaffected by historical or other factors. In other words, patriarchy in non-Western contexts is untouched by historical change and political agendas (Narayanan 1997: 49–52). Such a treatment replicates both colonialist and contemporary Hindu fundamentalist representations of religious traditions as fixed and unchanging. Colonialists represented India as a land infested with barbaric practices, incapable of change. Hindu fundamentalists have defended it by constructing an idealized Hinduism that confined women to traditional roles.

Although Julia Leslie and Mary Daly differ in that the former sees women as active agents and the latter as victims, they both essentialize *satī*. I find some of Uma Narayanan's critique of *satī* equally applicable to Leslie. Both see it as an unchanging and eternal aspect of the tradition and in their approach, there is little room for the "politics of tradition formation" or the construction of *satī* as tradition.[12] In other words, their approach leaves the concept of tradition "unproblematized" and this results in "a simplistic, ahistorical, and apolitical" interpretation of *satī* (Narayanan 1997: 61). Daly completely overlooks historical and contextual variations in the practice of *satī*, whereas Leslie shows awareness of these factors but does not interact with them or draw out their implications in her representation of Roop Kanwar as an active agent of her destiny. Leslie discusses Roop Kanwar's *satī* without sufficiently contextualizing it. She gives a brief historical background and an account of how Rajputs perceive Roop Kanwar's *satī* without taking into serious consideration how Rajasthan's religious, economic, political, and historical factors (both past and present) can affect the perception, appropriation and the construction of *satī*. While Leslie's approach results in a blurring of history, Daly's approach results in the "erasing of history." Religious beliefs, cultural and social practices appear to be static or fixed and divorced from vested economic and political interests. As Uma Narayanan points out:

> "Religion" also appears in these analyses as a set of beliefs and practices unconnected to a variety of economic interests and political agendas that might underlie and contribute to changes in its beliefs and practices. What results is not merely an intellectually inadequate picture of religion as an evolving social institution, but a picture of religion that plays an important role in a "colonialist stance" toward Third-World contexts.
> (1997: 52)

Liberating texts: Roop Kanwar's *satī* from *Śrīvaisnava* and other textual perspectives

Having looked at the hermeneutical implications of Leslie's use of a strongly biased patriarchal treatise to show that *satī* is empowering for most Hindu women, I now wish to draw attention to other liberating texts and women's voices within the tradition that offer a more positive image of women. Leslie is not unaware of the voices of protest over *satī*, but she chooses a non-liberative patriarchal text to construct women as positive agents – *satī* as "victor." In the process, other voices are silenced and Hindu patriarchy is homogenized and frozen. Here I take a brief look at some *Śrīvaiṣṇava* patriarchal texts within the *bhakti* (devotional) tradition, which offer a liberating image of women.[13] The aim of the exercise is not to replace one patriarchal text with other similar texts, rather it is to show that Hindu patriarchy is not monolithic but complex and that there are significant divergences within patriarchal representations of woman.

Liberating texts within the *bhakti* tradition hold views on *satī* different from that of Tryambaka. For example, there are some *Śrīvaiṣṇava* texts that contain liberative images of women. Seen from a *Śrīvaiṣṇava* textual perspective, Roop Kanwar has chosen a path, *satī*, that is not allowed by that tradition. Katherine Young looks at the text, *Śrīvaiṣṇava Samayācāra Niṣkarṣa* ("the Essence of *Śrīvaiṣṇava* Normative Behaviour"), by Piḷḷailokamjīyar (composed probably between the end of the sixteenth and the eighteenth centuries), which contains a lengthy discussion on *satī* and widowhood from a *Śrīvaiṣṇava* standpoint. Śrīvaiṣṇava women are not to choose the path of *satī*; their salvation is not tied up with that of their husbands. Where orthodox brahminical texts consign women to rebirth, *Śrīvaiṣṇava* texts see women as entitled to salvation in their own right. Young writes: "All real Śrīvaiṣṇava women, whether brahmin or non-brahmin, are *prapannas* [devotees] and therefore desirous of salvation and consequently are not to practice *satī* of any form" (1996: 256). A *Śrīvaiṣṇava* woman who chooses to become a *satī* "is not really a Vaiṣṇava" (ibid.: 256). Widowhood is seen in more positive terms than those envisioned by Tryambaka, as Young explains:

> The position of widowhood also seems to be considerably more liberal among some Śrīvaiṣṇavas than the prevailing brahmanical norms. Teṉkalai women [those in a sect within Śrīvaiṣṇavism], for example, do not shave their heads ... More importantly, the Teṉkalai widow is considered auspicious, for it is believed that her husband has gone to supreme Heaven (i.e., Vaikuṇṭha). This contrasts with the categorical inauspiciousness of the Hindu widow who has been viewed (perhaps after the tenth century until recently) as an ogress or a witch who caused her husband's untimely death.
>
> (1996: 256).

There are other *Śrīvaiṣṇava* texts which contain liberating images of women. Young looks at another text, *Śrīvaiṣṇava Tīpikai*, which, although it shares some of the orthodox brahminical norms outlined in Tryambaka's manual on the behavior of women, offers some positive views of women. They are required to "share the Śrīvaiṣṇava realm of sectarian learning along with men," affirm their sectarian identities, and, like their male Śrīvaiṣṇava counterparts, "to cultivate various qualities such as knowledge, devotion, indifference to worldly objects, control, compassion, forbearance, and being without ego, wealth and desire" (Young 1996: 277). Another influential *Śrīvaiṣṇava* text, *Śrīsaṇḍilya-viśiṣṭa-parama-dharma-śāstra*, places emphasis on the "husband's responsibility ... to turn his whole household toward the supreme Lord (rather than to demand or assume that a woman must treat her husband as god according to the conservative brahminical code of *strīdharma*") (ibid.: 279). My point is that the prevalence of such texts within the Hindu tradition, despite their patriarchal orientation, offers a more positive view of women than Tryambaka's Sanskrit manual. Their existence also indicates that brahminical patriarchy, however oppressive it may have been, has not always been static or permanently frozen.

One can add a list of other dynamic voices that challenge Tryambaka's views on *satī*. Bāṇa, a well-known Sanskrit poet and scholar (625 CE), points to the futility of following one's husband in death: "This following of another to death is most vain! It is a path followed by the ignorant! It is a mere freak of madness, a path of ignorance … To the dead man it brings no good whatever. For its is no means of bringing him back to life, or heaping up merit, or gaining heaven for him, or saving him from hell, or seeing him again, or being reunited with him."[14] Medhātithi, the tenth-century chief commentator of Manu, takes a fierce stance against widows becoming *satīs*. Such a practice is seen as contrary to *dharma* and the *dharma* of *kṣatriya* (warrior) and scriptural injunctions. Furthermore, he recommends the remarriage of widows in some circumstances. No doubt his views were controversial even in his time. While Medhātithi protests loudly against immolation, Manu is silent about it. The Śākta sect denounces the practice of immolation. The *Mahānirvāṇa Tantra* is strongly opposed to women burning with their husbands. It declares in no uncertain terms: "A wife should not be burnt with her dead husband. Every woman is the embodiment of the goddess. That woman who in her delusion ascends the funeral pyre of her husband, shall go to hell."[15] If we are to see *satī* in the light of the *Bhagavad-gītā*, which sets a high value on *niṣkāma karma* (actions done without any desire for their fruits or reward), then any action that is reward-oriented becomes an inferior mode of action. The nineteenth-century Hindu reformer Rammohan Roy challenged the defenders of *satī* by pointing out that the *Gītā* entitled women to salvation, and therefore there was no reason to consign them to a lower mode of action (Sharma *et al.* 1988: 67–72). By contrast, Tryambaka's recommendation of the path of *satī* for women denies women the right to salvation on their own terms. In other words, women's salvation is viewed in terms of reunion with their husbands, whereas men's salvation is seen in terms of release from *saṃsāra*, the cycle of birth, death, and rebirth.

Liberating female texts and voices

I would now like to draw attention to an eighteenth-century liberating text, *Radhika Santwanam* ("Appeasing Radhika"), by Muddupalani, an accomplished and honored Telugu poet, scholar and courtesan at the Thanjavur court of the Nayaka King Pratapasimha, who ruled between 1739 and 1763. This text stands in sharp contrast to the eighteenth-century Sanskrit treatise by

Tryambaka of the Thanjavur court of the Maratha kings. Women attached to this court were highly accomplished in art, music, dance, and literature and were held in high esteem by their rulers. Muddupalāni offers a lively and contrasting image of women in her erotic and controversial epic dealing with the love of Rādhā and Krishna, which shows Rādhā taking the initiative in love-making (Tharu and Lalita 1993: 8). In contrast to Tryambaka's patriarchal treatise on the behavior of women, in this epic woman is not the subservient wife or lover. In *bhakti* (devotional) and literary works it is not uncommon to find women expressing spiritual longing in sensual terms. Unlike orthodox brahminical treatises which have little room for women's sensuality, Indian esthetic tradition allows a legitimate display of nine *rasas* (meaning "essence") or basic emotions such as love, pleasure, anger, or joy. In evoking *śṛṇgara rasa*, Muddupalani was acting in accordance with or conforming to the classical esthetic theory, which allows an affirmation of women's sensuality. This text is especially significant in view of the fact that the eighteenth century was seen as an age of darkness in need of reform. Although the eighteenth and nineteenth centuries were characterized by economic and political decline, they also witnessed creativity and refinement in other areas such as art, literature, music, and religion.[16] In fact, the eighteenth-century [in Thanjavur] was seen as "the golden age of Telugu literature" and other arts such as dance music, painting, and sculpture flourished (ibid.: 1993: 6). A reprint of Muddupalani's work in 1910 was banned by the British government, as some parts of the epic were deemed to be obscene and therefore "would endanger the moral health of their Indian subjects" (Tharu and Lalita 1993: 4) Like the British government and some Indian translators, Tryambaka, too, would have found Muddupalani's epic objectionable. Such an erotic piece of work was offensive to both brahminical and patriarchal colonial thinking. My purpose in drawing attention to this text is to bring to the fore alternative voices in the contemporary period, voices which tend to get overlooked and delegitimized in favor of a particular androcentric text.

Yet another liberating image is that of the well-known sixteenth-century *bhakti* saint Mīrābaī, from Rajasthan, who is particularly relevant to a discussion on *satī*. Mīrābaī did not choose to become a *satī* on the death of her husband, but challenged conventional definitions of gender, caste, family, honor, and shame – a sharp contrast to Roop Kanwar, also from Rajasthan, who "became" a *satī* in the twentieth century. Rajput women were expected to defend and uphold the honor of their men. Mīrābaī was part of the Rajput community. Although she was from a royal family, she ignored social norms and moved freely with those from the margins, content to live out her ardent devotion to her god Kṛṣṇa, whom she looked upon as her husband while refusing to look upon her human husband as a god.

The ideology of *bhakti* challenges the orthodox brahminical rulings on women. Madhu Kishwar and Ruth Vanita write: "The ideology of *pativratā*, whereby a woman's salvation lies in unquestioning devotion to her husband, comes into active conflict with the ideology of *bhakti* when the *bhakta* is a woman. Apart from the flouting of secular and religious authority in which all the *bhaktas* have, to some extent, to engage, the woman *bhakta* has also to flout the absolute authority of the husband and his family over her life, since she now acknowledges a higher authority" (1989: 91–2). *Bhakti* saints such as Mīrābaī, Akka Mahādevī, and others challenge the conventional ideal of *pativratā*. One may argue that they have substituted the divine lord for their human husbands, but there is a significant difference in that the divine husband is not seen as a patriarchal monarch. These women poets and saints have opened up an alternative path for women who may not want to follow the traditional *pativratā* ideal. As Nancy Martin points out:

> By her example, Mira offers the possibility of a life lived for God and not for men and a way to approach the divine directly. Through her narrative she offers an interpretive framework for women's self understanding and for social acceptance or at least tolerance of women who choose to live as she did. Though decidedly religious and circumscribed within the bounds of existing social structures, this space created by Mīrābaī allows for spiritual and personal growth; for the cultivation of talents, education, and leadership; and for the creation of a life beyond that of wife and mother for women.
>
> (1996: 39–40)

For a more traditional example, one can turn to Śārāda Devī, wife of Sri Rāmakrishna Paramahaṃsa (a nineteenth-century Bengali saint), who followed the path of *strīdharma*, but did not become a *satī*. Rāmakrishna looked upon her as spiritual partner, taught her the sacred mantras and how to initiate people into them. After his death, she became the spiritual guide to Rāmākrishna's disciples, both monks and laypeople.

Such examples illustrate that the notion of *strīdharma* need not be confined to traditional definitions. These women poets and saints offer an alternative path to that of *satī*. In not opting for *satī,* they were not being untrue to their tradition or themselves. Contemporary women scholars, such as Madhu Kishwar, who challenge conventional definitions of feminine behavior and the *satī* ideology, are seeking to redefine and reinterpret feminine roles. It appears that Julia Leslie's hermeneutical strategy allows little room for reinterpretation of traditional roles. In other words, women's *śakti,* power, is confined to roles that conform to brahmanical norms. In fact *śakti* calls into question oppressive, gender-based assumptions and allows for varied legitimate ways of expressing Hindu womanhood. Hindu goddesses such as Kālī and Durgā challenge conventional constructs of an ideal wife and provide an alternative role model for Hindu women, one that is positive and and challenging. Liberating texts such as *Devī Māhātmyam* ("Glorification of the Goddess") affirm *śakti* as the ground and center of all creation and existence.

Such a text which has both textual and popular appeal (for both men and women) provides an empowering and positive construct of the feminine.[17]

Concluding remarks

The issue of *satī* has largely to do with representational politics. First of all, no representation can claim to be authentic, for it involves an element of interpretation and reinterpretation and is affected by the interpreter's own location, and by historical, contextual, and political factors. Furthermore, one's reading is informed and determined by one's methodological and conceptual framework, in terms of which one discusses particular events. One cannot rule out how a representation would be read by others, and even a well-intentioned representation can create a favorable ground for ideological agendas to be affirmed or contested.

My main concern is not who represents whom (although that is important) but what purpose is served by the representation of Roop Kanwar as a positive construct. Unlike most Western representations, which see the subaltern woman as a victim, Julia Leslie perceives her as a positive agent, which is commendable but at the same time problematic. Her notion of positive construct has more to do with women as self-sacrificing agents of their destiny (willingly or unwillingly) than with women who resist or who express their devotion differently.

The question of agency is a complex one, as can be discerned from Indian feminist discourse on *satī*. Spivak speaks of the impossibility of constructing or recovering the subjectivity of the subaltern female whereas Lata Mani and Sunder Rajan try to establish the subjectivity of the female (however imperfect). Mani constructs women as subjects from the accounts of widow-burning, and Sunder Rajan defines subjectivity in terms of the "pain" women go through but universalizes the subjectivity of the subaltern.[18] In different ways, all three show the difficulty of constructing a meaningful subjectivity of the subaltern.

Leslie is engaged in recovering the agency of Roop Kanwar, an effort that poses more questions than it answers. She maintains the agency of the subaltern at the conceptual and ideological level – *satī* as an autonomous agent – while condemning the practice. As I have shown, the notion of *satī* as "victor" does not offer anything new but only serves to confirm what patriarchy wants to hear: that women's *śakti,* or power, lies in their capacity for self-sacrifice. We hear not the voice of Roop Kanwar but Leslie's – how she reads the silenced subaltern. We hear the voices of witnesses and others who honor Roop Kanwar as a true *satī*, but their testimony is not interrogated and is seen as confirming Leslie's predetermined thesis – *satī* as "victor." Furthermore, the iconography of Roop Kanwar is not her own representation but one that is constructed for her and represents the ideology of others. In other words, she is spoken for and therefore silenced. It is this silence one is asked to investigate. Spivak directs Western feminists and others engaged in recovering the voice of the subaltern to address their own connivance in the construction of subalternity (Spivak 1993: 91). Witnesses may affirm Roop Kanwar as a true *satī*, a free agent shaping her own destiny, but that does not necessarily make her one. In other words, for whom is she a positive agent? What is the purpose of recovering the agency of the subaltern woman? Leslie's concept of agency would suit well the interests and agendas of pro-*satī* campaigners who see the woman as a free agent in the matter of *satī*, but it would be detrimental to Indian feminist goals. Although Leslie is keen to see Hindu women in their own terms, her benevolence for the subaltern turns out to be problematic in that she ends up endorsing patriarchal values and norms. She simultaneously enables and disenables women in the process of affirming the subjectivity of the subaltern.

Leslie does not problematize the notion of "good" or "virtuous" woman but takes it for granted as the norm for all Hindus. She perpetuates a particular notion of ideal woman as being universal and authentic, although she is aware that not all Hindu women subscribe to it. She does not seem to take into account how *satī* is socially, historically, and politically constructed, nor the relation between religious beliefs and ideologies. In other words, Leslie takes an ahistorical approach to discuss a complex issue. Her hermeneutical method results in essentializing and fixing *satī* as authentic tradition, thus ignoring other ideological factors that have contributed to the perpetuation of *satī* ideology. Her representation thereby reinforces essentialist and orientalist conceptions of Hindu women.

Although Leslie's main concern is women as active agents, "Suttee or *satī*: victim or victor?" turns out to be more about text and *satī* as tradition. In other words, it is more about brahminical textual perspectives on women's wifely duty and devotion, and the relevance of these perspectives for contemporary Hindu women than about how women challenged or resisted them. In this respect Leslie appears to be recreating some aspects of the nineteenth-century Hindu-colonial debate over *satī*, in which women were not central to the debate. Whereas colonialists and nationalists used texts to argue whether the practice had any scriptural warrant, Leslie uses an eighteenth-century text on the wifely duties of women in order to endorse the *satī* ideal. I do not doubt her genuine intention to understand Hindu women but her hermeneutical strategy leaves us with a homogenized patriarchy to cope with. Furthermore, it would certainly provide ammunition for those who would welcome the resurrection of Tryambaka's views on *satī* as embodying the Hindu ideal of wifely duty. Leslie's strategy also tends to replay the tradition-versus-modernity debate which trivialized feminists' struggle with Hindu fundamentalists over the *satī* issue. In seeing *satī* as the ideal norm regardless of a lack of uniform assent to it, Leslie makes it a timeless aspect of the Hindu tradition. In positing *satī* as tradition, Leslie tends to leave little negotiating space for those who interrogate or problematize *satī*.

While some of her Western counterparts have been engaged in saving "brown women from brown men" (Spivak 1993: 92), Leslie seems to be engaged in entrusting brown women to brown men. In other words, Leslie seems to be engaged in recovering for Hindu women their long-cherished patriarchal norms and values. As with the eighteenth-century orientalists, she turns her attention to the classical past where she locates an "idealized" image of Hindu woman in the pages of a remote text and relocates Hindu women within the patriarchal household of the orthodox pundit Tryambaka. To use her own words, she relies on an "unusual text" and uses it as an example to demonstrate that *satī* has not lost its appeal and continues to empower women in traditional India. In doing so, she fixes and freezes an idealized notion of womanhood as the norm. There appears to be no room for models at variance with the notion of *satī* as outlined by Tryambaka. Leslie offers a monolithic concept of conjugal relationship. In privileging and universalizing a particular manifestation of Hindu patriarchy, she blurs internal diversity and silences other liberating texts and humanizing voices, both male and female, are silenced.

Women who consciously or unconsciously internalize patriarchal expectations of feminine behavior and definitions of ideal woman may feel the need to affirm *satī,* but their act of veneration should not lead us to assume that *satī* has always been a religiously inspired act. Furthermore, the notion of *satī* as "virtuous woman" can be used to legitimize and perpetuate patriarchal expectations and goals. Devotion to one's husband, wife, friend, or country is to be appreciated, but when this "devotion" is used to indoctrinate or manipulate, or to con women into believing that *satī* is the most appropriate means of demonstrating their virtuousness, then something is fundamentally wrong. More often than not, when occasional instances of *satī* take place, mythological and scriptural examples of ideal womanhood tend to be reinforced and reclaimed. Women have been coping for a long time with oppressive ideologies and situations, and they have always tried to make a virtue out of adversity. Therefore, to make a case for Roop Kanwar as a positive construct, does not say anything significantly new, nor does it generate new questions; it only confirms women's ability to endure suffering. Furthermore, such a hermeneutic strategy reinforces Tryambaka's patriarchal conception of what it means to be a "good" or "virtuous" woman. We need to move on.

(This chapter has its genesis in a paper presented to the Department of Religious and Theological Studies at Lund University, Sweden. It was subsequently published as "Single text and scripting *satī*: a postcolonial perspective" (Sugirtharajah 1999a). The current version is enlarged and theoretically more nuanced and is reprinted with kind permission of the *Journal of Feminist Studies in Religion*, where it first appeared (2001; 17 (1): 5–32.)

Chapter 6

Conclusion

This concluding chapter has two parts: the first draws attention to how some aspects of orientalist and missionary constructions are being replicated in postcolonial contexts. The second part highlights some hermeneutical issues that have been raised in this volume. These issues revolve around the concept of religion, the textualization and representation of Hinduism, and the need for postcolonial theorists to take religion seriously. Also, in order to demonstrate how varied and complex European constructions of Hinduism are, I draw attention to the differing theological and ideological concerns undergirding them.

Replicating orientalist constructions

As in the colonial context, Hindus in diaspora[1] are faced with the question of what it means to be a Hindu. Responses to it have been largely dictated from the outside and have become part of Hindu self-definition. Hindus in both colonial and postcolonial environments tend to draw on European orientalist constructions of the glorious past in order to contest negative portrayals of Hinduism and to acclaim its high status. Both orientalists and Hindus are engaged in constructing an idealized picture of Hinduism – the difference being that nineteenth-century Hindus such as Rammohan Roy and Dayānanda Saraswatī were divesting Hinduism of its images and refashioning what they saw as a pure form of Hinduism, whereas *bhakti*-oriented sectarian Hindus in diaspora are restoring temple Hinduism. The diasporic landscape is dotted with Hindu temples, testifying to the vitality of iconic Hinduism. What Western orientalists and Protestant missionaries loathed (the worship of images) has now become part of the religious landscape of the West; what they saw as "degenerate Hinduism" has now become one of the visible markers of Hindu identity in the diaspora. Moreover, temple worship, which was seen as detrimental to social and economic progress, has proved to be an economically profitable enterprise in India and the diaspora, rather than a liability.

In redefining Hinduism, some Hindu proponents for the tradition are still influenced by, and at times compromised by, orientalist representations of Hinduism. They tend to make selective use of Western conceptual categories in order to make Hinduism comprehensible and less strange to outsiders. Ironically, Hindus are using more or less the very same tools used by Western scholars of Hinduism in order to clear up misconceptions and present a homogenized view of Hinduism. What is conspicuous is that Hindus living outside India are now drawing on the Western orientalist conception of religion as a unified category in order to make Hinduism intelligible to both insiders and outsiders. The booklet, *An Introduction to Hinduism*, prepared by the National Council of Temples (UK), and the book *Explaining Hindu Dharma: A Guide for Teachers* (Prinja 1996) prepared by British Hindus, are cases in point. Both are produced with a view to rectifying misrepresentations of Hinduism and presenting an "authoritative" introduction to the tradition. In so doing, a loosely knit tradition with a variety of beliefs and practices is forced into a narrow conceptual framework, thus making Hinduism appear as a unified system with all its heterogeneous aspects intact.

There are diverse Hindu organizations in India and the diaspora, each representing a particular version of Hinduism and each directly or indirectly shaping the construction of the tradition and Hindu identity. Currently, there are varied Hindu voices speaking for Hinduism, such as the Vishwa Hindu Parishad (VHP), Rashtriya Sevak Sangh (RSS), the National Council of Hindu Temples (NCHT), the National Students Forums (NSF) and religious movements such as the Ramakrishna Mission, International Society for Kṛṣṇa Consciousness (ISKCON), Swaminarayan, Satya Sai Baba, and others. These various organizations are a disparate group, competing with each other and at times even contradicting each other. They come out of different cultural, political, social, and hermeneutical contexts, but the undergirding principle which binds them together is the desire to project an acceptable face of Hinduism. If in the colonial period British colonialists and missionaries saw themselves as moral and social reformers of Hindu society, various Hindu organizations and religious sects in the diaspora now see their role as revitalizing and affirming Hindu religion and culture. Disaporic environments have become fertile sites for these Hindus to present themselves as champions of Hindu *dharma*. Since the 1990s there has been a growing consciousness of Hindu identity in the West. Hindu organizations and movements are making themselves visible in the public domain through websites focused on Hinduism, through conferences, seminars, and youth camps, through Hinduism and language classes, through festivals and the preparation of Hindu resource material for religious education teachers. The interesting aspect of this hermeneutical enterprise is that some Hindus are keen to speak for themselves rather than be spoken to or spoken on behalf of.[2]

New orientalists: fashioning a monolithic Hinduism

My main concern is not with the history of these aforementioned organizations but with illustrating how they promote and mediate orientalist constructions of Hinduism. One of the marks of orientalism is the construction of Hinduism as devoid of any heterogeneous voices. In nineteenth-century colonial India, Hindus such as Rammohan Roy and Dayānanda Saraswatī used orientalist constructions of the golden past in order to challenge missionary denunciations of Hinduism. Now a high-profile guru-centered Vaiṣṇava *saṃpradāya* (tradition) such as Swaminarayan,[3] which has a large Gujarati following both in India an the diaspora, draws on Western orientalist affirmations of Hinduism. A conspicuous case in point is the exhibition *Understanding Hinduism*, held in the magnificent Swaminarayan temple in north London. The exhibition guidebook sings the praises of Hinduism's splendid achievements in numerous fields ranging from mathematics to literature and science. It is a neat little book, giving a brief historical introduction, followed by a simplified statement of Hindu beliefs. In other words, the guide is a tailor-made introduction to Hinduism and to the Swaminarayan tradition, one that blurs internal diversity and complexity and represents Hinduism in a monolithic fashion. Such an idealized representation of Hinduism speaks to the Hindu minority in the diaspora, especially the young who constantly face stereotypical images of Hinduism, thus enabling them to take pride in their ancient culture.

What is interesting is that a minor Gujarati sectarian sect which claimed non-Hindu status in India has now become a transnational movement, and seeks to speak for all Hindus. It has now become an agent of Hindu mission in diaspora, proclaiming a unified Hinduism. It sees itself as a global representative of the entire Hindu tradition and custodian of its moral, spiritual, and cultural values. Although the sect has its own set of scriptures, it now seeks to highlight its Vedic roots. As Mukta points out: "From being a religious sect based on scriptures outside of the Vedas, the North London Swaminarayan temple has now become a prime exponent of the Vedic tradition, situated within a configuration which valorizes a specific glorious history" (2000: 460).[4]

Textualizing Hinduism

One of the features of orientalism is an overt textualization of Hinduism. In nineteenth-century British India, Hindus used orientalist affirmations of Vedic Hinduism in order to counteract negative Western conceptions and attitudes towards Hinduism. Now Hindus in the diaspora are turning to religious movements such as the International Society of Kṛṣṇa Consciousness (ISKCON)[5] to seek validation for their own tradition. ISKCON has made imaginative use of Western hermeneutical tools in order to package

Hinduism in a form that speaks to young British Hindus. It represents a Western style of Hinduism that is embedded in the Hindu *bhakti* tradition. It has mastered the art of translating and disseminating knowledge about Kṛṣṇa to a Western audience. The significant factor about ISKCON is that its founder, Swami Prabhupada, saw his mission as bringing the message of Kṛṣṇa to the West, and being a translator himself, he was able to render into English the teachings of Kṛṣṇa. While the Baptist missionaries, as we have seen, translated Sanskrit texts into vernacular languages and into English in order to prove the primacy of Christian texts, Swami Prabhupada and his followers were engaged in translating Hindu texts into English in order to proclaim the universality of the message of Kṛṣṇa. Early orientalists such as Warren Hastings and Jones undertook translation of Hindu texts in order to serve the needs of the colonial government, and the Protestant missionaries, to further the cause of missionary enterprise. Unlike Western orientalists like Max Müller, who have little regard for any Hindu text other than the Veda, the Hare Kṛṣṇas affirm *bhakti* texts which are the basis of ISKCON.

ISKCON has the trappings of a Semitic religion inasmuch as it has a founder, an incarnate deity (Kṛṣṇa), a set of teachings, and so forth. It owes its origin not to a mythological founder but to a sixteenth-century saint, Chaitanya of Bengal, and it was brought to the West by Swami Prabhupada, the founder of ISKCON. It has a strong missionary zeal to spread the message not in the form of a creed but in the form of a *mantra* – the chanting of the Hare Kṛṣṇa mantra as a means to *mokṣa*, liberation. If Farquhar and Müller were eager to proclaim Christ to Hindus, the Hare Kṛṣṇas are eager to proclaim Kṛṣṇa to both non-Hindus and Hindus alike. ISKCON affirms a devotional form of worship centered around Kṛṣṇa which the nineteenth-century Protestant orientalists and missionaries derided and for whom, as we have seen, any expression of ardent or ecstatic devotion, *bhakti*, was a mark of effeminacy. Müller and Farquhar would be horrified to witness their own people turning to "temple" Hinduism, venerating iconic images and expressing passionate devotion in an "effeminate" style on the streets of Oxford and London.

The resurgence of politicized Hinduism

Another characteristic of orientalism is that it faults the Other as being the cause of the degeneration of Hinduism. Just as orientalists such as Jones and Müller advanced the notion that Muslim invasion caused the degeneration of Hinduism, present-day Hindu revivalists see Islam as a threat to Hinduism. There is currently a resurgence of political forms of Hinduism (not something entirely new) which tend to collapse multitudinous traditions into a manageable system, one that transcends caste, sectarian, and other differences. Both in India and the diaspora, Hindutva ideologues are politicizing

Hinduism and promoting allegiance to it. The Vishwa Hindu Parishad (VHP), an international organization of Hindus, is trying to forge a monolithic Hinduism – a unitary system with a unitary vision to be shared by all Hindus.[6] The literature on the Hindutva issue is copious and is growing fast. Scholars in various academic disciplines are engaged with this contentious yet highly significant issue, requiring a more comprehensive treatment than the scope of this volume allows.[7]

The VHP's discourse on oneness or unity is based on its notion of India as a sacred land that has been the victim of foreign invasions, Muslim rule and conversion to Islam, and proselytizing Christian activities. Contemporary Hindu nationalists and revivalists tend to draw on the Western orientalist thesis in order to restore Hinduism to what they see as its original state of purity. The VHP and allied organizations emphasize the need to recover the lost glory and sanctity of Hinduism and defend, strengthen, and protect Hindu *dharma* against alien forces.

It is ironic that in its 1993 celebration of the centenary of the Parliament of World Religions held in Chicago, the VHP should hail Vivekānanda as "a champion of militant Hinduism," although he did not favor the kind of militancy espoused by contemporary Hindu nationalists. My point is that whatever Vivekānanda might have said, he certainly did not ask Hindus to demolish places of worship, whether Hindu or Muslim. As Tapan Raychaudhuri points out: "It is difficult to imagine him as the ideological ancestor of people who incite the ignorant to destroy other people's places of worship in a revanchist spirit" (1998: 16). Vivekānanda has become "a central icon in Hindu nationalist discourse, and yet the Ramakrishna Mission he founded … has tended to remain outside of the fold of Hindu nationalism" (Bhatt and Mukta 2000: 411).

In constructing a monolithic Hinduism and a Hindu India, the VHP sees itself as continuing and fulfilling the task initiated by Hindu nationalists in nineteenth-century British colonial India. In so doing, it is replicating orientalist formulations and Western notions of modernity – constructing India as a unified nation. Hindus under imperial rule forged a unified India in order to fight for *Swaraj*, or home rule. In contrast, Hindu nationalists are now constructing a narrow vision of nationhood – Hindu India – in order to defend and protect Hindu *dharma* from secular forces, and from Christians and Muslims whom they fear will weaken it. While the VHP rejects secularism, it does not hesitate to embrace other signs of modernity (capitalism, technology, and science). As King states: "It is somewhat ironic, therefore, to find that the very Hindu nationalists who fought so vehemently against British imperialist rule themselves accepted the homogenizing concepts of 'nationhood' and 'Hinduism', which ultimately derived from their imperial rulers" (King 1999: 107).

The VHP seems to be much concerned with minority Hindus in the diaspora, in order to create a sense of Hindu spiritual nationalism among them.

The image of India as a spiritual homeland is constantly invoked, and such an image appeals to Hindus in the diaspora who feel like second-class citizens. It seeks to mobilize Hindus in the West through its worldwide conferences such as the Virat Hindu Sammelan at Milton Keynes in 1989, and the World Vision 2000 conference in Washington DC in 1992. Such conferences promote the notion of Hindu India and a monolithic Hinduism which does not speak to all Hindus. It is ironic that the VHP and other Hindu organizations replicate nineteenth-century orientalist constructions of Hinduism as a unified system of beliefs and practices, in order to advance their own political agendas.

Reframing Hinduism and forging an identity

Religion is increasingly becoming a marker of identity among young British Hindus in the West. Whereas nineteenth-century Hindu "reform" movements were redefining, "reforming" and constructing a "pure Hinduism" in the face of missionary and colonial vilification, Hindu students in the diaspora are concerned not so much with reforming Hinduism as with forging a Hindu identity in the face of minority status in Western contexts. They are in the process of constructing or reformulating Hinduism in British terms in order to affirm their identity. They define their identity not necessarily in terms of allegiance to a set of beliefs, although that may play some part. Being in the early stages of discovering themselves and their religion, young British Hindus are, at this stage, affirming a cultural rather than a narrow religious identity.[8] They are keen to mobilize Hindus from various linguistic backgrounds across the United Kingdom – Gujarati, Tamil, Punjabi, Bengali, and other Hindus under one banner, fostering a sense of Hindu nationalism though not the kind advocated by Hindutva ideologues. They are not so much concerned with the recreation of the glorious period of a bygone era as with reframing Hinduism in terms to which they can relate.

Concluding remarks

I should like to draw attention to some hermeneutical insights that arise from this work. First, the very concept of religion and religions is problematic in that it is not free from Western Christian theological presuppositions and is inextricably bound up with colonialism and modernity.[9] To put it another way, the investigation and theorizing of religion is very much a Western enterprise, and the theoretical and methodological presuppositions undergirding it have been applied to the study of Hinduism and other religions. Implicit in the modern category of "religion," and in what Müller calls the "science of religion" or the comparative study of religions, is a hermeneutical exercise which posits Christianity as a rational religion, and in terms of which other religions are assessed. Put concisely, the Enlightenment notion of religion is treated as a universally applicable category.

Second, the Enlightenment construction of religion is heavily grounded in scripture, to the exclusion of other non-textual sources. Orientalists and missionaries approach Hindu texts with their own biblical presuppositions, and their translation of Hindu texts is informed by a search for the Ur text.[10] Both orientalists (Jones and Müller) and missionaries (Ward and Farquhar) adopt a textualized approach to Hinduism, each one presenting Hinduism from his differing theological stance. As we have seen, orientalist and missionary constructions of Hinduism are not homogeneous, and their conceptual frameworks are grounded in various Christian theological suppositions. It is particularly through the prism of biblical monotheism that orientalists and missionaries interpret and evaluate Hinduism. Jones situates Hinduism within the biblical time-framework and thus asserts the primacy of biblical revelation. Whereas Jones finds in Hinduism a distorted version of biblical monotheism, Müller locates in it an infantile monotheism which has yet to grow into full maturity. For William Ward, Hinduism is devoid of a living monotheistic god and therefore has no salvific value. Jones views Hinduism in the light of the Mosaic view of history as recorded in Genesis, and Müller adopts an evolutionary approach, but both scholars, in different ways, use Protestant monotheism as a yardstick for evaluating Hinduism. As with Müller, Farquhar, too, subscribes to an evolutionary view of religion which holds Christianity as the fulfillment of Hinduism. For Jones, the answer to cultural and religious diversity is to be found in the monogenetic view of history recorded in Genesis, whereas for Müller and Farquhar the solution is to be found in an evolutionary view of religion which sees Hinduism finding fulfillment in Christianity. By contrast, for William Ward, Hinduism is totally the "Other" which needs to be purged of its demonic power, and this he believes could be achieved by proclaiming the gospel to the "heathens."

While Ward represents Hindu women as hapless victims of a barbaric tradition, Julia Leslie offers a contrasting image of Hindu women – as "active agents." Leslie's reading of *satī* as "empowering" for some Hindu women challenges both Ward's and Mary Daly's representation of *satī* as pathetic victims. Her portrayal of Roop Kanwar as a positive agent is laudable but at the same time problematic in that she takes an ahistorical approach to *satī*. Leslie seems to be more concerned with exploring the "religious ideology" that informs *satī* than with the relation between beliefs and ideologies. As do both Western and Indian orientalists and colonialists, Julia Leslie, too, relies on the Sanskrit textual tradition in her discussion of *satī*. In privileging an archaic patriarchal treatise on Hindu women, other liberating texts and voices tend to get silenced, and the result is a homogenized patriarchy and an idealized notion of *satī*.

While one cannot totally avoid or overcome the conceptual categories through which other cultures are seen, a problem arises when these categories are seen as having universal validity and application. Orientalists and missionaries not only privilege male-dominated Sanskrit texts but also read textual prescriptions as descriptions of actual reality. What has been demonstrated is that the kind of Hinduism constructed by orientalists and missionaries has more to do with questions posed by the Enlightenment than with how Hindus themselves have approached their tradition. Western scholars of Hinduism "search for universal and unifying foundations such as the principle of rationality, a common human nature underlying cultural diversity and the development of a neutral or objective framework and methodology for discerning such universalist principles" (King 1999: 44). Other dominant features of the Enlightenment are a linear notion of history and the notion of progress, by which criteria non-Western cultures are measured. Since the nineteenth century Hindu thinkers such as Rammohan Roy, Dayānanda Saraswatī, Vivekānanda, Radhakrishnan, and others have been appropriating in varying degrees and ways the Enlightenment conception of religion. For example, like Müller, Dayānada Saraswatī privileges the Veda as the only authentic text of Hindus, and he rejects image worship and constructs a pristine form of Hinduism based on the Veda. But unlike Müller who treats the Veda as an infantile document, Dayānanda Saraswatī projects the Veda as rational and scientific and thereby claims a superior status for it. Since the so-called Hindu renaissance there has been a tendency to construct Vedānta as the religion of Hindus, in response to Western critiques of Hinduism. In doing so, Hindus are replicating orientalist affirmations of Vedānta as the essence of Hinduism.

Religion, to the ordinary Hindu, is not simply confined to texts or to a prescribed set of beliefs. It includes these aspects yet it encompasses a wide variety of other areas such as art, dance, music and folklore; post-Enlightenment scholars of religion, however, take little note of these non-textual domains. There is a marked reluctance to shift the focus from texts. Even a cursory glance at some of the current introductory material on Hinduism reflects a predominantly text-oriented approach.[11] It is largely through the lens of brahminical textual and ritual traditions that Hinduism is perceived. In other words, textual Hinduism is given primary consideration.

Third, there is a hermeneutical issue concerning the interface between reason and imagination. A significant conceptual category that informs orientalist and missionary constructions of Hinduism has to do with the juxtaposition of "reason" and "imagination" as both contrasting and complementary categories. As we have seen in Western oriental thought, India is associated with "imagination" and Europe with "reason." Moreover, imagination is linked with the feminine and reason with the masculine. It is in the light of this conceptual framework that Hinduism is interpreted and appropriated. Both orientalists and missionaries see Hinduism as lacking the "world-ordering rationality" of Western thought. In other words, Hinduism is seen in Western feminine categories. It is likened to a "sponge," "a jungle," lacking any discernible order. It is seen as chaotic and wild, requiring careful pruning and the introduction of "a certain degree of rationality into it" (Inden 1992: 86). As already noted, orientalists such as Jones are not dismissive of the "feminine" but relegate it to the poetic realm; he seems to be at ease with exploring the feminine in poetry rather than in religion. While missionaries such as William Ward and Utilitarians such as James Mill denounce Hinduism for its "effeminacy," orientalists treat effeminacy as a mark of immaturity. For Jones and Müller, imagination signifies a state of childhood, or, to use Inden's words "an inferior form of reason that attempts theoretical thought but can do so only by the use of sensual images ..." (ibid.: 94) Since the European Enlightenment, India has come to represent, for Western orientalists, the feminine self of Europe. Hinduism continues to provide a convenient hermeneutical site for the orientalist search for their own "primitive" self. To put it another way, Hinduism represents the feminine elements that have been suppressed within European culture and projected on to it. What we see here is a feminization of Hinduism in terms of European conceptions of the feminine. For Western orientalists the feminine signifies a state of immaturity, and for missionaries it is a mark of moral depravity. By contrast, in Hindu philosophical thought – in *Sāṃkhya* philosophy – the feminine *prakṛti* (nature) is seen as an active and dynamic principle, and the masculine (*puruṣa*) is assigned a passive role. *Śakti*, the divine feminine power, is already latent in the masculine, and without the activating power of *śakti*, the masculine (*Śiva*) is rendered powerless. These concepts, *puruṣa* and *prakṛti* and *Śiva* and *śakti* indicate complementarity of the masculine and the feminine, although in some instances the former or the latter may be given primacy. Western feminization of Hinduism has little to do with the empowerment that the term *śakti* connotes: rather it implies a lack that can only be rectified by masculinizing Hinduism. In other words, Hinduism needs to be stripped of its idolatrous practices which render it effeminate, and be guided by the sons of the Enlightenment. The fact is, such a hermeneutical exercise facilitates intellectual colonization.

Fourth, what the study has demonstrated is that orientalists and missionaries privilege Sanskrit texts and the Sanskrit language. While missionary orientalists such as William Carey learnt Sanskrit in order to undermine Hindus texts – to show that they are "sacred nothings" – Jones, once his interest in the language was kindled, was eager to explore and present the literary treasures of the Hindu world to the West. Jones prided himself upon saying that he "spoke the language of Gods," whereas Carey, although he admired the language, disliked Hindu literature and disassociated language from literature and religion. Jones spoke endearingly of Sanskrit literature whereas Carey denounced it. While Jones was domesticating Hindu mythological texts and making them palatable for his European audience, Carey was keen to place Hindu mythological texts alongside the Gospel in order to deflate Hindu texts. Carey introduced a heavily Sanskritic curriculum at

Serampore College to serve this purpose, but he came under severe attack for doing so. The introduction of Sanskrit came to be seen as sanctioning idolatrous practices rather than challenging them, to which Carey responded by stating: "The people do not venerate the language for the idolatrous ideas it contains, but the ideas for the dress they wear ... Instead of pulling down the temple around which the worshippers are assembled, let us displace the idol, and present for the veneration of the people, a new and legitimate object of regard, arranged in new vestments" (in Young 1981: 35). Furthermore, Carey used Sanskrit as a tool for conversion. "If this College be conducted with due vigour," Carey states, "it may be made the Christian Benares, and the tide of Sungskritu literature be turned completely on the side of Christianity" (ibid.). Jones, too, saw language as a means of conversion but was less optimistic about winning converts:

> We may assure ourselves, that neither Muselmans nor Hindus will ever be converted by any mission from the Church of Rome, or from any other church; and the only human mode, perhaps, of causing so great a revolution will be to translate into *Sanscrit* and *Persian* such chapters of the Prophets, particularly ISAIAH, as are indisputably Evangelical, together with one of the Gospels, and a plain prefatory discourse containing full evidence of very distant ages, in which predictions themselves, and the history of the divine person predicted, were severally made publick; and then to quickly to disperse quietly the work among the well-educated natives; with whom if in due time it failed of producing very salutary truth by its natural influence, we could only lament more than ever the strength of prejudice, and the weakness of unassisted reason.
>
> (Jones 1799a: 279–80)

Fifth, the overall theme of the volume has to with the representations of the "Other," representations which do not take place in a vacuum. There has been a tendency to view the encounter between the East and the West in terms of intellectual and cultural exploration, thus underplaying the political and economic domination of the West over the people of Asia. Edward Said is one of the foremost literary critics to draw attention to this factor in his book *Orientalism* (1978) and in subsequent publications. Although orientalism has become a loaded and contentious term, it is still very useful in examining varied discourses, whether they be literary, political, religious, or philosophical. Orientalism has been useful in uncovering a variety of perplexing Western attitudes and conceptions of the East as well as Eastern conceptions of the West.

One of the future tasks of postcolonialism should include theorizing religion and examining how it operates in a multi-cultural postcolonial context. Postcolonial theorists have shown a great reluctance to interrogate religion; scholars in the field of postcolonial studies have theorized about literature, art and history, but not religion. In other words, postcolonialism has not adequately addressed the question of religion and how it operates in a postmodern world. Postcolonial theorists have drawn attention to colonialism and its impact on culture, history, and politics but not on religion, despite the fact that its pioneers and theorists such as Frantz Fanon, Albert Memuni and Edward Said come from the Islamic world where religion is not divorced from everyday life.

Postcolonial discourse shares the secular assumptions and biases present in other discourses. Despite religion being a significant aspect of most non-Western cultures, postcolonial theorists have not taken on board its potency. For example, Gandhi used religious resources to challenge and subvert colonialism. In Latin America, liberation theologians have utilized religion to champion the cause of the poor. In present-day India, religion is being used to promote a narrow nationalism and religious fundamentalism. The future of postcolonialism depends on its ability to address how religion affects and shapes societies, for religion in one form or another continues to surface even in secular environments.

To sum up briefly, India, its religion, its sacred texts, and its language (Sanskrit) became the object of the orientalists' gaze. Orientalists saw themselves as "discovering" India's ancient past and as enlightening the Hindu elite with their newly discovered knowledge. Orientalists, in studying the ancient Sanskrit texts, came to textualize, restructure, and domesticate them. The orientalist enterprise was aimed at transforming a disparate tradition into a tightly knit uniform body of texts mainly to serve the administrative needs of the colonial government. Although different in many respects, both orientalists and missionaries believed in the superiority of the Western civilization, and saw colonialism as beneficial to the natives. Where they differed was that the orientalists saw themselves as restoring to Hinduism its lost purity, whereas the missionaries saw themselves as bringing Christian enlightenment to Hindus who were in darkness. Both, in different ways, were engaged in the process of reforming and civilizing Hindus and their traditions.

I should like to emphasize that it is not the aim of this volume to discredit the work of orientalists and missionaries, whose erudite scholarship and serious engagement with Sanskrit texts is not in dispute. What the present volume has tried to do is take issue with what these orientalists and missionaries did with the material and how they managed to fashion or construct a Hinduism that was in line with their own theological and ideological presuppositions. They not only domesticated Hinduism to meet their own purposes but were engaged, wittingly or unwittingly, in "civilizing the natives" and educating Hindus about what these scholars perceived to be "true" or "real" Hinduism. What I have attempted to show is that Western constructions of Hinduism are complex – constructions fraught with ambivalences, contradictions, denunciations and idealizations. In short, orientalists and missionaries produced a Hinduism largely of their own "imagining."

Notes

Introduction

1 The term "goes back to the Vedic texts and referred to non-Sanskrit speaking people often outside the caste hierarchy or regarded as foreign and was extended to include low castes and tribals. Foreigners, even of high ranks, were regarded as *meleccha*" (Thapar 1993: 78).
2 See also Savarkar 1989. It forms the title of his book *Hindutva – who is a Hindu?*, published in 1923. For a brief discussion of the term *Hindutva* and the distinction between Hinduism and *Hindutva*, see Lipner's article "On 'Hindutva' and 'Hindu-Catholic', with a moral for our times" in *Hindu-Christian Studies Bulletin*, vol. 5, 1992. See also Sharma 2002: 1–35.
3 For further discussion of this contentious term, see Lorenzen 1999: 630–59, Doniger 1991: 35–41, Hawley 1991: 20–33, and Fitzgerald 1990: 101–18. Also see Malik 2001: 10–31, von Stietencron 2001: 32–53, Thapar 2001: 54–81, Frykenberg 2001: 82–107, King 1999: chapter 5, and the special issue of *The Journal of the American Academy of Religion* 2000: 68 (4).
4 There are a number of volumes which deal with the subject. For a convenient entry into the origin, background, key practitioners, and debates from within and outside the field, see Ashcroft *et al.* 1989, Gandhi 1998, McLeod 2000, and Quayson 2000. For clarification of terms, see Ashcroft *et al.* 1998. For issues, themes, and future direction of the discourse, see Schwarz and Ray 2000, Chrisman and Parry 2000, Lopez 2001, and Goldberg and Quayson 2002. For anthologies, see Williams and Chrisman 1994, Ashcroft *et al.* 1995, Mongia 1996, and Childs and Williams 1997. For application of the theory for specific disciplines, see Majid 2000 for Islam and Cohen 2000 for the Middle Ages. There are journals dedicated specifically to postcolonial issues – *Postcolonial Studies: Culture, Politics and Economy,* and *Interventions: International Journal of Postcolonial Studies.*
5 Said 1985, 1993.
6 Bhabha 1994.
7 Spivak 1993, 1999.
8 See King 1999 and Bilimoria 2000: 171–207.

1 William Jones: making Hinduism safe

1 Although Jones was not the first person to uncover the linguistic affinity between Sanskrit and Greek and Latin, he arrived at his formulation independently, and he brought to public knowledge the value of comparative philology. Jones insisted upon a common origin for all peoples, but he did not use linguistic affinity to establish a connection between language and race. With the development of comparative philology, however, linguistic affinity came to be equated with racial identity in the works of the German orientalist Max Müller. See Mukherjee 1968: 91–3.

2 Jones first translated *Śakuntalā* into Latin, and then from Latin into English. It was published in 1789 as *Sacontalá or The Fatal Ring.*
3 For various aspects of Jones' life and work, see the following: Mukherjee 1968, Cannon 1990, and Murray 1998.
4 Also known as *Mānava Dharmaśāstra* or *Manusmṛti* in Sanskrit, and attributed to Manu, although it contains the views of several authors. Probably composed during the first two centuries of the common era, it is concerned with the *dharma* (duty) of men and women, of various castes, rules of conduct, morality, and law, and encompasses a wide range of subjects from pollution and purification to politics and administration.
5 See Rocher 1994: 220–21.
6 For a further account of Jones in relation to Romanticism, see Mukherjee 1968: 42–8 and Drew 1987: chapter 2.
7 Viṣṇu is also known by other names but Jones has chosen the epithet "Nārāyaṇa" meaning "moving on the waters." Viṣṇu in Hindu iconography is portrayed reclining on the coiled body of a seven-hooded snake, *Ananta Śeṣa,* which serves as his couch and floats on the vast ocean, signifying a complete state of absorption before the next cycle of creation begins. The term *Ananta* means "endless" referring to cosmic time, and *Śeṣa* means "the remainder," and it is from that which remains that creation comes about.
8 For other editions and compilation of Jones' work, see Cannon 1979 and 1993.
9 "On the Gods of Greece, Italy, and India" (1784: hereafter GGII). Jones also admits that this comparison is perhaps superficial, partly because of his brief residence in India and partly because of lack of leisure for his literary pursuits. For the text see Jones 1799a and Marshall 1970: chapter 6.
10 Letter dated Calcutta, 22 June 1784.
11 GGII.
12 Third Anniversary Discourse.
13 GGII.
14 See also Mukherjee 1968: 104.
15 GGII.
16 GGII.
17 GGII.
18 GGII.
19 GGII.
20 GGII.
21 GGII.
22 GGII.
23 GGII.
24 GGII.
25 GGII.
26 GGII.
27 Placing Hindu *yugas* within a biblical time-framework, Jones declares: "We may here observe, that the true History of the World seems obviously divisible into *four* ages or periods; which may be called, the first, the *Diluvian*, or purest age … next, the *Patriarchal*, or pure age … thirdly, the *Mosaick*, or less pure, age; from the legation of MOSES, and during the time, when his ordinances were comparatively well-observed and uncorrupted; lastly, the *Prophetical*, or *impure*, age beginning with the vehement warnings given by the Prophets to apostate Kings and degenerate nations" (Jones 1799a: 244).
28 Third Anniversary Discourse.
29 Third Anniversary Discourse.
30 "On the literature of the Hindus." With regard to Charles Wilkins' translation of the *Gītā*, Jones took a Protestant line of thinking. He found Wilkins' translation exemplary but hoped that it could have been more verbatim. Comparing Wilkins' translation of the *Gītā* with the original Sanskrit, Jones remarks: "But, as a learner, I could have wished that it had been still

more literal, and that the verses had been numbered, and everything put in the Sanscrit printed in Italicks, like our excellent translation of the Bible" (Cannon 1990: 259).

31 As Rosane Rocher points out: "It was not until German romanticism and nineteenth-century German philology, with their emphasis on *Ur-literatur*, the very first and original sources, that the Vedic *saṃhitās* became a primary focus of interest" (1994: 227).

32 GGII.

33 Letter to Charles Wilkins, 24 April 1784.

34 Speaking of his romantic admiration for the *Bhagavadgītā*, Jones wishes that Wilkins' translation of it was more literal (Cannon 1990: 259).

35 Letter to Warren Hastings, 7 January 1785.

36 "On the literature of the Hindus."

37 Third Anniversary Discourse.

38 Third Anniversary Discourse.

39 GGII.

40 See Halbfass 1988: 56.

41 GGII.

42 Letter to Earl Spencer, 4 September 1787.

43 GGII.

44 GGII.

45 GGII.

46 GGII.

47 For these and other hymns, with a helpful introduction, see Franklin 1995: 98–179.

48 See Majeed 1992: 22–24.

49 Letter to Earl Spencer, 17 August 1787.

50 Correspondence with the Government of Fort William.

51 Correspondence with the Government of Fort William.

52 Letter to the first Marquis of Cornwallis, 19 March 1788.

53 Charge to the Grand Jury, at Calcutta, 10 June.

54 In his letter to Thomas Yeates, dated 7 June 1782, Jones remarks: "The constitutional or public law is partly unwritten, and grounded upon immemorial usage, and partly written or enacted by the legislative power, but the unwritten or common law contains the true spirit of our constitution: the written has often most unjustifiably altered the form of it: the common law is the collected wisdom of many centuries, having been used and approved by successive generations ... the unwritten law is eminently favourable, and the written generally hostile to the absolute rights of persons" (Teignmouth 1804: 211–12).

55 Correspondence with the Government of Fort William, 1785. "If we had a complete Digest of Hindu and Mohammedan laws, after the model of Justinian's inestimable Pandects compiled by the most learned of the native lawyers, with an accurate verbal translation of it into English; and if copies of the work were reposited in the proper offices of the Sedr Divani Adalat, and of the Supreme Court, that they might occasionally be consulted as a standard of justice, we should rarely be at a loss for the principles, at least, and rules of law applicable to the cases before us, and should never perhaps be led astray by the Pandits or Maulavis, and who would hardly venture to impose on us, when their imposition might be easily detected" (Jones 1799b: 74–5).

56 See also Spivak's "Can the subaltern speak?" (1993: 76–7).

57 See also Cohn 1996: 68–72.

58 For Rocher's view on Jones' relation with pundits as a colonial administrator and oriental scholar, as well his attitude to law, see Rocher 1994: 236–40.

59 Correspondence with the Government of Fort William.

60 See Thapar 1999a: 199.

2 Max Müller: mobilizing texts and managing Hinduism

1 For biographical details, see Müller 1976. For an appreciation of Müller's life and work, see Prabhananda 2001.

2 For a detailed treatment of the role of the *Ṛg Veda* in the work of Müller, see Neufeldt 1980.

3 Unlike Darwin, Müller does not see human evolution as beginning with the beast, but with the child. In his letter to the Duke of Argyll dated 22 February 1880, Müller states that he holds "that Man was evolved, not however from a beast, but from a child, which actually represents a stage much lower than the highest beast, but potentially a stage out of the reach of any beast" (Müller (1902b: 81).

4 Although Müller regards the Veda as having nothing to do with modernity, when the modern form of communication, the microphone, was invented, he used it, and recited the oldest Sanskrit hymn, the *Ṛg Veda*, in order to sanctify and give the Veda a ritual welcome (ibid. 1902b: 48–9).

5 In a similar vein, he writes to the Duke of Argyll: "that if the religion of India could be brought back to the simple form which it exhibits in the Veda, a great reform would be achieved" – but this alone will not suffice. In his view the Veda lacks "the high and pure and almost Christian morality of the Buddha" but the redeeming fact is that "as far as the popular conceptions of the deity are concerned, the Vedic religion, though childish and crude, is free from all that is so hideous in the later Hindu Pantheon" (Müller 1902a: 362). Similarly in his letter to Professor Deussen of Kirk, Müller speaks of making Vedānta intelligible both to Europeans and Indians (ibid.: 399).

6 The term *Ārya* is a European construct and has both inclusive and exclusive meanings. Trautmann draws attention to the significance of the Aryan construct in British and non-British contexts. In the British setting, the term Aryan includes both British and Indians, as can be seen in the English translation beneath the Sanskrit inscription in the Old Institute in Oxford: "This Building, dedicated to Eastern sciences, was founded for the use of Aryas (Indians and Englishmen) by excellent and benevolent men desirous of encouraging knowledge" (Trautmann 1997: 5). By contrast, in the European setting, the phrase "for the use of Aryas" could exclude Jews, gypsies and colored people. Trautmann points out: "Yet both senses of *Arya* or *Aryan*, the inclusive one of the Oxford inscription and the exclusive one of the ideologists of racial hatred, come from different perspectives on the same construct, the idea of an Aryan people, (whether conceived as a race or not ...)" (ibid.).

7 For further discussion, see Nandy 1991 (1988): 23–5.

8 Dayānanda Saraswatī dispensed with the Hindu pantheon of gods and goddesses. He turned away from image worship at the age of fourteen. When he was observing an all-night fast and vigil in honour of Śiva, he wondered whether the "hideous emblem of Shiva in the temple was identical with Mahādeva (the great god) of the scriptures, or something else." He told his father that he could not "reconcile the idea of an omnipotent, living God, with this idol, which allows mice to run upon its body, and thus suffer its image to be polluted without the slightest protest" (de Bary 1988: 630).

9 Müller's idealized portrayal of the Hindu character was no doubt a morale booster for Hindus at a time when they were being denounced. For a list of quotations attesting to the truthfulness of Hindus, see Müller 1892: 63. Here are a couple of quotations that Max Müller draws upon. Warren Hastings on Hindus: "They are gentle and benevolent, more susceptible of gratitude for kindness shown them, and less promoted to vengeance for wrongs inflicted, than any people on the face the earth; faithful, affectionate, submissive to legal authority (ibid. 1892: 60). Bishop Heber on Hindus: "The Hindus are brave, courteous, intelligent and most eager for knowledge and improvement; sober, industrious, dutiful to parents, affectionate to their children, uniformly gentle and patient, and more easily affected by kindness and attention to their wants and feelings than any other people I ever met with" (ibid.).

10 Müller speaks of his personal experience of Hindu pundits: "During the last twenty years, however, I have had some excellent opportunities of watching a number of native scholars under circumstances where it is not difficult to detect a man's true character, I mean in literary work and, more particularly, in literary controversy" (Müller 1892: 63).

11 For Mill both the past and present state of Hindus were equally corrupt, requiring colonial intervention.

12 See *Speeches by Lord Macaulay with His Minute on Education* in Young 1935.

13 Debendranath Tagore, who succeeded Rammohan Roy, gave up the infallibility of Veda in favour of intuition as the guiding principle of the Samāj.

14 See van der Veer 2001: 111.

15 Warren Hastings was highly impressed on reading Wilkins' draft translation of the *Bhagavadgītā*, and made a deliberate attempt to publicize it in Britain. He hoped that by showing that Indians were not a savage race but had a sublime text such as the *Gītā*, he could win the support of the British public for an oriental mode of government (see Marshall 1970: 180).

3 William Ward's "virtuous Christians, vicious Hindus"

1 Ward's four-volume text, *A View of the History, Literature, and Mythology of the Hindoos* has a complicated history. The volumes I have used were published at different times: volumes 1 and 2 were published in 1817, and 3 and 4 were published in 1820. For a brief account of the publication history of Ward's text, see Mani 1998: 215n. For a comparison of the first edition of Ward's *Account of the Writings, Religion and Manners of the Hindoos* (1811) with the last edition of the same work under the title *A View of the History, Literature and Mythology of the Hindoos* (1822), see Mani 1998: 122–40.

2 See Potts 1967.

3 Müller also critiques James Mill, who drew on Ward's *Hindoos* in order to firm up his negative evaluation of Hindus. See Müller 1892: 42–4.

4 For further discussion on *satī*, see chapter 5 in this volume.

5 Lata Mani compares "the status of *satī* in Ward's *Hindoos* and journal writings with its subsequent representation in the *Missionary Register*." See Mani 1998: 140–51.

6 See Panikkar 1995: 35–7.

4 Decrowning Farquhar's Hinduism

1 For a discussion of "inclusivism" in Christian theology of religions, see Race 1983: chapter 3.

2 For Farquahar's religious and intellectual background, see Sharpe 1965, chapter 4. For nineteenth-century Protestant attitudes to Hinduism, see chapter 1 in the same volume.

3 See Farquhar's "Missionary study of Hinduism" in Sharpe 1963: 126–7.

4 A similar process is replicated in the Hindu writings of contemporary Hindus such as Vivekānanda and Radhakrishnan who see monistic Vedāntic thought as encompassing the truth of other religions. Unlike the missionaries, they did not seek converts or deny the truth in different religions but saw these truths as relative, finding their final consummation in the formless and eternal truth of the *Vedānta*. While missionaries were projecting Christianity as the unique religion with a universal message, nineteenth-century Hindu reformers such as Rammohan Roy and Swami Dayānanda Saraswatī were formulating a Hinduism that would answer such challenges.

5 See Farquhar's "Missionary study of Hinduism" in Sharpe 1963.

6 For different tellings of the *Rāmāyaṇa*, see Richman 1991 and 2000.

5 Courtly text and courting *satī*

1 For William Ward's views on *satī*, see chapter 3.

2 Colebrooke 1801: 716–22.

3 See Hawley 1994: 11–15 for a fuller account of the varied shades of meaning of *satī*, . While *satī* in Sanskrit refers to the woman, suttee (coined by the British) refers to the rite of widow immolation.

4 See Dehejia 1994: 50. There are many versions of the goddess Satī myth in the *Purāṇas*, which have little to do with the practice of *satī*. Satī, the daughter of Dakṣa, was an earlier incarnation of Parvatī and the wife of Śiva. In one version the grief-stricken Śiva, carrying the corpse of Satī, roams the earth. Both Satī and Śiva's grief demonstrate their devotion to each other, but in the practice of *satī*, we never hear about the devotion of the husband to his wife.

5 As Radha Kumar points out: "Recent historical research suggests the nineteenth century sati abolition movement might have created the myth of an existing practice where none existed. Not only was sati neither common nor widespread, it could never be either continuously, for its truth lay in being heroic or exceptional. The only example we appear to have of a widespread incidence of sati is in the early decades of the nineteenth century in Bengal, where there seemed to have been more than one incident of sati a day, even after Bentinck had outlawed it in that province. Some doubt has been cast on these figures, the bulk of which were collected at the height of the sati abolition movement, and in a province ruled by the chief British opponent of sati, William Bentinck. They do not specify, for example, what kinds of distinctions were made between suicide by widows and sati, and it is possible that a combination of ignorance and the desire to prove the gravity of sati as a problem might have led administrators to transpose from the former category into the latter" (Kumar 1993: 9).

6 See also Narayanan 1997: 73–80 and Tully 1991: 210–36.

7 The deification of *satī* – the notion of *satī* becoming a goddess – seems to have gained importance in the latter part of the second millennium CE. It was particularly related to the heroic ideal of the warrior or kṣatriya. The followers of the *Śākta* sects in eastern India were totally against this practice and deification of *satī*, as they saw a female as an embodiment of the goddess. Furthermore, they saw women who chose *satī* as going to hell. This notion challenged the *kṣatriya* ethic. As Thapar points out: "This contradiction of the kṣatriya ethic has its own interest as a statement of opposition particularly as it comes from those who were initially regarded as being of lesser status but constituting the larger percentage of people. Possibly this kind of opposition nurtured the compensatory notion of a sati being converted into a goddess, a notion which seems to have gained currency in the later second millennium AD" (1988: 17).

8 The *Dharmaśāstras,* composed during the first two centuries of the common era, are concerned with rules of conduct, morality, and law. The ambivalent attitude to women in the law books are attributed to Manu (the author of the *Mānava Dharmaśāstra*), under whose name are found heterogeneous legal perspectives from different periods. In the *Dharmaśāstras*, women are accorded dependent status as daughters, wives, and mothers. While wifely devotion is glorified, a woman's sexuality is seen as an obstacle to man's spiritual pursuits.

9 Although Leslie speaks about the relation between text and social reality, and the need to look at women's voices in anthropological and historical surveys in the concluding part of *The Perfect Wife: The Orthodox Hindu Woman according to the Strīdharmapaddhati of Tryambakayjvan* (Leslie 1989: 325–9), she does not give any serious attention to these issues in "Suttee or *satī*." She points out that exclusive preoccupation with one particular text does not rule out alternative frameworks, but her choice of the text itself leaves little room for constructive discussion or empowerment. Furthermore, the text is used in such a way that *satī* is essentialized and given a timeless quality.

10 Mayo 1927.

11 For Narayanan's well articulated, detailed and perceptive critique of Mary Daly's representation of *satī* see pp. 43–68. For Narayanan's views on Katherine Mayo, see pp. 56–8. My critique of Julia Leslie's representation of *satī* has resonances with Uma Narayanan's analysis of Daly's views on *satī*.
12 See Lata Mani (1993b: 87–118), and also Thapar who gives an excellent historical survey of *satī*, drawing attention to factors that contributed to the construction of *satī* as tradition (1988: 14–19).
13 *Bhakti* movements challenged rigid caste structures, brahmin authority, and ritualism. Although the impact of *bhakti* movements was not all that visible at the social level, women were accorded a greater freedom in the religious domain in certain strands within the *bhakti* tradition. Women saints and poets play a significant role in various *bhakti* traditions, and some *bhakti* literature has women authors.
14 Cited in Vidya Dehejia (1994: 53).
15 Quoted in Romila Thapar (1988: 17).
16 It is commonly held that the eighteenth century was a "dark age" for India, and that the nineteenth-century social and reform movements were the result of the introduction of Western education and and European thought. Without trivializing the Western impact, in his book Panikkar shows that there were dissenting voices (heterodox sects) in most parts of India in the eighteenth century before the British intervention, who challenged some Hindu practices that had become corrupt. See K. N. Panikkar (1995: 34–6).
17 See Coburn 1998: 29–48.
18 See Spivak (1993), Mani (1993a) and Sunder Rajan (1990: 1–23).

6 Conclusion

1 For a detailed account of Hindus in the diaspora, see Vertovec 2000 and Rukmani 1999.
2 See the *Journal of the American Academy of Religion* 2000; 68 (4).
3 See Williams 2001 for a detailed account of the history of the Swaminarayan movement. One of the forms of Hinduism which is making a significant global impact in the diaspora is Swaminarayan Hinduism, a small religious and social reform movement of Vaiṣṇava *saṃpradāya*, founded in the western state of Gujarat by Swami Sahajanand or Swaminarayan in early nineteenth-century British India. It is a particular form of *bhakti* Hinduism with a marked ethnic identity and strong puritanical streak. A sectarian movement with its own gurus and teachings, it has become a transnational movement and seeks to speak for all Hindus. It has unquestionably put down roots in the diaspora, catering to the cultural, spiritual, moral, and spiritual needs of the Gujarati communities settled in the UK, USA, Canada, Australia, and other places including non-Western countries.

Swaminarayan, the founder, was no stranger to the British. The picture of the historic meeting in Rajkot in 1890 between Sir John Malcolm (the then British Governor of Bombay) and Swaminarayan graces most Swaminarayan temples, including the one in north London – a testimony to the cordial relations between the colonizer and the colonized. Both shared a common vision in that they were keen to "reform" Hindu society and saw themselves as initiators of social change. Swaminarayan emerged as a social and religious reformer at a time of great social and political change in British India. Sir John Malcolm found in him an ally and the former saw British rule as divine providence. Swaminarayan was no stranger to Christian missionaries either. The Anglican Bishop Heber was greatly impressed by Swaminarayan's ethical teachings and his commitment to social and religious reform. The British left India in 1947, but the Swaminarayans have come to stay in Britain.
4 Mukta points out: "The particular caste *sampradaya* became evident in the period following Independence, when the APS went to court to ensure that they were categorized as a specific movement which fell outside of the 'Hindu' fold, so that it would remain exempt from the Harijan Temple Entry Act of 1947." Shastri Yagna Purushottamdas was engaged

"in a legal battle to have the Swaminarayan sect declared as: 'entirely different from the vast majority of other Hindu temples where Hindus in general have a legal right to go'" (Mukta 2000: 459). However this was not granted on the grounds "that Hinduism is a religion not only based on the Vedas but other scriptures as well" (ibid.).

5 See Knott 1986 for a clear account of the origin, growth, beliefs and practices of the Hare Krishna Movement. Hindu response to Hare Krishna has gone through various phases of suspicion, ambivalence, and partial acceptance to acknowledgement. For many Hindus, Bhaktivedanta Manor has now become a place of worship and pilgrimage. For some Hindus in the diaspora, ISKCON has become a mouthpiece for Hindus, putting across the teachings of Hinduism to the wider public. Whether Hare Krishnas call themselves Hindus or not is immaterial. The point is the roots of ISKCON lie in the *bhakti* tradition and its founder being an Indian guru makes it a legitimate tradition.

6 The Vishwa Hindu Parishad (World Hindu Council), which was founded in Bombay in 1964, has chapters worldwide, in the USA, Canada, the UK, and other parts of Europe, and in many other non-Western countries. It was founded with aim of uniting Hindus of all the sects and sub-sects of Hindus under a globalized monolithic category, *Hindutva*.

7 As Tanika Sarkar points out: "Modern Hinduism, over 200 colonial and post-colonial years, has systematically tried to absorb the public and political spheres within this fold; and that in fact this only continues its age-old practice of being closely connected with political processes in pre-colonial times" (Sarkar 2001: 271). See also Bhatt and Mutkta 2000: 407–40, van der Veer 1994.

8 See Raj 2000: 535–56.

9 See Smith 1962; "Disciplining religion" in King 1999: 40–1; "A human tragedy or the divine retribution" in Balagangadhara 1994: 307–17. There are relatively few books on Hinduism as such by Hindu scholars, and most of them have been produced in response to Western critiques. Radhakrishnan's *The Hindu View of Life* is a case in point. Radhakrishan tends to see Hinduism in terms of the Vedāntic model, one that was adopted by early Western orientalists and later replicated and amplified by Hindu thinkers.

10 The question of an Ur text has never been an issue for Indian translators. For example, the many retellings of the *Rāmāyaṇa* are not necessarily variant readings of the "original" text, but each telling (both oral and written) is unique while at the same time it is related to other tellings. What matters is not the "original" but how it has been transformed by the creative imagination of the various translators and narrators. As A. K. Ramanujan remarks: "In this sense, no text is original, yet no telling is a mere telling – the story has no closure, although it may be enclosed in a text" (1991: 46).

11 Narayanan draws attention to these factors in her recent essay "Diglossic Hinduism: liberation and lentils" (Narayanan 2000: 779) in *Journal of the American Academy of Religion*.

Bibliography

Ashcroft, Bill (2001) *On Post-Colonial Futures: Transformations of Colonial Culture*, London: Continuum.

Ashcroft, Bill, Griffiths, Gareth, and Tiffin, Helen (1989) *The Empire Strikes Back: Theory and Practice in Post-colonial Literatures*, London: Routledge.

Ashcroft, Bill, Griffiths, Gareth, and Tiffin, Helen (1995) *The Postcolonial Studies Reader*, London: Routledge.

Ashcroft, Bill, Griffiths, Gareth, and Tiffin, Helen (1998) *Key Concepts in Post-Colonial Studies*, London: Routledge.

Aurobindo, Sri (1971) *The Secret of the Veda*, vol. 10., Pondicherry: Sri Aurobindo Ashram.

Aurobindo, Sri (1984) (1915) *Swami Dayananda*, Pondicherry: All India Books.

Balagangadhara, S. N. (1994) *"The Heathen in His Blindness:" Asia, the West and the Dynamic of Religion*, Leiden: E. J. Brill.

Banerjee, Sumanta (1989) *The Parlour and the Streets: Elite and Popular Culture in Nineteenth Century Calcutta*, Calcutta: Seagull Books.

Bhabha, Homi K. (1994) *The Location of Culture*, London: Routledge.

Bhatt, Chetan and Mukta, Parita (2000) "Hindutva in the west: mapping the antinomies of diaspora nationalism," *Ethnic and Racial Studies* 23 (3).

Bilimoria, Purushottama (2000) "A subaltern/postcolonial critique of the comparative philosophy of religion," *Sophia* 39 (1).

Cannon, Garland (ed.) (1979) *Sir William Jones: A Bibliography of Primary and Secondary Sources*, vol. 7., Amsterdam: John Benjamin B. V.

Cannon, Garland (ed.) (1970) *The Letters of William Jones*, vol. II. Oxford: Clarendon Press.

Cannon, Garland (1990) *The Life and Mind of Oriental Jones: Sir William Jones, the Father of Modern Linguistics*, Cambridge: Cambridge University Press.

Cannon, Garland (1993) *The Collected Works of Sir William Jones*, London: Curzon Press. Reprint of the 1807 edition, 13 vols. London: John Stockdale and John Walker.

Carey, William (1818) *A Grammar of the Bengalee Language*, 4th edn with additions, Serampore: Mission Press.

Carman, John and Narayanan, Vasudha (1989) *Tamil Veda: Piḷḷaṉ's Interpretation of the Tiruvāymoḻi*, Chicago: University of Chicago Press.

Carrier, James G. (ed.) (1995) *Occidentalism: Images of the West*, Oxford: Clarendon Press.

Chakravarti, Uma (1993) "Whatever happened to the Vedic *Dasi*? Orientalism, nationalism and a script for the past" in Kumkum Sangari and Sudesh Vaid (eds) *Recasting Women: Essays in Colonial History*, New Delhi: Kali for Women.

Chatterjee, Margaret (1983) *Gandhi's Religious Thought*, Basingstoke: Macmillan.

Chatterjee, Partha (1993) *The Nation and its Fragments: Colonial Postcolonial Histories*, Princeton: Princeton University Press.

Chaudhuri, Nirad C. (1974) *Scholar Extraordinary: The Life of Professor Rt. Hon. Friedrich Max Müller, PC*, London: Chatto and Windus.

Childs, Peter and Williams, Patrick (1997) *An Introduction to Post-Colonial Theory*, London: Prentice-Hall.

Chrisman, Laura and Parry, Benita (2000) *Postcolonial Theory and Criticism*, Cambridge: D. S. Brewer.

Coburn, Thomas B. (1998) "Devī: the great goddess," in S. J. Hawley and D. M. Wulf (eds) *Devī: Goddesses of India*, Delhi: Motilal Banarsidass.

Cohen, Jeffrey Jerome (ed.) (2000) *The Postcolonial Middle Ages*, London: Macmillan.

Cohn, Bernard S. (1996) *Colonialism and its Forms of Knowledge: The British in India*, Princeton: Princeton University Press.

Colebrooke, Henry (1801) "On the duties of a faithful Hindu widow" in *Supplemental Volumes to the Works of Sir William Jones*, London: G. G. and J. Robinson.

Coomaraswamy, Ananda K. (1909) *Essays in National Idealism*, Madras: G. A. Natesan.

Daly, Mary (1984) *Gyn/Ecology: The Metaethics of Radical Feminism*, London: Women's Press.

de Bary, Theodore Wm (1988) *Sources of Indian Tradition*, Delhi: Motilal Banarsidass.

Dehejia, Vidya (1994) "Comment: a broader landscape", in J. S. Hawley (ed.) *Satī the Blessing and the Curse: The Burning of the Wives in India*, New York: Oxford University Press.

Derrett, M. and Duncan, J. (1968) *Religion, Law and the State in India*, London: Faber and Faber.

Devi, Maitreyi (1994) *It Does Not Die: A Romance*, Chicago: University of Chicago Press.

Doniger, Wendy (1991) "Hinduism by any other name," *The Wilson Quarterly* 15 (3).

Drew, John (1987) *India and the Romantic Imagination*, Delhi: Oxford University Press.

Ellsberg, Robert (1991) *Gandhi on Christianity*, Maryknoll: Orbis Books.

Farquhar, J. N. (1903) *Permanent Lessons of the Gita*, Madras: The Christian Literature Society.

Farquhar, J. N. (1912) *A Primer of Hinduism*, London: Oxford University Press.

Farquhar, J. N. (1913) *The Crown of Hinduism*, London: Oxford University Press.

Farquhar, J. N. (1917) *Gita and Gospel*, Madras: The Christian Literature Society.

Farquhar, J. N. (1920) *An Outline of the Religious Literature of India*, London: Oxford University Press.

Farquhar, J. N. (1929) *Modern Religious Movements in India*, London: Macmillan.

Fitzgerald, Timothy (1990) "Hinduism and the 'World Religion' fallacy," *Religion* 20 (2).

Franklin, Michael J. (ed.) (1995) *Sir William Jones: Selected Poetical and Prose Works*, Cardiff: University of Wales Press.

Freeman, Kathryn (1998) "'Beyond the stretch of labouring thought sublime:' Romanticism, post-colonial theory and the transmission of Sanskrit texts," in *Orientalism Transposed: The Impact of the Colonies on British Culture*, J. F. Codell and D. S. Macleod (eds) Aldershot: Ashgate.

Frykenberg, Robert E. (2001) "The emergence of modern Hinduism as a concept and as an institution: a reappraisal with special reference to South India," in G. Sontheimer and H. Kulke (eds) *Hinduism Reconsidered*, New Delhi: Manohar.

Gandhi, Leela (1998) *Postcolonial Theory: A Critical Introduction*, Edinburgh: Edinburgh University Press.

Goldberg, David Theo and Quayson, Ato (2002) *Relocating Postcolonialism*, Oxford: Blackwell Publishers.

Griffiths, Jay (1999) *Pip Pip: A Sideways Look at Time*, London: Flamingo.

Halbfass, Wilhelm (1988) *India and Europe: An Essay in Understanding*, Albany: State University Press.

Hawley, John Stratton (1991) "Naming Hinduism," *The Wilson Quarterly* 15 (3).

Hawley, John Stratton (1994) "Introduction" in J. S. Hawley (ed.) *Satī, the Blessing and the Curse: The Burning of the Wives in India*, New York: Oxford University Press.

Hodgen, Margaret T. (1964) *Early Anthropology in the Sixteenth and Seventeenth Centuries*, Philadelphia: University of Pennsylvania Press.

Inden, Ronald (1992) *Imagining India*, Cambridge MA and Oxford: Blackwell.

Jones, William (1799a) *The Works of Sir William Jones in Six Volumes*, vol. I., edited by Anna Maria Jones, his wife, London: G. G. and J. Robinson.

Jones, William (1799b) *The Works of Sir William Jones in Six Volumes*, vol. III., edited by Anna Maria Jones, his wife, London: G. G. and J. Robinson.

Jones, William (1799c) *The Works of Sir William Jones in Six Volumes*, vol. IV., edited by Anna Maria Jones, his wife, London: G. G. and J. Robinson.

King, Richard (1999) *Orientalism and Religion: Postcolonial Theory, India and "The Mystic East,"* London: Routledge.

Kishwar, Madhu and Vanita, Ruth (1989) "Poison to nectar: The life and work of Mīrābaī" *Manushi*, 10th anniversary issue 50–52.

Knott, Kim (1986) *My Sweet Lord: The Hare Krishna Movement*, Wellingborough: The Aquarian Press.

Kumar, Radha (1993) *The History of Doing: An Illustrated Account of Movements for Women's Rights and Feminism in India 1800–1990*, Delhi: Kali for Women.

Leslie, Julia (1989) *The Perfect Wife: The Orthodox Hindu Woman According to the Strīdharmapaddhati of Tryambakayajvan*, Delhi: Oxford University Press.

Leslie, Julia (1992a) "Introduction" in Julia Leslie (ed.) *Roles and Rituals for Hindu Women*, Delhi: Motilal Banarsidass.

Leslie, Julia (1992b) "Suttee or satī: victim or victor?," in Julia Leslie (ed.) *Roles and Rituals for Hindu Women*, Delhi: Motilal Banarsidass.

Lipner, Julius (1992) On "Hindutva" and a "Hindu-Catholic" with a Moral for our Times, *Hindu-Christian Studies Bulletin* 5.

Loomba, Ania (1993) "Overworlding the 'Third World'" in P. Williams and L. Chrisman (eds) *Colonial Discourse and Post-colonial Theory: A Reader*, New York: Harvester Wheatsheaf.

López, Alfred J. (2001) *Posts and Pasts: A Theory of Postcolonialism*, Albany: State University of New York Press.

Lorenzen, David N. (1999) "Who invented Hinduism?," *Comparative Studies of Society and History* 41 (4).

McGann, Jerome J. (1993) "Introduction" in McGann, J. I. (ed.) *The New Oxford Book of Romantic Period Verse*, Oxford: Oxford University Press.

McLeod, John (2000) *Beginning Postcolonialism*, Manchester: Manchester University Press.

Majeed, Javed (1992) *Ungoverned Imaginings: James Mill's History of British India and Orientalism*, Oxford: Clarendon Press.

Majid, Anouar (2000) *Unveiling Traditions: Postcolonial Islam in a Polycentric World*, Durham: Duke University Press.

Malik, Aditya (2001) "Hinduism or three-thousand-three-hundred-and-six-ways to invoke a construct," in G. Sontheimer and H. Kulke (eds) *Hinduism Reconsidered*, New Delhi: Manohar.

Mani, Lata (1993a) "The female subject, the colonial gaze: reading eyewitness accounts of widow burning", in T. Niranjana, P. Sudhir, and V. Dhareshwar (eds) *Interrogating Modernity: Culture and Colonialism in India*, Calcutta: Seagull.

Mani, Lata (1993b) "Contentious traditions: the debate on sati in colonial India," in Kumkum Sangari and Sudesh Vaid (eds) *Recasting Women: Essays in Colonial History*, Delhi: Kali for Women.

Mani, Lata (1998) *Contentious Traditions: The Debate on Sati in Colonial India*, Berkeley: University of California Press.

Marshall, P. J. (1970) *The British Discovery of Hinduism in the Eighteenth Century*, Cambridge: Cambridge University Press.

Marshman, John C. (1859) *The Life and Times of Carey, Marshman and Ward: Embracing the History of Serampore*, vol. 2, London: Brown, Green, Longman and Roberts.

Martin, Nancy (1996) "Mīrābaī inscribed in text: embodied in life" in Rosen, S. J. (ed.) *Vaiṣṇavi: Women and the Worship of Krishna*, Delhi: Motilal Banarsidass.

Mayo, Katherine (1927) *Mother India*, London: Jonathan Cape.

Mehta, R. (1983) *The Dialogue with Death: Sri Aurobindo's Savitri, A Mystical Approach*, Delhi: Motilal Banarsidass.

Mongia, Padmini (1996) *Contemporary Postcolonial Theory: A Reader*, London: Arnold.

Mukherjee, S. N. (1968) *Sir William Jones: A Study in Eighteenth-Century British Attitudes to India*, Cambridge: Cambridge University Press.

Mukta, Parita (2000) "The public face of Hindu nationalism", *Ethnic and Racial Studies* 23 (3).

Müller, Max F. (1868) *Chips from a German Workshop*, vol. I. *Essays on the Science of Religion*, London: Longman, Green.

Müller, Max F. (1875) *Chips from A German Workshop*, vol. IV. *Essays Chiefly on the Science of Language*, London: Longman, Green.

Müller, Max F. (1878) *Lectures on the Origin and Growth of Religion as illustrated by the Religions of India*, London: Longman, Green.

Müller, Max F. (1879) "Preface" in Müller, Max. F (ed.) *The Sacred Books of the East*, vol. I. Oxford: Clarendon Press.

Müller, Max F. (1884) "Introduction" in Müller, Max. F (ed.) *The Sacred Books of the East* vol. XV. Oxford: Clarendon Press.

Müller, Max F. (1892) *India: What Can it Teach Us? A Course of Lectures delivered before the University of Cambridge*, London: Longman, Green.

Müller, Max F. (1901a) *Collected Works of the Right Hon. F. Max Müller. Last Essays: Second Series XVII: Essays on Language, Folklore and Other Subjets*, London: Longman, Green and Co.

Müller, Max F. (1901b) *Collected Works of the Right Hon. F. Max Müller. Last Essays: Second Series XVIII: Essays on the Science of Religion*, London: Longman, Green and Co.

Müller Max F. (1902a) *The Life and Letters of the Right Honourable Friedrich Max Müller edited by his wife*. vol. I. London: Longman, Green and Co.

Müller, Max F. (1902b) *The Life and Letters of the Right Honourable Friedrich Max Müller edited by his wife*, vol.II. London: Longman, Green.

Müller, Max (1976) *My Autobiography*, Delhi: Hind Pocket Books.

Murray, Alexander (ed) (1998) *Sir William Jones 1746–94: A Commemoration*, Oxford: Oxford University Press.

Murthy, Anantha U. R. (1992) "Search for an identity: a viewpoint of a Kannada writer" in Sudhir Kakar (ed.) *Identity and Adulthood*, Dehli: Oxford University Press.

Nandy, Ashis (1991) *The Intimate Enemy: Loss and Recovery of Self Under Colonialism*, Delhi: Oxford University Press.

Narayanan, Uma (1997) *Dislocating Cultures: Identities, Traditions, and Third World Feminism*, New York: Routledge.

Narayanan, Uma (2000) "Diglossic Hinduism: liberation and lentils," *Journal of the American Academy of Religion* 68 (4).

National Council of Hindu Temples (U.K.) *Hinduism: An Introduction to the World's Oldest Living Religion*, Leicester (n.d.).

Neufeldt, Ronald W. (1980) *F. Max Müller and the Ṛg-Veda: a Study of its Role in his Work and Thought*, Columbia: South Asia Books.

Oldenburg, Veena Talwar (1994) "The Roop Kanwar case: feminists' responses," in J. S. Hawley (ed.) *Satī the Blessing and the Curse: The Burning of the Wives in India*, New York: Oxford University Press.

Panikkar, K. N. (1995) *Culture, Ideology, Hegemony: Intellectuals and Social Consciousness in Colonial India*, New Delhi: Tulika.

Panikkar, Raimundo (1964) *The Unknown Christ of Hinduism*, London: Darton, Longman and Todd.

Potts, Daniel E. (1967) *British Baptist and Missionaries in India 1793–1837: The History of Serampore and Its Missions*, Cambridge: Cambridge University Press.

Prabhananda, Swami (2001) *Max Müller and his Contemporaries*, Kolkota: The Ramakrishna Institute of Culture.

Prakash, Gyan (1999) *Another Reason: Science and the Imagination of Modern India*, Princeton: Princeton University Press.

Prinja, Nawal, K. (ed.) (1996) *Explaining Hindu Dharma: A Guide for Teachers*, Norwich: Religious and Moral Education Press (RMEP) for Vishwa Hindu Parishad.

Quayson, Ato (2000) *Postcolonialism: Theory, Practice or Process*, Cambridge: Polity Press.

Race, Alan (1983) *Christians and Religious Pluralism*, London: SCM Press.

Radhakrishnan, S. (1998) (1927) *The Hindu View of Life*, Delhi: Harper Collins.

Raj, Dhooleka Sarhadi (2000) "Who the hell do you think you are? Promoting religious identity among young Hindus in Britain," *Ethnic and Racial Studies*: 23 (3).

Ramanujan, A. K. (1991) "Three hundred Rāmāyaṇas: five examples and three thoughts on translation" in P Richman (ed.) *Many Rāmāyaṇas: The Diversity of a Narrative Tradition in South Asia*, Berkeley: University of California Press.

Ravindran, V. (1996) "The unanticipated legacy of Robert Caldwell and the Dravidian movement", *South Indian Studies* 1 (1).

Raychaudhuri, Tapan (1988) "Swami Vivekananda's construction of Hinduism" in William Radice (ed.) (1998) *Vivekananda and the Modernization of Hinduism*, Delhi: Oxford University Press.

Richman, Paula (ed) (1991) *Many Rāmāyaṇas: The Diversity of a Narrative Tradition in South Asia*, Berkeley: University of California Press.

Richman, Paula (ed.) (2000) *Questioning Rāmāyaṇas: A South Asian Tradition*, New Delhi: Oxford University Press.

Rocher, Rosane (1994) "British orientalism in the eighteenth century: the dialectics of knowledge and government," in A. C. Breckenridge and Peter van der Veer (eds) *Orientalism and Postcolonial Predicament*, Delhi: Oxford University Press.

Rukmani, T. S. (1999) *Hindu Diaspora: Global Perspectives*, Montreal: Concordia University Press.

Said, Edward W. (1985) *Orientalism*, Harmondsworth: Penguin.

Said, Edward W. (1993) *Culture and Imperialism*, London: Chatto and Windus.

Sarkar, Tanika (2001) *Hindu Wife, Hindu Nation: Community, Religion and Cultural Nationalism*, Bloomington: Indiana University Press.

Samartha, Stanley J. (1974) *The Hindu Response to the Unbound Christ*. Inter-Religious Dialogue Series 6, Madras: The Christian Literature Society.

Savarkar, V. D. (1989) (1923) *Hindutva: Who is a Hindu?* 6th edn. Bombay: Veer Savarkar Prakashan.

Schwab, Raymond (1984) *The Oriental Renaissance: Europe's Discovery of India and the East 1680-1880*, New York: Columbia University Press.

Schwarz, Henry and Ray, Sangeeta (eds) (2000) *A Companion to Postcolonial Studies*, Oxford: Blackwell.

Sen, Keshub Chunder (1980) (1871) *Keshub Chunder Sen in England: Diaries, Sermons, Addresses and Epistles*, Calcutta: A Writer's Workshop Book.

Sharma, Arvind (2002) "On Hindu, Hindustan, Hinduism and Hindutva", *Numen: International Review for the History of Religions* 49 (1).

Sharma, A., Ray, A., Hejib, A. and Young, K. K. (1988) *Sati: Historical and Phenomenological Essays*, Delhi: Motilal Banarsidass.

Sharpe, Eric J. (1963) *J. N. Farquhar: A Memoir*, Calcutta: YMCA.

Sharpe, Eric J. (1965) *Not to Destroy But to Fulfil: The Contribution of J. N. Farquhar to Protestant Missionary Thought in India before 1914*, Uppsala: Gleerup.

Sharpe, Eric J. (1985) *The Universal Gītā: Western Images of the Bhagavadgītā*, London: Duckworth.

Shri Swaminarayan Mandir, Exhibition: *Understanding Hinduism*, London. (n.d.)

Sijie, Dai (2001) *Balzac and the Little Seamstress*, New York: Anchor Books.

Sinha, Mrinalini (1995) *Colonial Masculinity: The "manly" Englishman and the "effeminate Bengali" in the Late Nineteenth Century*, Manchester: Manchester University Press.

Smith, Cantwell W. (1962) *The Meaning and End of Religion*, New York: Macmillan.

Spivak, Gayatri Chakravorty (1990) *The Post-colonial Critic: Interviews, Strategies, Dialogues*, (ed.) S. Harasym. London: Routledge.

Spivak, Gayatri Chakravorty (1993) "Can the subaltern speak?" in P. Williams and L. Chrisman (eds) *Colonial Discourse and Postcolonial Theory: A Reader*, New York: Harvester Wheatsheaf.

Spivak, Gayatri Chakravorty (1999) *A Critique of Postcolonial Reason: Toward a History of Vanishing Present*, Cambridge: Harvard University Press.

Spurr, David (1993) *The Rhetoric of Empire: Colonial Discourse in Journalism, Travel Writing and Imperial Administration*, Durham: Duke University Press.

Srivastava, Sushil (2001) "Situating the Gentoo in history: European perceptions of Indians in early phase of colonialism", *Economic and Political Weekly* 36 (7).

Sunder Rajan, Rajeswari (1990) "The subject of sati: pain and death in the contemporary discourse on sati", *Yale Journal of Criticism* 3 (2).

Sunder Rajan, Rajeswari (1993) *Real and Imagined Women: Gender, Culture and Postcolonialism*, London: Routledge.

Sugirtharajah, Sharada (1997) "Women in Hinduism" in P. Bowen (ed.) *Themes and Issues in Hinduism*, London: Cassell.

Sugirtharajah, Sharada (1999a) "Single text and scripting *satī*: a postcolonial perspective," *Svensk religionhistorisk årsskrift* 8: 53–9.

Sugirtharajah, Sharada (1999b) "Virtuous Christians, vicious Hindus: a postcolonial look at William Ward and his Hinduism," *Studies in World Christianity* 5 (2).

Sugirtharajah, Sharada (2001) "Courtly text and courting *satī*," *Journal of Feminist Studies in Religion* 17 (1): 5–32.

Teignmouth (Lord) (1804) *Of the Life, Writings, and Correspondence of Sir William Jones*, London: John Hatchard.

Thapar, Romila (1988) "In history," *Seminar* 342.

Thapar, Romila (1993) *Interpreting Early India*, Delhi: Oxford University Press.

Thapar, Romila (1994) *Cultural Transaction and Early India: Tradition and Patronage*, Delhi: Oxford University Press.

Thapar, Romila (1996) *Time as a Metaphor of History: Early India*, Delhi: Oxford University Press.

Thapar, Romila (1999a) *Śakuntalā: Texts, Readings and Histories,* New Delhi: Kali for Women.

Thapar, Romila (1999b) "Some appropriations of the theory of Aryan race relating to the beginnings of Indian history" in D. Ali (ed.) *Invoking the Past: The Uses of History in South Asia*, New Delhi: Oxford University Press.

Thapar, Romila (2000) "Interpretations of Indian history: colonial, nationalist, post-colonial" in P. R. de Souza (ed.) *Contemporary India: Transitions*, New Delhi: Sage.

Thapar, Romila (2001) "Syndicated Hinduism" in G. Sontheimer and H. Kulke (eds) *Hinduism Reconsidered*, New Delhi: Manohar.

Tharu, S. and Lalita K. (1993) "Introduction" in S. Tharu and K. Lalita (eds) *Women Writing in India: 600 BC to the Present, vol. I.* Delhi: Oxford University Press.

Thomas, M. M. (1969) *The Acknowledged Christ of the Indian Renaissance*, London: SCM Press.

Trautmann, Thomas R. (1997) *Aryans and British India*, Berkeley: University of California Press.

Tully, Mark (1991) *No Full Stops in India*, New Delhi: Viking.

Vaid, Sudesh and Sangari, Kumkum (1991) "Institutions, beliefs and ideologies: widow immolation in contemporary Rajasthan," *Economic and Political Weekly*, April 27.

van der Veer, Peter (1994) *Religious Nationalism: Hindus and Muslims in India*, Berkeley: University of California Press.

van der Veer, Peter (2001) *Imperial Encounters: Religion and Modernity in India and Britain*, Princeton: Princeton University Press.

Vertovec, Steven (2000) *The Hindu Diaspora: Comparative Patterns*, London: Routledge.

von Stietencron, Heinrich (2001) "Hinduism: on the proper use of a deceptive term," in G. Sontheimer and H. Kulke (eds) *Hinduism Reconsidered*, New Delhi: Manohar.

Ward, William (1817a) *A View of the History, Literature, and Mythology of the Hindoos*, vol. I. London: Black Parbury and Allen.

Ward, William (1817b) *A View of the History, Literature, and Mythology of the Hindoos*, vol. II. London: Black Parbury and Allen.

Ward, William (1820a) *A View of the History, Literature, and Mythology of the Hindoos*, vol. III. London: Black Parbury and Allen.

Ward, William (1820b) *A View of the History, Literature, and Mythology of the Hindoos*, vol. IV. London: Black Parbury and Allen.

Williams, Patrick and Chrisman, Laura (ed.) (1994) *Colonial Discourse and Post-colonial Theory: A Reader*, New York: Harvester Wheatsheaf.

Williams, Raymond Brady (2001) *An Introduction to Swaminarayan Hinduism*, Cambridge: Cambridge University Press.

Young, G. M. (1935) *Speeches by Lord Macaulay with his Minute on Indian Education*, London: Oxford University Press.

Young, J. C. (2001) *Postcolonialism: A Historical Introduction*, Oxford: Blackwell.

Young, Katherine K. (1996) "Theology does help women's liberation: Śrīvaiṣṇavism, a Hindu case study" in S. J. Rosen (ed.) *Vaiṣṇavi: Women and the Worship of Krishna*, Delhi: Motilal Banarsidass.

Young, Richard Fox (1981) *Resistant Hinduism: Sanskrit Sources on Anti-Christian Apologetics in Early Nineteenth-century India*, Vienna: Institute for Indology, University of Vienna.

Index